GLOBAL SECURITY WATCH
IRAN

A Reference Handbook

Thomas R. Mattair

PRAEGER SECURITY INTERNATIONAL

Westport, Connecticut · London

Library of Congress Cataloging-in-Publication Data

Mattair, Thomas R.
    Global security watch—Iran : a reference handbook / Thomas R. Mattair.
        p. cm. — (Global security watch, ISSN 1938–6168)
    Includes bibliographical references and index.
    ISBN 978–0–275–99483–9 (alk. paper)
1. Iran—Foreign relations—United States. 2. United States—Foreign relations—Iran. 3. National
Security—Iran. 4. National Security—United States. 5. National Security—Middle East. I. Title.
DS274.2.U6M38   2008
327.55—dc22   2008007312

British Library Cataloguing in Publication Data is available.

Library of Congress Catalog Card Number: 2008007312
ISBN-13: 978–0–275–99483–9
ISSN: 1938–6168

First published in 2008

Praeger Security International, 88 Post Road West, Westport, CT 06881
An imprint of Greenwood Publishing Group, Inc.
www.praeger.com

Printed in the United States of America

The paper used in this book complies with the
Permanent Paper Standard issued by the National
Information Standards Organization (Z39.48–1984).

10 9 8 7 6 5 4 3 2 1

To my mother and in memory of my father
Veritas

Contents

Preface

One of the most serious subjects in international politics today is Iran. There is widespread concern about Iran's nuclear programs and about Iran's role in Iraq, the Persian Gulf, and the Arab-Israeli conflict. There is also considerable debate about how successful or unsuccessful diplomacy, economic sanctions, or war will be in addressing these concerns about Iran.

Understanding Iran's intentions is a great challenge. Does Iran seek nuclear weapons? Would Iran wage war with them? Does Iran seek to be the unquestioned power in Iraq and the Persian Gulf? Is Iran unalterably opposed to Israel? The answers to these questions are not entirely clear. Understanding Iran's capabilities is considerably easier. In time, Iran does have the capability to build nuclear weapons. Iran already does have the military, economic, and political assets to threaten its neighbors. Iran's acquisition of nuclear weapons would certainly enhance Iran's threat. Reacting to Iran's capabilities by assuming that Iran has the worst intentions, however, could motivate Iran's leaders to adopt the worst intentions. It could possibly be a self-fulfilling prophecy. Regardless of the difficulty, therefore, efforts to understand Iran's intentions could be crucial. The fact that there has been so little diplomatic contact between the United States and Iran has been a major handicap in this regard. New diplomatic efforts that focus on only one or two issues should be expanded to include every issue at dispute between Iran, its neighbors in the region, and the world's major powers. This could provide an opportunity to learn what Iranian leaders really want.

This book attempts to explain how Iran and the world have come to a dangerous state of affairs. It traces the history of interactions that have led to grievances and mistrust in Iran and in its neighbors and major world powers. It argues that diplomacy is necessary, but does not promise that diplomacy will be successful.

The real interests of Iran and these other states may be irreconcilable, and war may be inevitable. But war will be costly, and diplomacy is a worthwhile effort.

The main chapters of this book concentrate on Iran's foreign relations and cover Iran's domestic politics only insofar as necessary to help explain Iran's foreign relations. Iran's domestic politics are covered in more detail, however, in the biographies of Iran's major leaders near the end of the book.

I could not have written this book if it had not been for the support I have received over the years. I learned a great deal from Professor George Lenczowski, admired his work, and valued his friendship during and after my years at the University of California, Berkeley. I received needed fellowship support from the Earhart Foundation in my early years of teaching and research at the University of Southern California, the University of California at Riverside, and Cornell University. I have also had generous support and friendly encouragement for my research from Shirley Merrill and Sandra Merrill. The Middle East Policy Council, and especially its Vice President Anne Joyce, enabled me to gain a firsthand knowledge of Washington. The Institute for Political and International Studies in Tehran hosted me for an illuminating conference and facilitated many meetings for me in Tehran with officials, academics, journalists, and merchants. The Emirates Center for Strategic Studies and Research enabled me to gain a firsthand knowledge of the Gulf. Throughout it all, I have enjoyed the great friendship of Randall N. Pratt, Jr., M.D., Captain, USN. Most importantly, Laura Stevens has given me a happy private life that makes it possible for me to devote time to public issues.

T.R.M.
Washington DC
March 2008

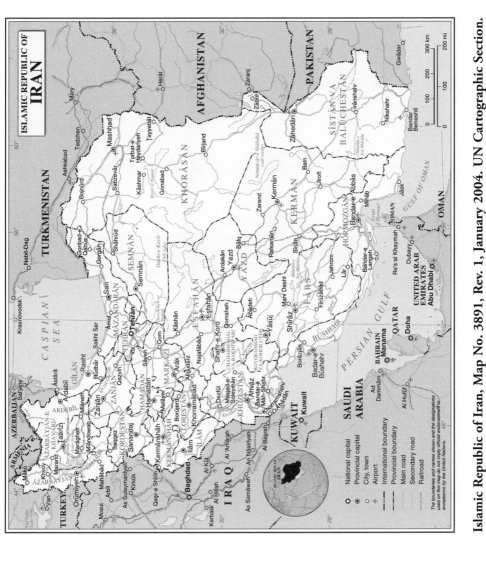

Islamic Republic of Iran, Map No. 3891, Rev. 1, January 2004. UN Cartographic Section.

CHAPTER 1

The History of Iran

Between 1500 BC and 900 BC, nomadic Aryan tribes from Central Asia began migrating south, eventually conquering the Elamites who had settled in southwest Iran *circa* 3000 BC. One of these tribes founded the Kingdom of Medes in northwest Iran. The other settled in southern Iran, and called it Iran, or Land of the Aryans. The Greeks later called it Persis, and so most Western histories refer to the land as Persia and the people as Persians throughout most of Iran's history.

By 550 BC the Persians, led by Cyrus the Great, conquered the Medes. Cyrus established the Achaemenid Empire, and he and his successors extended it over what is now known as Iran and as far as the Mediterranean coast of North Africa, Egypt, Palestine, Phoenicia, Asia Minor, areas of southeastern Europe, Armenia, Syria, Mesopotamia, Afghanistan and to the Indus river in what is now Pakistan. The religion of the Persians was Zoroastrianism, based on the prophet Zoroaster's teachings about a supreme god called Ahura Mazda, or "the wise spirit." The Persian's greatest city, Persepolis, was built *circa* 500 BC by Darius I, who established himself as the Achaemenid "King of Kings," ruling over his provinces, or satrapies, through his princes, or satraps. Darius' forces invaded Greece in 490 BC and were defeated by the Athenians at Marathon. His son, Xerxes, sent forces that defeated the Spartans at Thermopylae in 480 BC, but his forces lost subsequent battles and were driven from southeastern Europe in the following year. The empire then began a long decline, and was finally conquered by the Macedonian Alexander the Great, whose Macedonian and Greek forces defeated the Persians in the Battle of Arbela, or Gaugamela, east of the Tigris river, in 331 BC.[1]

After Alexander's death, his general Seleucid established the Seleucid dynasty in about 313 BC, and it ruled Persia and carried out Alexander's vision of bringing Greek culture to Persia during the next century. In 250 BC, the Parthians, from southeast of the Caspian Sea, took control over Persia. By 235 BC, they began expanding and establishing the Arsacid Parthian Empire, which stretched from southwest Asia to Asia Minor. They fought numerous wars against the Romans in the west, defeating forces under Marc Antony of the Roman Republic in 36 BC, and losing to the forces of the Emperor Trajan of the Roman Empire in AD 116. They also fought wars against the Kushans in the east, in what is now Afghanistan, Pakistan, and northwestern India. After four hundred years, the Parthians were overthrown in AD 224 by a Persian, Ardashir, who established the Sassanid dynasty, which restored Persian rule over Persia, and ruled for another four hundred years. The Sassanids continued to fight the Kushans. They also continued to fight with the Roman Empire, taking Mesopotamia and Syria from them in the early decades of their rule, and continuing to fight wars after the Roman Emperor Constantine I accepted Christianity in the AD 300s. In about AD 550, Sassanid forces had marched as far as Constantinople, the capital of the East Roman Empire, or Byzantine Empire, where they were defeated, leading to their retreat toward Persia. The Sassanid dynasty finally fell when Arab armies following Islam, the new monotheistic religion revealed by the Prophet Muhammad and worshipping Allah, invaded Persia in AD 637, defeating Persian forces at the decisive Battle of Nehavend in AD 642, and converting its people to the new religion.

Persia then splintered into numerous principalities governed for centuries by Arab Muslim rulers, or caliphs. Upon the death of the fourth caliph, Ali, who was Muhammad's son-in-law, there was a succession struggle that divided Islam into two major sects, Sunnism and Shiism. The Shias, many of them Persians, insisted that rightful rule could only be exercised by the descendants of Ali. They resisted the Umayyad dynasty of caliphs that began ruling from Damascus in AD 660, who were accepted by Sunnis. When Ali's son Husayn was defeated at the Battle of Karbala in AD 680 by the Umayyad Caliph Yazid I, it was a political victory for Sunnis, but Shias have commemorated Husayn as a martyr and revered him as an imam, a spiritual leader endowed with the highest understanding of Allah, until this day. Shia belief also gives tremendous importance to the Twelfth Imam, Muhammad al-Mahdi, also known as the Mahdi, or the Guided One, and as the Hidden Imam. Shia Islam holds that Allah took the Twelfth Imam into hiding in AD 939 and that he will someday return to usher in an era of justice until the second coming of Jesus, and the Day of Judgment, and the end of the world.[2]

The Umayyad caliphate ruled from AD 660 to 749, and the Abbasid caliphate then ruled from AD 750 until 1258 from their capital in Baghdad. But the Abbasid caliphate soon began to decay and in the mid-900s a Persian Shia dynasty, the Buwayids, ruled as viceroys in Baghdad, thus ruling over Persia from 945 until 1055. The Seljuks, who were Central Asian Turkmen from Turkestan, or what is now Turkmenistan and Uzbekistan, and who were also Sunnis, then exercised real power as sultans under the Abbasid caliphs from 1055 until 1194, thus ruling over Persia. They were followed briefly by other Turkmen tribes. In 1217, Genghis Khan's Mongol tribal armies, from what is now Mongolia, Manchuria, and Siberia, invaded Persia, destroying many of its cities, and later overthrowing the Abbasids in Baghdad in 1258. The Mongol Empire's actual rule over Persia was brief, with Persia invaded and ruled again in the late 1300s by the Mongol Turkman Tamerlane, from Turkestan. Mongols and Turkmen fought among themselves in Persia during most of the 1400s.

A new era began in 1501, when the Safavids, an Azeri Turkish tribe from the northwestern area called Azerbaijan, defeated the Mongols and established a dynasty that ruled Persia for two hundred years, beginning with the rule of Shah Ismail Safavi.[3] Shah Ismail established Shia Islam as the official state religion, and it was during this era that Shiism actually spread throughout Persia and became the dominant sect. As it developed, political authority was wielded by the shahs, while religious authority resided in the Shia clerics who instructed the faithful. Shah Ismail fostered Shiism in part because of his faith and in part to consolidate an empire that could counter the strength of the Sunni Turkmen tribes in Central Asia and the Sunni Mughal Empire in India as well as the Sunni Ottoman Turks to the west. The Ottoman Turks had overthrown the Byzantine Empire in 1453 and established the Ottoman Empire in 1517. They ruled over Anatolia, or what is today Turkey, and the Arab world, and their capital Constantinople was the seat of the Sunni Islamic caliphate. During the first years of Shah Ismail's rule, Portuguese naval explorers began to enter the Persian Gulf and establish control over its commerce, ushering in an era when Europeans were the real powers in the Gulf. Shah Abbas Safavi, who ruled from 1587 until 1629, and who established Isfahan as his capital, thwarted invasions by the Ottoman Empire and also thwarted advances by Turkmen tribes from Central Asia. Even with the help of the British East India Company's naval fleet, however, he was not able to drive the Portuguese from the Gulf, although Arab tribes from Oman succeeded. This was followed, however, by Dutch, French, and British penetration of the Gulf.

In 1722, Sunni tribes from Afghanistan invaded and overthrew the Safavids. In the 1730s, Nadir Shah, a Sunni Turkman tribesman from Persia's northeastern province of Khorasan, drove the Afghans from Persia and conquered Afghanistan. He also invaded India, capturing Delhi in 1739. He also made expeditions in the Gulf, seizing Bahrain in 1736 and briefly establishing garrisons elsewhere along the Arab coast and as far as Muscat on the Oman coast until Arab tribes and fleets and the mutinies of his own forces, many of them Arab sailors, drove him out. He was assassinated in 1747 by his own aides. In that same year, his Afghan general Ahmad Shah established Afghanistan's independence. Persia was ruled briefly by Nasir Khan in the 1750s and by Karim Khan Zand, from the Kurdish Zand tribe, from 1757 until 1779. Both of them tried to establish Persian control along the Persian coast, but Arab tribes from the Arab coast of the Gulf competed and eventually established their own rule in numerous ports along the Persian coast. From the death of Karim Khan Zand in 1779 until 1794, there was a struggle for control of Persia between the Kurdish Zand tribe and the Qajars, a Turkmen tribe that had converted to Shia Islam and settled in the region south of the Caspian Sea. The Qajars prevailed over the Zands and established the Qajar dynasty in 1794, establishing their capital in Tehran. They would rule Persia until 1925.

Throughout the 1800s and much of the 1900s, Persia's fate was shaped by the competition among European powers for influence in the region. In the early 1800s, the British, who controlled the commerce of their empire in India, were also establishing their naval predominance in the Persian Gulf and their predominance over the commerce and trade of the Gulf region, including Persia. The British were determined to thwart competition from Napoleonic France, and the Qajar Shah, Fath Ali, was concerned about Tsarist Russian expansion south toward the Caucasus. Thus, in 1800, Britain and Persia concluded the Malcolm Treaty of Alliance, in which the Shah agreed to exclude France from commercial activity in Persia and Britain agreed to protect Persia against foreign aggression. When Shah Fath Ali sensed British ambivalence about upholding its agreement, he sought an alliance with France in the Treaty of Finkelstein, but he lost confidence in it when Napoleon and Tsar Alexander I began to reconcile their differences. Britain, recognizing the possibility of a Franco-Russian invasion of India, and wanting to prevent Russian expansion south through Persia in the direction of the Gulf and India, quickly negotiated a Treaty of Alliance with Persia in 1805. When Napoleon invaded Russia in 1812, however, Britain was primarily concerned about French advances. Britain, therefore, attempted to reconcile with Russia and did not protect Persia against Russian territorial demands. Thus, in 1813, in the Treaty of Gulistan, Persia ceded its territory in the Caucasus, including Baku, to Russia, and recognized Russian dominance in the Caspian Sea. When Napoleon's invasion failed and British concerns subsided, Britain negotiated a new alliance with Persia in the Treaty of Tehran in 1814. Nevertheless, when Russia invaded Persia in 1826, Britain acquiesced, and Persia ceded its territory north of the Aras river to Russia in the Treaty of Turkomanchai in 1828.[4]

After losing this territory in the Caucasus, Persia made unsuccessful attempts in the 1830s to recapture its lost territories in northwestern Afghanistan, and Russia assisted Persia because it would mean further movement toward the British Empire in India. When Persia, under Shah Nasr ed-Din, finally captured the strategic fortress of Herat in northwest Afghanistan in 1856, Britain declared war on Persia. British naval forces landed at several ports on the Persian coast of the Persian Gulf, where Persia did not exercise real authority, and compelled Persia to withdraw from Afghanistan and recognize Afghanistan's independence in the 1857 Anglo-Persian Treaty of Paris.

In the following decades, Russia expanded throughout Central Asia. Moreover, from the late 1860s on, Russia expanded in Transcaspian areas claimed by Persia, taking control of what is now Turkmenistan and establishing another boundary with Persia along the Atrek river in 1881. Russia's advances led Britain to maintain Afghanistan as a buffer to protect the British Empire in India, and this led to the negotiations of boundary agreements with Russia and Afghanistan's other neighbors. Britain and Persia reached agreement on the Persian-Afghan boundary in 1892.

In the meantime, British efforts to expand their growing commercial dominance of the Persian Gulf region throughout all of Persia seemed successful when in 1872 Baron Julius de Reuter secured an economic concession from Shah Nasr ed-Din, which included the right to build a railroad connecting the Persian Gulf with the Caspian Sea. Russia's displeasure with this agreement, and Russia's steady military advances, led the Shah to cancel this agreement in 1873. Reuter appealed to the British government, and after years of negotiation, Persia agreed to new economic concessions to Britain in 1889. One established the Imperial Bank of Persia and the other established the Imperial Tobacco Company of Persia. Russia also demanded and secured economic concessions to establish a bank and to build a railroad in Persia's northwest province of Azerbaijan. Russia also fanned a popular boycott of tobacco, leading to the cancellation of that concession and the payment of financial damages to the British concessionaires. Russia also extended loans to Persia, obtaining Persian customs revenues and increased political influence in return. Nevertheless, in 1901, Persia granted an oil concession to an Australian, William Knox D'Arcy, covering all of Persia except for the five provinces along the northern border with Russia. In the meantime, from the late 1880s on, Persia attempted to expand its authority to its coast along the Persian Gulf, and along the Arab coast as well, and over various islands in the Gulf, in part to assert more authority over trade in the Gulf. When Persia acquired two warships from Germany in 1885, Persia began to gain the naval capability to do this. In response, the British undertook to thwart Persian efforts along the Arab coast and to assert the historical claims of Arab tribes to islands in the Gulf throughout the late 1800s and early 1900s.

In 1906 and 1907, popular demands for reform, led in part by Persia's merchant class, often called the bazaar, led Shah Mozaffer-ed Din to accept a constitution, establishing a parliament, or Majlis, and limiting royal authority. Britain favored this, but Russia regarded it as a threat. In 1907, Britain and Russia, both concerned about the rise of Imperial Germany, reached the Anglo-Russian agreement, in which Britain recognized a Russian sphere of influence in Persia's northern provinces and central regions, including the capital Tehran, Russia recognized a British sphere of influence in Persia's southeastern provinces of Sistan and Baluchistan, and both recognized Persia's southwest as a neutral zone. Russia then encouraged the new Shah, Mohammed Ali, to abrogate the new constitution in 1908. Domestic opposition forces, encouraged by Britain, and led by the Bakhtiari tribe from the south, marched on Tehran and overthrew the Shah in 1909. His son, Sultan Ahmed Mirza, a minor, assumed power and the constitution was restored. In the meantime, in 1908, oil was discovered in Persia's southwest province of Khuzistan, in the neutral zone, and the Anglo-Persian Oil Company was established to exploit this oil. In 1914, on the eve of World War I, the British Admiralty acquired the controlling share of the company, which provided much of their oil supplies.

The growing influence of Britain and Russia in their country in the years before the outbreak of World War I alarmed Persians. They began to see a relationship with Imperial Germany as a means of containing British and Russian influence. Persia professed official neutrality, but in 1915, Germany secured a secret alliance with Persia's prime minister, agreeing to guarantee Persia's independence and territorial integrity and to provide Persia with funds and arms. Germany also established relations with Persia's Swedish-officered Gendarmerie Corps and Persia's armed ethnic tribes in an effort to promote a revolt against Russian and British interests, and in particular to sabotage the Anglo-Persian Oil Company. Russian troops in Persia's northern provinces threatened to march on Tehran, and the government prepared to move from Tehran to Isfahan, but the British and Russians persuaded Shah Ahmed to stay and his cabinet stayed with him. Pro-German members of parliament left, set up a rival government in the west in Kermanshah, and entered an alliance with Germany by the end of 1915. Their acceptance of some Turkish forces of the Ottoman Empire, an ally of Germany but a traditional rival of Persia, undermined their popularity.

In light of these developments, British military forces from Mesopotamia were sent to guard the Anglo-Persian Oil Company's interests in Persia's southwest and a British military mission landed at the Persian Gulf port of Bandar Abbas, organized a local force called the South Persia Rifles, and marched into the interior fighting and defeating German-influenced gendarmerie and ethnic tribes. Persia's Russian-officered Cossack Brigade also moved south to Isfahan to meet with them. German influence in southern and central Persia was thus effectively defeated by 1917. In Persia's east, Britain and Russia had established the East Persia Cordon to prevent the war from spreading into Afghanistan, but a German-Ottoman mission successfully eluded British and Russian capture and crossed Persia into Afghanistan, where by 1916 they ultimately failed to rally the emir to any real action. In Persia's northwest province of Azerbaijan, a largely Turkish-speaking province, Ottoman Turkish and Russian forces battled each other throughout the war, with the Ottomans advancing in 1918 in the wake of the Russian Revolution and the desertions in the Russian forces.

At the end of World War I, British troops were stationed throughout Persia. Britain saw Persia as a buffer between the new Soviet Union and the British Empire in India, made sure that Persia was not included at the Paris Peace Conference in 1919, and insisted on an Anglo-Persian treaty in 1919 that would essentially make Persia a protectorate of Britain. When the Majlis was unwilling to ratify the treaty, however, Britain was not willing to impose it by force and began withdrawing its troops from Persia in 1920. Meanwhile, even after communist Soviet Red forces chasing counterrevolutionary White forces landed on Persia's Caspian Sea coast and helped local forces establish the Soviet Republic of Gilan inside Persia in 1920, the Soviet Union was still able to secure a treaty of friendship with Persia in February 1921. In this treaty, the Soviet Union renounced all privileges and concessions Tsarist Russia had obtained in Persia, but secured the right to send Soviet forces into Persia if it became a base for foreign aggression, for example, British aggression, against the Soviet Union. One week before this was signed, an officer in Persia's Cossack Brigade, Reza Khan, who had dismissed the brigade's Russian officers and replaced them with British officers, marched on Tehran and seized power in a coup. When British forces then withdrew from Persia in April 1921, the Soviets also withdrew their forces from Gilan in October. A Persian military expedition then toppled the Soviet Republic of Gilan in 1922 and restored Persian control there.

By 1923, Reza Khan became prime minister and forced Shah Ahmed to leave the country. In 1925 Reza Khan became Shah Reza Pahlavi, replacing the weak Qajar dynasty, beginning a new Pahlavi dynasty, and eventually restoring the name Iran as the official name of the country in 1936. He sought to liberate Iran from British and Soviet influence, to establish Iran's independence and control over its territory, and to develop Iran's economy, and believed that establishing a strong central government buttressed by strong armed forces and a modern civil bureaucracy was the best means to do so. Under Shah Reza, Iran's Majlis was a weak institution, Iran's liberal intellectuals and conservative clergy were sidelined, and Iran's communists were imprisoned or forced underground. He built an army that asserted his control over ethnic and tribal areas in Gilan, Azerbaijan, Kurdistan, and oil-rich Arab Khuzistan. He also built a navy that asserted his control over Iran's coast along the Persian Gulf, numerous islands in the Gulf, and taxes on trade through Iran's Gulf ports. He developed Iran's infrastructure of transportation and communications, particularly the construction of the Trans-Iranian Railway that linked the Caspian Sea and the Persian Gulf. He established the National Bank of Iran and promoted industrial development and foreign trade. He introduced socioeconomic reforms, including the French judicial system, secular education, and the unveiling of women, all of which challenged the traditional influence and role of the Shia clergy. In 1936, he officially named the country Iran, rejecting the Greek term Persia.

In Iran's relations with its neighbors, Shah Reza entered into a treaty of friendship in 1926 with Afghanistan, an independent state composed of many ethnic tribes and led by a reform-minded emir. He also entered into a treaty of friendship with the new modernizing secular republic of Turkey under Kemal Ataturk, which had replaced the defeated Ottoman Empire after World War I. He then resolved boundary disputes with Turkey along Iran's northwest borders in 1932. In 1937, he entered into the Saadabad Pact, an agreement calling for nonaggression and cooperation with Afghanistan, Turkey, and Iraq. Iraq had emerged into eventual independence under the Arab Hashemite dynasty from the ruins of the former Ottoman Empire.

Iran's relations with the major world powers were more difficult. Shah Reza alienated the Soviet Union by attempting unsuccessfully to grant oil concessions in Iran's northern provinces to British and American firms, despite a prohibition in the 1921 friendship treaty with the Soviet Union from granting concessions renounced by the Soviets to any other country. The Soviets successfully used the importance of their import-export trade with Iran to press for advantages in fishing rights in the Caspian Sea. Shah Reza also had numerous disagreements with Britain. Iran renounced the special legal immunities, or "capitulations," granted to British subjects in Iran, and Iran denied British air flights over its Persian Gulf coast to India. In 1928, however, Iran granted some legal protections to British residents and allowed Britain's Imperial Airways the right to fly over Iran's Persian Gulf coast. Iran also asserted claims to Bahrain as well as Abu Musa and the Tunbs, islands in the Persian Gulf that were ruled by Arabs who had entered into protection treaties with the British in the late 1800s, and Britain insisted on defending the Arab rule over these islands. In 1932, Iran cancelled the AIOC's (Anglo-Iranian Oil Company) concession, demanding a greater share of the company's profits, but after the dispatch of British warships and submission of the case to the League of Nations, Britain and Iran reached a bilateral agreement in 1933. This agreement provided Iran with more profits and provided Britain with an additional sixty-year commitment from Iran. As part of his effort to reduce the influence of the Soviet Union and Britain in Iran, Shah Reza forged relations with their competitor Germany. German advisers played a significant role in the development of Iran's economic infrastructure, and Germany became a major foreign trade partner of Iran. When Adolf Hitler came to power in 1933, these economic relations increased and diplomatic relations stressed the common Aryan character of the German and Iranian nations.

When World War II began in 1939, Iran again professed neutrality, but was pro-German and even increased its trade with Nazi Germany, which had entered into the Hitler-Stalin Pact with the Soviet Union in 1939. When Germany invaded the Soviet Union in 1941, however, Britain and the Soviet Union became allies, and they both saw Iran and its Trans-Iranian Railway as the best transit route for providing British and allied war supplies to the Soviet Union. When Iran refused their request to expel the German advisers who could have sabotaged this supply effort, British and Soviet troops invaded Iran, with Soviet troops occupying the northern provinces and British troops occupying the rest of the country. Britain and the Soviet Union forced Shah Reza to abdicate, his son Mohammad Reza became the new shah, a pro-Allied cabinet was installed, and Iran entered into a Tripartite Treaty of Alliance with Britain and the Soviet Union, with both foreign powers promising to withdraw their forces from Iran within six months of the end of the war. After the United States entered the war in late 1941, it sent noncombatant forces to Iran to oversee the provision of lend-lease supplies to the Soviet Union and to Iran as well. Once again, hoping to counter British and Soviet influence, Iran invited American advisers to help Iran reorganize its finances, economy, army, police, and health care.

During their wartime occupation of northern Iran, the Soviets supported the reemergence of the Iranian Communist Party, the Tudeh Party, or the "Masses" Party. The Soviets also promoted the idea of a separatist Azerbaijan and supported Kurdish tribes as well. British forces guaranteed the continued operation of the AIOC in the southwest, and Britain supported a nationalist party, Eradeye Melli, or "National Will," to counter the Tudeh Party. U.S. President Franklin D. Roosevelt, while meeting in Tehran with British Prime Minister Winston Churchill and Soviet Premier Josef Stalin in December 1943, secured their agreement to release a communiqué, expressing their "desire for the maintenance of the independence, sovereignty, and territorial integrity of Iran," but neither Britain nor the United States effectively resisted the activities in northern Iran of their wartime ally the Soviets. In 1944, the Soviets demanded an oil concession to cover the northern provinces, and Britain and the United States were seeking oil concessions in the southeast. The United States accepted the Iranian prime minister's opposition to new concessions, but Soviet complaints and pressure led to the resignation of the prime minister. During this episode, a nationalist leader, Dr. Muhammad Mossadeq, led the Majlis in passing a law demanding parliamentary approval of all foreign oil concessions, and this was a harbinger of what Iran's postwar oil policy would be. Iran was about to embark on another effort to limit foreign influence over its affairs.

NOTES

1. For a multivolume series on Iran's history, see W. B. Fisher, ed., *The Cambridge History of Iran* (Cambridge: Cambridge University Press, 1968).

2. For a recent study of Shia Islam, see Vali Nasr, *The Shia Revival: How Conflicts within Islam Will Shape the Future* (New York and London: W.W. Norton and Company, 2007).

3. For an account of Iran's foreign policy over the following four hundred years, see Rouhollah K. Ramazani, *The Foreign Policy of Iran: A Developing Nation in World Affairs, 1500–1941* (Charlottesville: The University Press of Virginia, 1966).

4. For additional accounts of this period, see George Lenczowski, *The Middle East in World Affairs,* 4th ed. (Ithaca and London: Cornell University Press, 1980).

CHAPTER 2

Iran under Shah Mohammad Reza Pahlavi

Shah Mohammad Reza Pahlavi was a fundamentally pro-Western leader who played a role in safeguarding Western interests in the Middle East, but he did have grievances regarding the history of foreign, including Western, intervention in Iran. This had included the Anglo-Russian rivalry over Iran in the nineteenth and twentieth centuries, culminating in the Anglo-Russian occupation of Iran during World War II and the forced abdication of his pro-German father by these British and Soviet occupation forces in 1941. He clearly resented Soviet occupation and pressure, was intent on resisting it, and saw his ties with Western powers as the key to achieving this. But he also resented what he saw as inequitable arrangements obtained by British and other Western governments and business firms in Iran and insufficient Western financial and military assistance to Iran. Thus, he became determined to assert what he considered Iran's rights and interests in its foreign relations and to establish Iran as an independent actor and a dominant power in the region. Like his father, he sought to limit Soviet and British influence, to obtain support from a third party, in this case the United States, to consolidate his power, to modernize Iran, and to turn Iran into an independent regional power.[1]

In 1941, when he succeeded his father, Shah Mohammad Reza Pahlavi was a reigning constitutional monarch, but not a fully ruling monarch. Iran was occupied, the conservative Shia clergy reemerged to challenge his father's secular judicial reforms, diverse tribal and ethnic groups had separatist ambitions, and the Tudeh Party worked with the occupying Soviet Red Army to promote communist goals. In December 1945, soon after World War II ended, the Tudeh worked with the Soviet Red Army to establish the Autonomous Republic of Azerbaijan. Soon thereafter Kurdish tribal and national figures established an independent Kurdish Republic with assistance from the Red Army. Soviet forces failed to abide by their obligation to withdraw from Iran within six months of the end of the war, i.e., in March 1946, until the Soviet Union had secured numerous concessions from Iran's prime minister. In particular, the Soviets insisted that Iran establish a joint Soviet-Iranian oil company to operate in the north, with a 51 percent interest for the Soviet Union and a 49 percent interest for Iran, and that Iran's prime minister name three Tudeh members to his cabinet. When Soviet forces did withdraw, in May 1946, after warnings from the United States, Iran gradually extricated itself from these concessions, the prime minister first dismissing the Tudeh cabinet ministers, then sending armed forces into Azerbaijan to topple the Tudeh regime there in December 1946, and finally with the parliament refusing to ratify the Soviet-Iranian oil agreement in October 1947. The Soviet Union hinted about sending its armed forces back into the north, used its radio outlets to appeal to Azerbaijanis and Kurds to break away from Iran, and boycotted Iranian exports. When an alleged Tudeh member attempted to assassinate the Shah in February 1949, Iran outlawed the party, declared martial law, and clashed with Soviet forces that crossed the border into Iran. As diplomatic and economic relations with the Soviet Union deteriorated, the Shah sought aid and assurances from the United States in order to counter Soviet pressure. He received modest military and economic assistance that he considered wholly inadequate, but did secure from President Truman a statement of a U.S. "desire for the maintenance of the independence and territorial integrity of Iran."[2]

In the early 1950s, Iran remained a constitutional monarchy where the parliament wielded real power. In March 1951, Iran's parliament, dominated by the nationalistic Dr. Muhammad Mossadeq and his National Front party, nationalized the British government-owned AIOC. This company had earned 200 million British pounds in profits in 1950 as opposed to £16 million in revenue for Iran, and had offered Iran only an additional £4 million when Iran had sought a new profit-sharing agreement. The nationalization of AIOC initially made Mossadegh a national hero, as it was an assertion of national independence and promised dramatically increased revenues. The Shah, who had been willing to accept AIOC's offer, reluctantly accepted Mossadeq as prime minister. AIOC shut down production and marketing of Iranian oil and pressed successfully for an international embargo of Iranian oil and this eventually led to Iran severing diplomatic relations with Britain in October 1952. This crisis led to the loss of Iran's leading role in oil production and export as Saudi Arabia, Kuwait, and Iraq emerged as major producers and competitors. It caused economic hardship in Iran, enabled the Tudeh Party to reemerge, and generated opposition to Mossadeq in the religious clergy and in his own National Front. As Mossadeq's support in the parliament eroded, he dissolved the body. Encouraged by Britain and the United States, the Shah then attempted to dismiss Mossadeq. When he refused and had the military detachment accompanying the Shah's emissary disarmed, the Shah left the country. Pro-Shah forces in the military directed by General Fazlollah Zahedi then quickly overthrew Mossadeq and restored the Shah to power in March 1953, in an operation that was planned and orchestrated by the British intelligence agency MI6 and the CIA.[3]

Iran secured a new international oil agreement that guaranteed Iran 50 percent of the profits of the extraction, refining, and marketing operations of a consortium of eight companies that replaced the AIOC, an agreement negotiated largely by the U.S. State Department. By 1965, Iran's annual revenue from oil exports reached $500 million. Iran also secured over $800 million in economic assistance and over $800 million in military assistance from the United States from the end of this crisis in 1953 until 1966. With the increased oil revenues and the U.S. aid, with aid from other Western powers, and with the support of Iran's military and security services, including its domestic intelligence apparatus, called SAVAK (National Organization for Information and Security), the Shah spent the following years thwarting Soviet subversion and pressure and consolidating power at the expense of the parliament. He transformed himself from a reigning to a ruling monarch, indeed an authoritarian monarch. By 1961, he dissolved the parliament; he brought it back in 1963 as a powerless institution. By early 1963, he introduced a socioeconomic reform movement called the White Revolution, which included a land reform program that reduced the land holdings of the landed aristocracy, thus reducing the socioeconomic base of their political power. Other elements of this reform program were the spread of literacy and the emancipation of women. As he was consolidating his authoritarian power and establishing these relations with the United States and introducing these reforms, however, the clergy was organizing itself as the major source of political opposition to his rule, which the clergy saw as a secular and tyrannical challenge to Shia Islam.[4]

The Shah's authoritarian rule and his relations with the United States and other Western powers, particularly Israel, were denounced by Ayatollah Ruhollah Khomeini. Indeed, by 1963 Khomeini's opposition to the Shah and his call for the army to overthrow the Shah led the Shah to warn the clergy against interference in politics. The Shah subsequently arrested Khomeini, leading to violent demonstrations that the Shah's security forces subdued with force and with casualties. Khomeini was deported and spent most of the next fourteen years in Najaf, a center of Shia study in southern Iraq, where he wrote and lectured about the importance of Islamic government and continued his criticisms of the Shah.[5]

Given the pressures Iran faced from the Soviet Union, with which Iran shared a 2000-kilometer border, and given the role that the United States and Britain had played in restoring the Shah to power and could play in financing Iran's economy and military and in containing the Soviet Union, it is not surprising that in 1955 Iran joined Britain, Turkey, Iraq, and Pakistan in a defense pact called the Baghdad Pact. Later that year, however, Egypt under President Nasser, who had overthrown the Egyptian monarchy in 1952, signed an arms deal with the Soviet-satellite state of Czechoslovakia, thus allowing the Soviet Union to advance its influence into the Arab world, a development that concerned the Shah greatly. He was also concerned about Afghanistan obtaining weapons from the Soviet Union in that same year. In 1959, Iran obtained a bilateral defense agreement with the United States and also joined Turkey, Pakistan, and Britain in the U.S.-sponsored CENTO (Central Treaty Organization). This was a defense pact that replaced the Baghdad Pact after the 1958 revolution in which radical pan-Arab military officers overthrew Iraq's Hashemite monarchy, precipitating Iraq's withdrawal from the Baghdad Pact, Iraq's entering into numerous agreements with Soviet bloc countries, and Iraq's development as a growing challenge to Iran.[6] As the Shah later explained, "If a country fails to secure its defenses, the communists play with it as a cat does with a mouse. During the Azerbaijan crisis, and again in Mossadegh's time, we Persians found ourselves in the unhappy role of the mouse. We resolved never again to be so unprotected."[7]

By the early and mid-1960s, however, the Shah was becoming more dissatisfied with U.S. economic and military assistance and embarked on what he called an "independent foreign policy," even normalizing relations with the Soviet Union. In 1962 he assured the Soviets that Iran would not permit Western missile bases to be established in Iran. In the mid-1960s, Iran signed numerous economic agreements with the Soviets. One of these agreements was for the joint construction of a pipeline to transport gas from Khuzistan in Iran's southwest to the Soviet Union. In 1966 and 1967, Iran purchased rifles, machine guns, trucks, armored personnel carriers, and antiaircraft guns from the Soviets. In part, this was an attempt to pressure Britain and the United States to be more forthcoming with military and economic support. And in part this was an attempt to reduce Soviet pressures in order to devote more attention to his ambitions in the Gulf. But he remained a strategic ally of the West and purchased most of his major weapons systems from the West once the West was willing to make the deals. He negotiated the purchase of two squadrons of F-4 Phantom jet fighter aircraft and other weapons to be financed by $250 million in loans from the United States in November 1967, one of many agreements with the United States and Britain over the next decade by which he modernized his military with purchases of jet fighters, air-to-air missiles, SAMs (surface-to-air missiles), tanks, a variety of naval vessels including hovercraft and other amphibious craft, patrol craft, fast attack craft, frigates, destroyers, and maritime patrol aircraft, as well as surface-to-surface missiles and helicopters.[8]

One of the Shah's most important foreign policy objectives was to establish Iranian dominance in the Persian Gulf. When the British announced in 1968 that Britain would withdraw its military forces from the Gulf in 1971, the Shah rejected a U.S. proposal for a joint defense scheme for the Gulf involving

CENTO and other external countries. He expressed only tepid interest in regional defense cooperation between Iran and the Arab Gulf states, thinking that Saudi Arabia and the smaller Arab emirates were not developed or secure enough to make an important contribution. He set out to make Iran the principal power in the Gulf and to discourage the establishment of any U.S. or Soviet military bases inside the Gulf as the British were withdrawing.[9]

Thus, the Shah's military programs in the late 1960s were designed in part to prepare for Britain's withdrawal from the Gulf. By the early 1970s, Iran had the region's most modern military and was the only littoral state that had a significant naval force in the Gulf. Iran's navy had bases at Bushire and Bandar Abbas, conducted military exercises in the waters of the Gulf with the air force and the army, and patrolled the waters and islands along Iran's long coastline, as well as much of the Gulf of Oman and the Indian Ocean.[10] The Shah's determination to assert Iran's military power in the Gulf and the Strait of Hormuz and on islands along the shipping lanes was certainly for defense of Iran's coast and mainland, and also because this was the principal outlet for Iran's oil and gas exports and also a major outlet for the oil exports of the Arab states of the Gulf. He was concerned that if islands along the shipping lanes were seized by unfriendly forces, they could use them as bases for disrupting shipping.[11]

It should be noted here that in addition to the Shah's strategic interests in the Gulf, he also wanted to assert Iran's claims to the oil resources in Gulf waters.[12] The international embargo of Iranian oil in the early 1950s, following the Iranian parliament's nationalization of AIOC, had allowed other producers and exporters of oil to emerge as major competitors to Iran. Thus, in 1959, Iran announced that its claim to the territorial sea off its coast and around islands under its sovereignty would be extended to twelve miles in order to extend its claim to potential offshore oil deposits in these areas. Then, during the 1960s, Iran negotiated median line agreements with Saudi Arabia and several other Gulf Arab states, agreements that demarcated the waters in which Iran and these other states would control islands and oil resources. By the mid-1960s, Iran's oil revenues of $500 million per year constituted 50 percent of the government's roughly $1 billion annual revenues, and Iran's oil concessions in the Gulf accounted for more than ten percent of Iran's oil production.[13]

The Shah had been concerned about radical pan-Arab nationalism and Soviet support for it since the 1950s. This ideology was championed by Egypt's President Nasser, who had overthrown the monarchy in 1952. He had acquired weapons from the Soviet bloc after 1955, intervened in North Yemen's 1962–67 civil war to support republican forces fighting royalist forces, and asserted the Arab character of the Gulf. It was also espoused by Iraq's Premier Abdul Karim Kassem, who had overthrown the monarchy in 1958, and his successors. Iraq now also acquired weapons from the Soviet bloc, asserted a claim to Iran's oil rich southwestern province of Khuzestan, which Iraq called Arabistan because of the Arab population there, challenged Iran's interests in the Arvand Rud water-way separating the two countries, which Arabs call the Shatt al-Arab waterway, and also asserted the Arab character of the Gulf.[14] This concern helps explain Iran's relations with Israel and with the conservative Arab states, and it helps explain Iran's policies in the Persian Gulf.

Iran had voted against the 1947 UN General Assembly Resolution recommending a partition of Palestine and the establishment of a Jewish state and a Palestinian state, believing that the establishment of a fully independent Jewish state would result in long-term Arab-Israeli conflict, but Iran eventually gave quiet *de facto* recognition to Israel after it won its independence in 1948. The Shah's desire to counter Nasser and other radical pan-Arab leaders in Iraq and elsewhere and their Soviet patrons was one reason for the Shah's willingness to develop quiet relations with Israel in the 1950s and 1960s. After the 1956 crisis over the Suez Canal, when Nasser's Egypt took control of this vital artery of world commerce, Iran helped finance the construction of an oil pipeline from Israel's port of Eilat on the Gulf of Aqaba to Ashkelon on Israel's Mediterranean coast. This provided Iran with an alternate route to ship its oil from the Persian Gulf to the Mediterranean Sea and lessened Iran's reliance on passage through Egypt's Suez Canal. It also facilitated Iranian oil sales to Israel. In 1965, Iran agreed to co-operate with Israel in providing funds, training, and arms to Iraqi Kurds fighting Iraqi government forces. This enabled the Shah to tie Iraqi forces down in their own north and to therefore deflect their challenge to Iran while he pursued his ambitions in the Gulf. In addition, the Shah saw his relationship with Israel as a means of cultivating the good will of the United States.[15]

As for the conservative Arab states, the Shah supported the royalist forces in North Yemen against the republican forces supported by Nasser's Egypt in the mid-1960s. Saudi Arabia, the largest of the conservative Arab states, was also able to support North Yemen's royalist forces. In this case, North Yemen was situated near the Bab el-Mandeb Strait, another strategic waterway for Iran. Once Iran's oil shipments passed through the Persian Gulf and the Strait of Hormuz, they headed for the Bab el-Mandeb Strait, which they passed through on their way into the Red Sea and then on toward the Mediterranean. During those same years, the Shah feared that the conservative small Arab shaikhdoms, or emirates, under British protection along the Arab coast of the Persian Gulf were also vulnerable either to Nasser's pan-Arab ideology or to aggressive subversion by him. Indeed, the Shah even considered Saudi Arabia vulnerable to this threat. Thus, the Shah viewed Nasser's withdrawal from North Yemen as critical.[16]

His concern about Nasser subsided, however, after Egypt's defeat by Israel in the 1967 war, when Israel captured Egypt's Sinai peninsula and Syria's Golan Heights, and also captured Palestinian East Jerusalem and the West Bank from Jordan and the Palestinian Gaza Strip from Egypt. Egypt's preoccupation with regaining the Sinai, and the Shah's expressions of support for Arab recovery of the Sinai and the other territories lost in this war, as called for in UNSC Resolution 242 of 1967, as well as the Shah's expressions of support for a Palestinian national home, led to Egypt's subsequent withdrawal from North Yemen and from Gulf affairs and bolstered the Shah's position in the Gulf. The Shah's concerns about Iraq were about to grow, however, as the radical pan-Arab Baath Party seized control of that state in 1968 and developed even closer ties with the Soviet Union, including periodic visits by Soviet naval vessels to Iraq's port of Umm al-Qasr. In addition, he was concerned about the growth of the PLO (Palestine Liberation Organization) and its support from the Soviet Union, and he complained that some of his domestic opponents received training in PLO camps. These concerns added to the Shah's conviction that Israel's occupation of Arab territories radicalized the Arab world and offered new opportunities for the Soviet Union, and he privately argued to Israel and to the United States that Israel should return these territories. Nevertheless, the Shah and Israel, both viewing Iraq as a threat, maintained their cooperative relations.[17]

The Shah's demand for the islands of Abu Musa and the Tunbs was one of the most contentious issues in the Gulf as Britain was planning its withdrawal from 1968 to 1971.[18] These islands lie along the strategic shipping lanes just to the west of the Strait of Hormuz in the Persian Gulf. As noted, the Shah stressed the strategic importance of these islands in protecting the sea-lanes and the threat that would be posed to the sea-lanes if radical forces were to seize these islands. This was a genuine concern, but not the only reason for demanding these islands from the emirates of Sharjah and Ras al-Khaimah. Indeed, Iran's Prime Ministers Hussein Ala and Asadollah Alam told the British in the 1950s and 1960s that Iran was interested in the islands because of the potential oil fields around them. In addition, the Shah also claimed that the islands had been the historic possessions of Iran, but that Britain had "seized" them late in the nineteenth century and claimed them for the emirates of Sharjah and Ras al-Khaimah. This was not a historically accurate assertion. He demanded that Britain "restore" Iranian control over the islands, he dismissed Arab arguments that the islands were the rightful possessions of Sharjah and Ras al-Khaimah, and he threatened to take the islands by force and to withhold diplomatic recognition of the Arab emirates that would be attaining independence after the British withdrawal if his demands were not met. The Shah also told the British that he had to obtain the islands because he would lose some domestic credibility if he agreed to Britain's request that he give up Iran's claim to Bahrain.[19]

In fact, the Shah was willing to abandon his claim to Bahrain and was using this as a bargaining chip to obtain British cooperation and Arab acquiescence in obtaining the islands for Iran. The Shah did yield Iran's claim to Bahrain and accepted the results of the April 1970 referendum in which Bahrainis chose to be an independent Arab state. He was dissatisfied with British efforts to find a compromise on the islands after his decision on Bahrain, and he threatened

to take them by force, as he had earlier, but after more than a year, British media-
tion did help Iran obtain a Memorandum of Understanding with Sharjah on Abu
Musa, which permitted Iranian forces to occupy the northern half of the island in
November 1971. When British mediation with Ras al-Khaimah did not succeed,
Iran's military forces occupied the Tunbs by force in the same month. The Shah
then granted official recognition to the new UAE (United Arab Emirates) in
December 1971.[20]

The Shah was also concerned that an insurgency in Oman's southwestern province of Dhofar could expand throughout the Gulf region. This insurgency was
supported by the PDRY (People's Democratic Republic of Yemen), i.e., South
Yemen, a Marxist-Leninist government that had come to power soon after the
British had withdrawn from South Yemen's port of Aden in 1967. This rebellion
was also supported by Baathist Iraq, which had growing ambitions in the Gulf, as
well as by the Soviet Union, the PRC (People's Republic of China), East Germany,
and even Fidel Castro's Cuba. The PDRY and the rebels, first known as the
Popular Front for the Liberation of the Occupied Arabian Gulf and later as the
PFLOAG (Popular Front for the Liberation of Oman and the Arab Gulf), had
stated their intention to "liberate" the small Arab Gulf emirates under British
protection. The Shah was concerned that the PDRY and the PFLOAG were the
kinds of subversive forces that might seize the emirates and the islands along the
shipping lanes and interfere with oil traffic, and he was concerned that Saudi
Arabia was vulnerable as well. The Shah's deployment of helicopter crews,
a combat brigade, and air force assets to Oman and his diplomatic efforts between
1973 and 1978, along with Saudi financial assistance, were decisive in helping
Oman subdue the rebellion in Dhofar and in cutting off its foreign support from
Iraq and others.[21]

The Shah was also concerned not only about the growing presence of the
Soviet navy in the Persian Gulf in the late 1960s and early 1970s, including
increasing Soviet naval visits to Iraqi ports as well as increasing Soviet arms
supplies to Iraq, but also about the growing Soviet naval presence in the Gulf
of Oman and in the Indian Ocean. His efforts to develop Iran's defenses from
the north of the Gulf through the lower Gulf and the Strait of Hormuz and
out into the Gulf of Oman and then into the Indian Ocean were intended to
counter this threat. Indeed, he began construction of a port at Chah Bahar
on Iran's coastline on the Gulf of Oman and planned for it to accommodate
Spruance-class destroyers he sought from the United States.[22]

Moreover, the Shah's concern about the Soviet-Indian Treaty of Friendship in
1971 and Soviet and Indian support for the independence of East Pakistan, or
Bangladesh, led the Shah to increase his financial assistance and military support
to his ally and India's rival Pakistan. His relations with India later improved, and
he even granted economic assistance to India in the mid-1970s, when it proved
to be neutral and not a client of the Soviet Union.[23] He was also concerned that

Afghanistan would ally with the Soviet Union and pose a threat to Pakistan, particularly after the royalist government of Afghanistan was overthrown in 1973 and replaced by a republic. He was relieved when the new government in Afghanistan followed a neutral course, and he extended economic aid to it, but was concerned again in 1978 when a Marxist coup brought a new government and new Soviet influence to Afghanistan.[24] He was also concerned that Soviet access to naval facilities at the port of Berbera in Somalia and then the Marxist coup in Ethiopia in 1974 offered the Soviets the opportunity to secure a foothold in the Horn of Africa, from which they could interfere with Iran's oil shipments. Indeed, when Somalia ejected the Soviets from Berbera in 1977 and the Soviets and Cubans poured military support into Ethiopia, he provided military support to Somalia.[25]

The Shah's control of the sea-lanes of the Gulf, his relations with conservative Arab states, and his concerns about radical pan-Arab states aligned with the Soviets influenced his policies during the October 1973 Arab-Israeli war, when Egypt and Syria launched a coordinated surprise attack against Israeli forces occupying Egypt's Sinai and Syria's Golan Heights, and when Israel regrouped and pushed Egyptian and Syrian forces back. He was pleased that Egypt's new president, Anwar Sadat, had expelled Soviet military advisers in 1972 and he did not want an Israeli victory that could enable the Soviets to reestablish these relations with Egypt or to strengthen the relations it already had with Syria, a pan-Arab Baathist state under Hafez Assad. Thus, he provided Egypt with emergency oil deliveries, transported Saudi forces to Syria, and allowed Soviet civilian aircraft to fly over Iran to deliver spare parts to the Arabs. But he did not want an Arab victory that would enable radical pan-Arab forces and their Soviet patrons to devote more of their energy to challenging Iran. Thus, he did not allow the Soviets to fly over Iran to deliver military equipment to Iraq, he did not cut oil supplies to Israel or join the Arab oil embargo against Israel's supporters, and he did supply Israel with some arms, including heavy mortars. Finally, he did not want a war that led to Soviet and American intervention and conflict in the region, and this was avoided. In the aftermath of the war, he continued to argue to the Israelis and to the United States that retention of the occupied territories could not provide Israel with security and that it should return them in exchange for recognition from the Arabs and international guarantees of its 1967 borders. Moreover, he argued that not only Palestinian national aspirations should be satisfied but also the PLO should be involved in Arab-Israeli negotiations.[26]

As the Shah became more powerful, he became more assertive. In early 1973, the Shah negotiated a new agreement with the international oil consortium that had been established in the early 1950s by which Iran established its full ownership of its oil industry and the consortium became only a service company. By late 1973, when major Arab oil producers implemented production cutbacks and embargoes to punish Western supporters of Israel during the October 1973 war, the Shah did not join them. Instead, he took advantage of the resulting reduced world oil supply to join with Venezuela to press the OPEC (Organization of Petroleum Exporting Countries) to set higher oil prices, resulting in the quadrupling of the price of a barrel of oil from about $3 per barrel in January 1973 to about $12 per barrel in December 1973. Despite supporting the political aims of the Arabs vis-à-vis Israel, the Shah seized this opportunity to greatly increase Iran's revenues. Indeed, when the major Arab oil exporters ended their production cutbacks and embargoes, they also reaped these higher revenues engineered by the Shah. Moreover, the Shah also made loans to Arab states that were not major oil producers, particularly Egypt, Jordan, and Syria. Despite being pro-Western, the Shah forced Western consumers of oil to pay the dramatically increased prices. Iran's revenue from oil exports thus grew from $1 billion in 1970 to $4 billion in 1973 to $20 billion in 1975. But Iran and the Arab oil producers now imported more from the West, in effect "recycling petrodollars." Indeed, the Shah entered into a $15 billion trade agreement with the United States in March 1975. Perhaps the most noteworthy aspect of this agreement was that the United States undertook to build eight nuclear reactors in Iran. The Shah had also signed a development agreement with France in 1974 which included a French commitment to build five nuclear reactors in Iran. He also signed an agreement with Germany for another nuclear reactor and the German firm Siemens began building it in Bushire.[27]

The Shah argued that Iran would use these nuclear reactors for civilian purposes, i.e., to produce electric power, but Akbar Etemad, who was the director of Iran's nuclear program under the Shah, has said that the Shah wanted the capability to develop nuclear weapons relatively quickly if Iran's regional competitors were doing so, and former Foreign Minister Ardeshir Zahedi has also said this.[28]

In 1975, with the Shah at the height of his powers and with Baathist Iraq fighting a difficult battle against Kurdish separatists supported by the Shah and the Israelis, the Shah negotiated a series of agreements that limited Iraq's influence in the region. He reached agreement with then Iraqi Vice President Saddam Hussein about the demarcation of the Iran-Iraq boundary along the Arvand Rud/Shatt al-Arab waterway in the March 1975 Algiers Accord. This agreement represented a concession by Iraq, which acknowledged the middle of the navigable channel, the thalweg, as the border, thus giving Iran increased use of the waterway. Iraq also agreed to accept the *status quo* in the Gulf and to end its support for the rebellion in Dhofar. In return, Iran agreed to end its support for the Kurdish separatists in Iraq, which thus denied Israel the ability to get its support to the Kurds, and which enabled Iraq to suppress the Kurds for the time being. As would be seen only a few years later, however, Iraq resented this concession on the Shatt al-Arab and sought to redress it when the Shah was removed from power in 1979.[29]

In early 1977, as Baathist Iraq was increasing its arms purchases from the Soviet Union, including the acquisition of Scud ballistic missiles, the Shah's request for U.S. Pershing ballistic missiles was denied by the new Carter administration, which was concerned about the potential for these missiles to carry nuclear warheads. This decision contributed to the Shah's concern that the Carter administration would not be a strong ally in deterring Soviet pressures. The Shah then entered into numerous arms-for-oil deals with Israel's Labor government. One of these deals involved a guaranteed supply of Iranian oil for Israel in return for Israeli modification of an Israeli surface-to-surface missile for Iran. This modification would extend the range of the missile and also replace American parts with Israeli parts so that U.S. permission for the arms transfer would not be necessary.[30]

In June 1977, when the Likud Bloc defeated the Labor Alignment for control of Israel's government, the Shah was alarmed that Likud's intention to build many new Jewish settlements in the West Bank would further radicalize the Arab world and provide further opportunities for the Soviets in the region. He supported Sadat's November 1977 visit to Israel and offer of peace, criticized Israel's subsequent negotiating positions, warned Israeli leaders about the prospects of Soviet support for another Arab-Israeli war, and argued that the Israelis should embrace Sadat's initiative. Nevertheless, he was concerned enough about the threats from Soviet-backed Baathist Iraq and from the Soviet Union itself to go forward with oil-for-arms deals with Israel in 1978. Israel even began construction of a missile assembly facility and a missile test site in Iran that would give Iran the ability to indigenously produce and test its own ballistic missiles and perhaps the possibility in the future to equip these missiles with nuclear warheads. Iran and Israel were careful not to reveal this activity to the United States.[31]

At the same time, however, in 1977 and 1978, the Shah faced a growing domestic opposition encompassing Shia clerics, former National Front leaders, merchants, intellectuals, unions, Tudeh Party followers, and many others. Resentments over the Shah's intolerance for political opposition and over the inequities and corruption associated with his rapid military modernization and industrial development converged. Cassette tape recordings of the exiled Ayatollah Khomeini's denunciations of the Shah were circulating in Iran's bazaars. The Shah alternately responded with tentative liberalization measures and displays of brutal military repression with many attendant casualties, but he could not subdue massive demonstrations and strikes throughout the country. He and his family left Iran in January 1979, never to return.[32]

THE MAJOR POWERS' POLICIES TOWARD THE SHAH'S IRAN

During World War II, British and Soviet troops occupied Iran because it was the most practical transit route for supplying the Soviet Union, an ally against

Nazi Germany, with weapons and other necessary supplies. The United States also sent noncombatant forces for this purpose. When the war ended, British and U.S. forces withdrew, but Soviet forces did not. The Soviet Union sought to develop long-term influence over Iran by supporting communist ethnic Azeris who established the Autonomous Republic of Azerbaijan and by supporting tribal leaders who established the independent Kurdish Republic, and by pressuring the government in Tehran to grant economic and political concessions to the Soviet Union.

The major objectives of U.S. foreign policy in the Middle East during the post–World War II era were to contain the expansion of the Soviet Union, maintain access to the oil resources of the region for the United States and its allies, and support Israel. President Truman viewed the Soviet Union as a direct threat to Iran and Turkey and to the region's oil resources and as an indirect threat to Greece. His private warning to the Soviets in 1946 that he was willing to use U.S. forces to resist the continuing presence of Soviet troops in Iran influenced the Soviet decision to withdraw them, and his administration's encouragement helped Iran dismantle the Soviet-supported republics in Azerbaijan and Kurdistan and repudiate the Soviet-Iranian oil concession. It can be noted here that the United States was the only state that possessed nuclear weapons at this time, giving Truman's warnings to the Soviet Union considerable weight. The Truman Doctrine, announced in March 1947, established a general policy of containment of the Soviet Union that was followed by all successive administrations until the dissolution of the Soviet Union in 1991.[33]

Britain was so weakened by World War II that it had informed the United States in February 1947 that it could no longer financially support Turkey and Greece, and later in the year, it turned the contentious issue of Palestine over to the United Nations and also relinquished its empire in India, accepting the independence of India and Pakistan. Nevertheless, Britain maintained its military, economic, and political presence in the Persian Gulf, ensured the flow of the region's oil to Western markets, and played a supporting role in U.S. efforts to contain Soviet advances in the Middle East.

The Truman and Eisenhower administrations were concerned about Iran's nationalization of AIOC in 1951 and the crisis that ensued. The United States initially encouraged Britain and Iran to negotiate a revised agreement, but Britain sought to protect its investment and was not willing to offer generous terms, and certainly not the 50–50 profit sharing agreements that American oil firms were negotiating in other countries. When this effort failed, when Iran nationalized the AIOC, and when Britain called for an international embargo of Iranian oil, American oil companies and the United States supported the embargo, thinking that Iran's nationalization of AIOC could establish a precedent that would lead to other countries nationalizing American oil companies. The British and the United States were also concerned that the ensuing crisis, and perhaps Mossadeq himself, could present the Tudeh Party, which now resurfaced, and the Soviet Union, which now had nuclear weapons and which supported Iran's nationalization as a blow against Western capitalist imperialism, with an opportunity to become the predominant powers in Iran. The British sought unsuccessfully to overthrow Mossadeq through their MI6 intelligence agency and finally persuaded the Eisenhower administration, which took office in January 1953, to authorize the CIA to instigate and lead Mossadeq's many domestic opponents in overthrowing him and restoring the Shah to power in August 1953, a covert mission called Operation Ajax. Britain and the United States were satisfied that they had safeguarded their economic and strategic interests. The United States even negotiated the creation of a new consortium in which American oil companies now participated, finally opening the Iranian oil industry to American firms.[34]

The modest U.S. economic and military assistance during the years of the Eisenhower, Kennedy, and Johnson administrations from 1953 through the mid-1960s, as well as U.S. sponsorship of CENTO and the U.S. bilateral defense agreement with Iran, were intended to shore up the ability of Iran to resist Soviet pressure and radical pan-Arab pressure and to foster closer commercial relations with Iran. While the Soviet Union protested these arrangements and offered its own economic and military assistance to the Shah, some of which he accepted in the mid-1960s, Soviet pressure was effectively contained. One legacy of U.S. intervention in 1953 and the subsequent U.S. economic and military support for the Shah, however, was a lingering resentment among many Iranians that was not anticipated by the United States and that would later undermine the U.S. position there. And Israel, which also saw Iran as a bulwark against the Soviets and pan-Arab adversaries as well as a check against conservative Arab adversaries, which shared intelligence about these threats with Iran, which received most of its oil supplies from Iran, which assisted along with the CIA in the training of the Shah's SAVAK, and which frequently and unsuccessfully sought official *de jure* recognition from Iran, would also later learn how deeply it was resented.

In January 1968, Britain's Labor government informed the United States that Britain planned to withdraw from the Gulf. Despite their competition for trade and investment opportunities in the Gulf region, successive U.S. administrations thought that the British military and political presence protected oil exports and conservative regimes against radical pan-Arab and Soviet threats. Therefore, President Lyndon Johnson asked Britain to maintain its military bases in the Gulf and to postpone its withdrawal.[35] The United States had maintained a small naval and air presence in Bahrain since 1949, and U.S. destroyers made occasional visits.[36] But the Johnson administration did not want the United States to assume the British role in the Gulf, in large part because the United States was involved in a costly and unpopular war in Vietnam. The administration proposed security groupings including Iran, Turkey, and Pakistan, which with

Britain were members of the U.S.-sponsored CENTO, as well as Kuwait and Saudi Arabia, for the post-British period, but Iran rejected this. Before long, the United States and Britain agreed that both would provide weapons and training primarily to Iran and secondarily to Saudi Arabia to enable these two Gulf states to defend themselves and to promote stability and Western interests in the region, a policy that became known as the "twin pillar" policy.[37]

For the Soviet Union, the British withdrawal decision signaled a desirable reduction of Western capitalist imperialist influence in Iran and the Gulf and an opportunity for the Soviet Union to increase its presence in the Gulf.[38] Only two months later, on May 12, Soviet naval vessels visited the Iraqi port of Umm al-Qasr, demonstrating the Soviet interest in increasing its influence in the Gulf region as the British prepared for their withdrawal.[39]

The United States and Britain were concerned about the May 1968 visit to the Gulf and to Iraq by Soviet naval vessels. When the Shah visited President Johnson in June 1968 to seek U.S. military sales to Iran, a joint communiqué noted that the President would continue to cooperate with the Shah's efforts to build a modern military to ensure the national security of Iran. Soon after the Shah's June 1968 visit, the United States began to deliver the F-4 Phantom jet fighters it had agreed to sell in November 1967.[40]

A year later, on July 25, 1969, U.S. President Richard Nixon announced the Nixon Doctrine, which called upon the U.S.'s Asian friends to assume more responsibility for their own defense. The United States would provide military and economic assistance, but would expect these countries to provide most of the manpower for their defense. In the case of South Vietnam, the major focus of this doctrine, this would be called "Vietnamization." The Nixon Doctrine would also be applied in the Gulf, where the administration now planned for Iran to play a key role in defending itself and the West's interests.[41] After the Shah's October 1969 visit to Washington, the United States and Britain agreed to a $1 billion defense program in which the United States would sell additional Phantoms and Britain would sell tanks and naval vessels to Iran.[42]

When Britain's Conservative Party took power in June 1970, they criticized the Labor Party's decision to withdraw from the Gulf. In the end, however, the Conservative policy on withdrawal would be the same as the Labor policy. In November 1970, the British, the United States, and Iran conducted joint naval exercises in the northern Gulf of Oman, to the east of the Strait of Hormuz. These exercises demonstrated the continuing British interest and the growing U.S. interest in the Persian Gulf, the Gulf of Oman, and the Indian Ocean, particularly in light of the increasing Soviet naval visits to these waters and the growing involvement of the Soviet Union throughout this region. Moreover, the PRC was interested in competing with the Soviet Union for influence in the region. These exercises also demonstrated that Britain and the United States were actively working with Iran to help prepare it to play its regional defense role after Britain's withdrawal.[43] Then on March 1, 1971, much to the Shah's satisfaction, Foreign Secretary Sir Alec Douglas-Home announced that British military forces would leave the Gulf by the end of the year, although Britain expected its navy to make regular calls at Gulf ports, expected its air force to retain its staging and overflight rights, and would offer friendship treaties and military training to the small emirates that would now see their protection treaties with Britain come to an end.[44]

In the meantime, President Nixon had decided late in 1970 to authorize additional military sales to Iran and Saudi Arabia.[45] U.S. arms sales to Iran's air force, army, and navy increased dramatically in 1971 and 1972. In February 1973, the administration concluded a $2 billion arms deal with Iran. Among other weapons systems, U.S. sales to Iran during the 1970s included F-5 and F-14 jet fighter aircraft.[46] The British also signed a £100 million contract for the sale of Chieftain tanks to Iran in May 1971 and Iran ordered more in 1975.[47]

When Britain did withdraw from the Gulf on December 1, 1971, it believed that it had made satisfactory arrangements for stability in the area and cooperation between Iran and the Arab states, and the United States agreed. Britain had assured the independence of Bahrain and its admission to the United Nations. It had supported the independence of Qatar and its admission to the United Nations as well. It had also assured the establishment of a federation of Arab emirates called the UAE, which was also admitted to the United Nations. Inasmuch as the Shah had consented to these developments, and inasmuch as Britain was not willing to use force to stop the Shah from seizing Abu Musa and the Tunbs, Britain's special emissary Sir William Luce attempted to mediate compromises on the status of these islands. He successfully mediated a compromise between Iran and Sharjah enabling the Shah to land forces on the northern half of Abu Musa. When Luce's mediation did not produce a compromise between Iran and Ras al-Khaimah, Britain acquiesced in the use of force by the Shah to seize the Tunbs. This British policy on these islands was a reversal of over a hundred years of British policy of asserting and defending the rights of Sharjah and Ras al-Khaimah to the islands against Persian and Iranian claims, and it thus constituted a stark recognition of the Shah's regional importance.[48]

Saudi Arabia and other conservative states of the Gulf, as well as Jordan and even Egypt, which was ruled by Sadat and was no longer in the radical pan-Arab camp, were uneasy about the Shah's power in the Gulf but acquiesced to his role, because they did think that Iran was a bulwark against the radical pan-Arab nationalists and the Soviets, which they also opposed. Saudi Arabia and the other conservative Arab states were generally satisfied with the outcomes in Bahrain, Qatar, and the UAE, and reluctantly acquiesced to the outcome on the islands, although the UAE sought to redress this. The radical pan-Arab states of Iraq, Libya, Algeria, and the PDRY, however, argued that Iran's ambitions in the Gulf were "imperialistic" and "expansionist" and that it would use its naval power and its occupation of the Tunbs and Abu Musa to interfere with Arab shipping through the Gulf and the Strait of Hormuz and to intervene in Oman and suppress the Dhofar revolution. Kuwait, a conservative Arab state, also expressed some concern, in part out of fear of Iraqi pressure.[49]

After the British withdrawal, the United States increased its support for Iran. In May 1972, President Nixon visited Tehran after his summit meeting in Moscow with Premier Leonid Brezhnev. The United States and the Soviet Union were establishing a détente that would enable both of them to contend with the rising PRC. One month earlier, however, in April 1972, the Soviet Union and Baathist Iraq had signed a fifteen-year treaty of cooperation. At the end of Nixon's May 1972 visit with the Shah, the United States and Iran issued a joint communiqué which said that the Gulf states had the primary responsibility for the security of the Gulf and that the United States would continue to cooperate with Iran in strengthening its defenses. Indeed, despite his interest in American-Soviet détente, Nixon agreed to the Shah's request for F-14 and F-15 fighter aircraft and also agreed to approve virtually all future Iranian requests for nonnuclear weapons. These aircraft would provide Iran with the capability to engage Soviet MiG fighters and to cope with the Iraqi challenge. Furthermore, Nixon agreed to provide financial support to the Iranian and Israeli efforts to aid Kurdish rebels in Iraq because it presented pro-Soviet Iraq with a challenge that would continue to divert its energies from the Gulf and Israel.[50] Moreover, the Nixon administration sold Iran an electronic surveillance system that allowed Iran to listen to the communications of its neighbors, including the Soviet Union, which had important military facilities within Iran's range. These and other military systems sold to Iran during the 1970s also required the United States to provide thousands of American military and civilian personnel for maintaining these systems and training Iranians to use them, thus giving the United States a significant supporting role within Iran. As noted previously, the Nixon administration would also approve substantial arms sales to Saudi Arabia, and this also entailed many American personnel in Saudi Arabia.[51]

The Nixon administration and the British also urged Iran and Saudi Arabia to cooperate and coordinate particularly in supporting Oman and the Yemen Arab Republic, i.e., North Yemen, against challenges from the PDRY, i.e., South Yemen, as well as Baathist Iraq, the Soviet Union, and others, particularly because the Nixon administration understood that Saudi Arabia was concerned about Iran's domination of the Gulf and was uncomfortable with Iranian military forces in Oman. While the United States and Britain were somewhat disappointed with the extent of Saudi-Iranian cooperation in the 1970s, they were pleased that Saudi financial contributions, Iranian military deployments, Iranian and Saudi diplomatic efforts, and the Sultan of Oman's domestic reforms helped to defeat the Dhofar rebellion, secure the regime in Oman, and deny the Soviets and the Chinese bases and influence in Oman.[52] On the other hand, the United States and Israel were disturbed that the Shah had ended his support for the Kurdish rebels fighting Saddam Hussein's regime in northern Iraq as part of the Algiers Accord in 1975, and the United States appealed to him to continue his support.[53]

It would later become clear, however, that Britain, the United States, Israel, and others had chosen to rely on the Shah's regional assistance and had acquiesced to his regional ambitions without fully understanding Iran's domestic politics. The Shah's Iran was also a candidate for domestic upheaval, and would later be overthrown and replaced by an Islamic regime that would pose a threat to the West, including a threat to shipping. Some of the West's leading scholars wrote that pressures for broader political participation in modernizing societies was a dilemma for modernizing monarchs, and some identified the growing professional middle class in Iran as a dissatisfied force, but few anticipated in the late 1960s and early 1970s that a revolution inspired by Iran's Shia clerics could overthrow the Shah's regime.[54]

In light of the Shah's role in promoting security in the region, the United States, Britain, and other Western powers acquiesced in the Shah's assertiveness on oil issues. The quadrupling of the price of a barrel of oil in late 1973 was reflected in substantially higher prices for Western consumers, painfully evident at gas stations around the United States, western Europe, and Japan, and the Nixon administration did duly protest to the Shah. At the same time, however, the Nixon administration and its successor, the Ford administration, which took over when Nixon resigned in August 1974, recognized that the United States could vigorously promote its exports to the oil producing countries and earn the dollars back, or "recycle petrodollars." More major arms sales to Iran, and the major trade deals, including the $15 billion U.S.-Iran trade agreement in 1975, which included the provision of nuclear reactors, were made with this in mind. British, French, and German deals with Iran were also made with this in mind.[55] It could even be noted here that the United States, France, and Germany did not question why a country as rich in oil and gas as Iran was would want to acquire nuclear reactors to produce electric power for civilian purposes and did not express concern that Iran might use this technology to develop nuclear weapons.

Moreover, the Shah's security role in the region led Israel to a grudging acceptance of the Shah's positions on the Arab-Israeli conflict after the 1967 war and the 1973 war. These positions frustrated Israeli leaders, but their view of the Shah's importance in deflecting Arab energies away from Israel led them to make serious efforts to maintain relations with him. Israel's Likud leaders even made efforts in 1977 and 1978 to persuade the Shah that they were open to negotiations on all issues, except that they would not negotiate with the PLO or accept what they called the establishment of a PLO state, although in fact they were committed to retention of the West Bank. They were even willing to supply the Shah with sophisticated weapons in 1978 despite his positions on the conflict.[56]

President Jimmy Carter and his administration were somewhat ambivalent about Iran under the Shah when they took office in 1977. Carter was an advocate of promoting human rights as a major objective of U.S. foreign policy and was dismayed that the Shah's intolerance for domestic political opposition resulted in human rights abuses. This concern was shared in particular by Secretary of State Cyrus Vance and many State Department officials. Yet Carter was impressed with the rapid economic development the Shah had promoted and the important strategic role the Shah played in the region. These views were shared in particular by the National Security Council and the Department of Defense. As domestic opposition to the Shah mounted in 1978, the Carter administration was handicapped by a lack of good intelligence about the opposition. The CIA, which relied on SAVAK more than its own limited contacts with the opposition in obtaining intelligence, reported in August 1978 that "Iran is not in a revolutionary or even a pre-revolutionary situation."[57] As the opposition did turn into a revolution, the U.S. Embassy in Tehran underestimated its significance in reports to Washington until almost the end.[58]

For all of these reasons, the Carter administration's policy was ambivalent. Carter called on the Shah to respect human rights and to introduce liberal reforms during 1977 and continued to do so as the revolution gained strength in 1978, urging the Shah to reach an accommodation with his opponents, and Carter was supported in this by Secretary of State Vance. This may have encouraged the Shah's opponents. Yet Carter also lent support to the Shah, even after the Shah's security forces had fired live ammunition on the rebelling population, causing considerable casualties, and Carter was supported in this by National Security Adviser Zbigniew Brzezinski and Secretary of Defense Harold Brown. This enraged the Shah's opponents. Brzezinski's interest in maintaining the Shah's rule was based in part on his concern that the Soviet Union would expand its influence into an unstable post-Shah Iran. The Soviet interest in the success of the revolution was demonstrated in a warning from Brezhnev to Carter in November not to interfere in Iran.[59]

In the final months of 1978, U.S. Ambassador to Iran William Sullivan and former Undersecretary of State George Ball recommended that the administration should negotiate with opposition leaders, including Khomeini, who they considered a moderate, and to consider calling on the Shah to transfer power to the opposition or abdicate. The White House rejected this, but when the Shah named the liberal opposition figure Shahpour Bakhtiar to be his prime minister, Carter sent General Robert Huyser to Iran to try to somehow ensure that Iran's military would be loyal to Bakhtiar if the Shah left the country. Then, the administration did call on the Shah to leave the country. When the Shah did leave, on January 16, 1979, after establishing a regency council to undertake his responsibilities, Bakhtiar could not retain power or the loyalty of the military in the face of Khomeini's return and establishment of an alternative government headed by Mehdi Bazargan. At that point, the Carter administration recognized the Bazargan government and began to conduct official relations with it.[60]

In the end, the Shah was swept from power by revolutionary forces led by Ayatollah Khomeini. The United States and other Western powers lost a strategic ally and would be faced with a new regime that soon posed a threat to their interests in the region. Given the nature and the strength of the opposition to the Shah in 1978 and 1979, there may have been no U.S. policy that could have prevented the revolution at that late date.

NOTES

1. See, for example, Lenczowski, *Middle East in World Affairs,* 181–82, 187–90, 200–1, 214–19.

2. Ibid., 182–84, 187–88.

3. See Mark Gasiorowski and Malcolm Byrne, eds., *Mohammad Mosaddeq and the 1953 Coup in Iran* (Syracuse, New York: Syracuse University Press, 2004). See also Ray Takeyh, *Hidden Iran: Paradox and Power in the Islamic Republic* (New York: Henry Holt and Company, 2006), 85–95. For an account by the top American CIA agent involved in this covert operation, see Kermit Roosevelt, *Countercoup: The Struggle for the Control of Iran* (New York: McGraw-Hill, 1979).

4. Robert Graham, *Iran: The Illusion of Power* (New York: St. Martin's Press, 1979).

5. Hamid Algar, "The Oppositional Role of the Ulama in Twentieth Century Iran," in *Scholars, Saints, and Sufis: Muslim Religious Institutions since 1500,* ed. Nikki Keddie (Berkeley, Los Angeles and London: University of California Press, 1972).

6. Lenczowski, *Middle East,* 200–3.

7. Mohammad Reza Shah Pahlavi, *Mission for My Country* (New York: McGraw-Hill, 1961).

8. For a summary of these various purchases and acquisitions, see Alvin J. Cottrell, "Iran's Armed Forces under the Pahlavi Dynasty," in *Iran Under the Pahlavis,* ed. George Lenczowski (Stanford, CA: Hoover Institution Press, 1978), 403, 407–13, 418–29.

9. For a comprehensive study of Iran's role in the Gulf region, see Thomas R. Mattair, *The Three Occupied UAE Islands: The Tunbs and Abu Musa* (Abu Dhabi: The Emirates Center for Strategic Studies and Research, 2005). See also Shahram Chubin and Sepehr Zabih, *The Foreign Relations of Iran: A Developing State in a Zone of Great-Power Conflict* (Berkeley: University of California Press, 1974), chap. 7. See also J.B. Kelly, *Arabia, the Gulf and the West* (USA: Basic Books, 1980), 54.

10. Again see Cottrell, "Iran's Armed Forces," 403, 407–13, 418–29.

11. See, for example, Rouhollah K. Ramazani, *The Persian Gulf: Iran's Role* (Charlottesville: University Press of Virginia, 1972), 89; Ramazani, *Iran's Foreign Policy, 1941–1973* (Charlottesville: University Press of Virginia, 1975), esp. 427; Ramazani, *The Persian Gulf and the Strait of Hormuz* (Alphen aan den Rijn: Sijthoff and Noordhoff, 1979), 72–75; Lenczowski, *Middle East,* 657; James Noyes, *The Clouded Lens: Persian Gulf Security and US Policy* (Stanford, CA: Hoover Institution Press, 1982), 18.

12. See, for example, Kelly, *Arabia,* 89.

13. Muhammad Morsy Abdullah, *The United Arab Emirates: A Modern History* (London: Hurtwood Press, 1994), 275.

14. Lenczowski, *Middle East,* 201.

15. Trita Parsi, *Treacherous Alliance: The Secret Dealings of Israel, Iran, and the United States* (New Haven and London: Yale University Press, 2007), 23, 53–54.

16. Lenczowski, *Middle East,* 632.

17. Ramazani, *Iran's Foreign Policy,* 404–6, 420–23; Abdullah, *United Arab Emirates,* 277–78; Parsi, *Treacherous Alliance,* 31, 33–34.

18. See Mattair, *Three Occupied UAE Islands.*

19. Ibid., esp. chaps. 3 and 9.

20. Ibid.

21. See Lenczowski, *Middle East,* 221–22. See also Noyes, *Clouded Lens,* 21, 37, 42, 69, 98.

22. See Ramazani, *Iran's Foreign Policy,* 348–52, 427–30, 435–38.

23. Graham, *Illusion of Power,* 64.

24. Lenczowski, *Middle East,* 219.

25. Ibid., 732–34.

26. Parsi, *Treacherous Alliance,* 44–48, 51–52, 70–71.

27. Lenczowski, *Middle East,* 218.

28. See Takeyh, *Hidden Iran,* 136.

29. Lenczowski, *Middle East,* 220–21.

30. See Parsi, *Treacherous Alliance,* 68–78.

31. See Ibid., 68–78, for a full account of this story. Some of the elements were reported in the *New York Times,* April 1, 1986.

32. For the Shah's account of his rule and of this revolution, see Mohammad Reza Pahlavi, *Answer to History* (New York: Stein and Day, 1980).

33. George Lenczowski, *American Presidents and the Middle East* (Durham, NC and London: Duke University Press, 1990), 7–21.

34. Ibid., 32–40. See also Gasiorowski and Byrne, *Mohammad Mosaddeq and the 1953 Coup in Iran.* See also Takeyh, *Hidden Iran,* 85–95. See also Roosevelt, *Countercoup.*

35. For a comprehensive study of the British withdrawal from the Gulf, see Mattair, *Three Occupied UAE Islands,* esp. chaps. 3, 9, and 10. See also Joseph Twinam, *The Gulf, Cooperation, and the Council: An American Perspective* (Washington DC: The Middle East Policy Council, 1992), 87; F. Gregory Gause, "British and American Policies in the Persian Gulf, 1968–1973," in *Review of International Studies* (Cambridge: Cambridge University Press, 1985), 258–59; and Glen Balfour-Paul, *The End of Empire in the Middle East: Britain's Relinquishment of Power in Her Last Three Arab Dependencies* (Cambridge, UK: Cambridge University Press, 1991).

36. Noyes, *Clouded Lens,* 55, 57–59; Twinam, *The Gulf,* 92–96. This was called MIDEASTFOR and consisted of a transport flagship and a C-131 transport aircraft.

37. Noyes, *Clouded Lens,* 56–57; Twinam, *The Gulf,* 88 and see footnote; Ramazani, *Iran's Foreign Policy,* 409–10; Chubin and Zabih, *Foreign Relations of Iran,* 237.

38. Ramazani, *Persian Gulf,* 105.

39. Chubin and Zabih, *Foreign Relations of Iran,* 72–74, 262–66. See also Mark N. Katz, *Russia and Arabia: Soviet Foreign Policy Toward the Arabian Peninsula* (Baltimore and London: The Johns Hopkins University Press, 1986), 178.

40. Ramazani, *Iran's Foreign Policy,* 363–65, and Cottrell, "Iran's Armed Forces."

41. Lenczowski, *American Presidents,* 116–19, 184; Noyes, *Clouded Lens,* 120–21.

42. Ramazani, *Iran's Foreign Policy,* 365–67.

43. Kelly, *Arabia,* 79, 83; Noyes, *Clouded Lens,* 59; Cottrell, "Iran's Armed Forces," 403.

44. Kelly, *Arabia,* 90–91.

45. Twinam, *The Gulf,* 87–88; Noyes, *Clouded Lens,* 55–58.

46. Ramazani, *Iran's Foreign Policy,* 367–69; Lenczowski, *Middle East,* 218; Cottrell, "Iran's Armed Forces," 418–27.

47. Kelly, *Arabia,* 92–93. See also Cottrell, "Iran's Armed Forces," 419.

48. Mattair, *Three Occupied UAE Islands,* chaps. 3, 9, and 10.

49. Ibid., chap. 7.

50. Ramazani, *Iran's Foreign Policy,* 356, 370. Lenczowski, *American Presidents,* 118–19. Parsi, *Treacherous Alliance,* 53–54.

51. Graham, *Illusion of Power,* 172. Noyes, *Clouded Lens,* 87.

52. Mattair, *Three Occupied UAE Islands,* 403–6.

53. Parsi, *Treacherous Alliance,* 54–58.

54. See Samuel Huntington, *Political Order in Changing Societies* (New Haven and London: Yale University Press, 1968), for a discussion of "the King's Dilemma." See James A. Bill, "The Patterns of Elite Politics in Iran," in *Political Elites in the Middle East,* ed. George Lenczowski (Washington DC: American Enterprise Institute, 1975), for a discussion of the professional middle class. See Nikki R. Keddie, "The Roots of the Ulama's Power in Modern Iran," in *Scholars, Saints, and Sufis,* esp. 229, for an assessment of the clergy.

55. Lenczowski, *Middle East,* 213–15.

56. Parsi, *Treacherous Alliance,* 72–78.

57. Lenczowski, *American Presidents,* 192, provides this quotation from Carter's memoirs.

58. Ibid., 185–92. For a comprehensive study, see Gary Sick, *All Fall Down: America's Tragic Encounter with Iran* (New York: Penguin Books, 1986). Sick was the top Iran officer at the National Security Council during this crisis.

59. Lenczowski, *American Presidents,* 193–96; Sick, *All Fall Down.*

60. Lenczowski, *American Presidents,* 194–99; Sick, *All Fall Down.*

CHAPTER 3

The Foreign Policy of the Islamic Republic of Iran

THE KHOMEINI YEARS

After coming to power in 1979, the clerical leaders of the Islamic Republic of Iran conducted a foreign policy very different from that of the Shah. Their policy toward the two superpowers was a policy of independence and nonalignment, called "neither East nor West." Most importantly, they challenged the United States, other major Western powers, their Arab allies, and Israel, who they saw as the "oppressors" of the world. Islamic Iran also saw the Soviet Union as an oppressor, but was not intent on confronting it directly. Islamic Iran sought to promote its version of Islamic government, or to "export the revolution," to the conservative family-ruled Gulf Arab Muslim states aligned with the West and to Lebanon, but it did not actively seek to export its revolution to the Muslim republics of the Soviet Union or to the secular, radical Arab Muslim states aligned with the Soviets and opposed to Israel, with the exception of Iraq.

The leaders of the Islamic Republic of Iran came to power with serious grievances regarding the history of foreign intervention in the area, particularly the history of U.S. and British policy toward Iran. This included the international embargo of Iranian oil after Iran nationalized the AIOC, and it included the MI6 and CIA involvement in overthrowing Prime Minister Muhammad Mossadeq and restoring the Shah to power in 1953, even though major figures from the clergy such as Ayatollah Abdolqasem Kashani were opposed to Mossadeq by 1953. Islamic Iran's leaders deeply resented the U.S. economic and military ties with the Shah, which enabled him to consolidate power and rule with an authoritarian hand, and the U.S. calls for the domestic reforms that the Shah undertook in the White Revolution in 1963. They also resented U.S. opposition to the revolution of 1978–79. Ayatollah Ruhollah Khomeini, the central figure in Iran's revolution and the leader of its government for the next decade, complained after returning to Iran from exile in January 1979 that:

> As for our own oil, it was given away to America and the others. It is true that America paid for the supplies it received, but that money was spent buying arms and establishing military bases for America. In other words, first we gave them our oil, and then we established military bases for them. America, as a result of its cunning (to which that man [the Shah] was also a party), thus benefited doubly from us. It exported weapons to Iran that our army was unable to use so that American advisers and experts had to come in order to make use of them. If the Shah's rule had (God forbid) lasted a few years longer, he would have exhausted our oil reserves in just the same way that he destroyed our agriculture.[1]

Islamic Iran's leaders were also aggrieved by the establishment of Israel in 1948 and the resulting displacement of Palestinians, seeing this as usurpation of sacred Islamic land by an illegitimate Zionist entity supported by Britain, the United States, and other major powers. Moreover, they have seen Israel as an agent of U.S. imperialism repressing Muslim populations in the region and threatening Islam itself. Thus, they were aggrieved by Israel's ties with the Shah, particularly that Israel's Mossad intelligence agency had helped to train the feared SAVAK agents that had repressed the Shah's opponents from the late 1950s until the revolution. They were also aggrieved by Israel's occupation of Arab land captured during the 1967 war. They were highly critical of Egypt's President Sadat's agreement to the Camp David Accord with Israel in 1978 and Egypt's peace treaty with Israel in 1979, even though Egypt recovered the Sinai peninsula lost in the 1967 war, as these agreements constituted Egypt's recognition of Israel's legitimacy as a state. After 1979, therefore, Iran's leaders considered it an Islamic duty to support opposition to Israel.[2] Indeed, Iran cut oil exports to Israel in 1979, broke diplomatic relations with Egypt, and supported Syria and other secular, radical Arab regimes that rejected Egypt's treaty with Israel. Nevertheless, Khomeini viewed PLO leader Yasser Arafat as a secular Arab nationalist and advised Arafat during his February 1979 visit to Iran that the PLO should adopt an Islamic orientation.[3]

Islamic Iran's anti-Western grievances led in turn to fears that the United States might seek to orchestrate a coup against the new Islamic Republic and led radical students to take U.S. Embassy personnel hostage in November 1979. Ayatollah Khomeini saw this as an opportunity for Iran to assert itself toward the United States, the "Great Satan," and to mobilize popular support for his efforts to consolidate his political power and that of the fundamentalist Islamic militant clerics around him and to marginalize the large array of liberal Islamic and secular political forces that had also taken part in the revolution. He thus endorsed the hostage-taking and their captivity for 444 days. During this time, he was able to sweep away the postrevolutionary provisional government led by the liberal

Islamist Prime Minister Mehdi Bazargan and other moderate democratic leaders, including secular National Front figures. This enabled him to establish a Shia theocracy with himself serving as the unelected Supreme Leader with constitutional authority to make Iran's foreign policy and to command its regular armed forces and its Islamic Revolutionary Guard Corps, an ideological military establishment also known as the Revolutionary Guards or Pasdaran. He sought to humiliate the United States, demanding an apology for previous U.S. interventions in Iran, pledges of no further U.S. interference in Iran's domestic affairs, and the return of the Shah and his assets, and also announcing that Iran would no longer sell oil to the United States. Despite the Islamic regime's concerns that the Soviet invasion of Afghanistan in December 1979 could result in pressures against Iran, whose armed forces were in disarray after the revolution, Khomeini maintained his demands against the United States, the only state that could actually deter Soviet advances. Khomeini would not authorize the release of the hostages until President Jimmy Carter was defeated in his reelection bid and President Ronald Reagan was formally inaugurated in January 1981.[4]

Iran's leaders sought to export the revolution to Iraq because Islamic Iran, a Shia theocracy, saw Saddam Hussein's secular, radical, Sunni, pan-Arab, Baathist, pro-Soviet regime as an ideological and geopolitical rival for power. Khomeini called on the Iraqi people to overthrow their regime and Iran encouraged, supported, and trained Saddam's domestic opponents, such as Iraq's Shia Hizb al-Dawa al-Islamiya (the Party of the Call to Islam), to overthrow him. In the face of this Iranian support for his opponents, and sensing an opportunity to overturn the territorial and political concessions he had made to Iran in the 1975 Algiers Accord, and perhaps sensing an opportunity to gain territories in Iran's oil-rich and Arab-inhabited Khuzistan province, Saddam Hussein abrogated the 1975 Algiers Accord and, after months of border skirmishes, his forces invaded Iran in September 1980, advancing toward Ahwaz, the capital of Khuzistan. Khomeini saw this war as another opportunity to consolidate the domestic power of Iran's fundamentalists and as an existential war that justified enormous human and material sacrifices, and he was bolstered by hundreds of thousands of Iranian volunteers and conscripts who headed for the war front, where they were able to stall Iraq and produce a stalemate by 1981. By September 1981, Iranian forces had repulsed Iraq's offensive against Iran's strategic oil port at Abadan, on Iran's side of the Arvand Rud/Shatt al-Arab river. Khomeini was therefore unwilling to end the war even when Iranian forces recaptured their strategic port at Khorramshar on the Arvand Rud river in May 1982, when they crossed the river into Iraqi territory in June 1982, and when remaining Iraqi forces subsequently withdrew from Iran. Iraq sought an end to the war at that point, but Khomeini sought the end of Saddam Hussein's regime. Iran launched repeated assaults against Iraq in the years after 1983, led by "human waves" of lightly armed young men and boys conscripted and infused with the idea of martyrdom and followed by tanks and artillery, and these assaults threatened Iraq's control over its Shia-inhabited south. Iraq repeatedly repulsed them with its superior armed forces and by using chemical weapons on the battlefield and launching air force attacks and ground-based missiles against Iranian cities, sometimes using chemical weapons. Iran did, however, destroy Iraq's Gulf oil terminal early in the war, forcing Iraq to export most of its oil via pipelines rather than through the Gulf; bombed Basra with its artillery throughout the war; seized some of Iraq's Majnoon oil installations north of Basra in 1984; captured some of Iraq's Fao peninsula in 1986; and occasionally launched retaliatory missile attacks against Baghdad and other cities. The loss of life in this eight-year long war was staggering, with estimates of more than one million Iraqis and Iranians killed.[5]

Early in this war, in 1981, the People's Mojahedin (Mojahedin-e Khalq or MEK or MKO), a Marxist-Islamic Iranian opposition movement, bombed Iran's Islamic Republican Party's headquarters, killing dozens of parliament and cabinet members, and subsequently bombed the prime minister's office, killing him and the president. This group received support and sanctuary from Iraq. During the war, Iran sought to strike at the MEK bases in Iraq. Iran supported Iraqi Kurdish opponents of Saddam's regime during the war. Iran provided refuge and training for Iraqi Shia parties that had fled Saddam's repressive measures even before the war broke out. In 1982, Iran brought a number of Iraqi Shia groups together in the newly created SCIRI (Supreme Council for the Islamic Revolution in Iraq) and trained them for guerrilla warfare and to establish an Islamic government in a post-Saddam Iraq. The previously mentioned al-Dawa party initially joined but later left, seeking more independence from Iran.[6]

Islamic Iran also condemned the rulers of Saudi Arabia and the other Gulf Arab states in 1979 and 1980, arguing that Islam rejected hereditary monarchies, and accusing them of corruption and of promoting Western values and interests. Islamic Iran's grievances against these conservative Sunni Arab regimes, which joined together to form the GCC (Gulf Cooperation Council) in 1981, grew during the Iran-Iraq War, as did Iran's grievances against Egypt, the United States, other Western powers, and the Soviet Union, largely because these states provided weapons, intelligence, funds, and other support to Iraq. Iran's efforts to export its revolution also continued. Iran supported the Shia Islamic Front for the Liberation of Bahrain, which made a failed coup attempt against Bahrain's Sunni Arab ruling family in 1981, and Iran may have been involved in numerous terrorist attacks in Kuwait and Saudi Arabia. Saudi Arabia, Kuwait, and other GCC states provided tens of billions of dollars to the Iraqi effort by the end of this war. The United States successfully orchestrated an arms embargo against Iran by most major powers for much of the time after 1983, forcing Iran to rely on the PRC and North Korea for most of its weapons, although the United States also secretly provided Iran with some weapons during this war. Nevertheless,

Iran's commercial trade with western Europe and Japan, and with the non-Arab Muslim and pro-Western states of Turkey and Pakistan, continued throughout this war.[7]

This issue of U.S. arms supplies to Iran during this war will be covered in more detail in the following chapter, but it deserves attention here as well. Despite Iran's hostility to Israel and the United States, Iran was willing to purchase desperately needed weapons from these despised sources in order to cope with the immediate challenge posed by war with Iraq. Iran reportedly acquired $500 million in weapons from Israel between 1980 and 1983, with the knowledge of the United States, and paid for these supplies by resuming Iranian oil exports to Israel. When this was publicized in 1981, Khomeini vigorously denied it, claiming it was Israeli and Iraqi propaganda designed to discredit Iran's Islamic leadership. Indeed, Iran publicly denounced Israel throughout this period, in part to maintain its anti-Israeli credentials in the Arab and Islamic world.[8]

In fact, these sales did not ameliorate Iran's opposition to Israel and the United States or temper Iran's desire to export its revolution. When Israel invaded Lebanon in June 1982 to drive the PLO and Syria out of Lebanon, and particularly to defeat the PLO not only as a military force but also as a political force, Iran played an important role in helping to build the Hezbollah (Party of God), the Lebanese Shia Islamic resistance to the invading Israeli forces and their Lebanese Christian allies. The Lebanese Shia community were the largest, most economically underdeveloped, and most politically underrepresented community in the country. Moreover, they were located primarily in southern Lebanon, and arguably had suffered the most from the Lebanese civil war that had been ongoing since 1975 and from the Israeli interventions against the PLO, many of those interventions taking place across Israel's northern border into southern Lebanon. In July, 1982, therefore, Iran sent 1,000 Revolutionary Guards as well as some intelligence agents and clerics to Lebanon's Syrian-controlled Bekaa Valley, and their recruiting, proselytizing, training, arming, and financing helped produce a Hezbollah militia that numbered perhaps 7,000 fighters by the end of the 1980s. For Iran, this was an opportunity not only to support resistance to Israel and the United States, but also to export its Islamic revolution to a Shia community in the Levant and to build a fundamentalist Islamic organization that was preferable to the secular Amal that had previously represented the Lebanese Shia, and preferable to Arafat's secular PLO, which supported Iraq in the war with Iran. Iranian financial support also permitted Hezbollah to develop a network of social services for the Shia community in the Bekaa, southern Beirut, and southern Lebanon.[9]

When the United States intervened in Lebanon in August 1982, first to oversee the departure of PLO forces from Lebanon and then to support Christian forces against Muslim and Druze forces, Hezbollah attacked the U.S. Embassy in Beirut in April 1983, killing 17 Americans in this suicide truck bomb attack, and then launched two more suicide attacks in Beirut in October 1983 that killed 241 Marines in their barracks and also killed 58 French servicemen. U.S. forces then withdrew from Lebanon in February 1984 and the civil war continued to rage. Hezbollah's attacks against Israeli forces still occupying Lebanon, including many suicide truck bombings, also led Israel to withdraw to a security zone in southern Lebanon by June 1985 and finally to withdraw from southern Lebanon in 2000. Hezbollah also was involved in the hijacking of TWA Flight 847 in June 1985 and took dozens of Americans, Europeans, and others in Lebanon hostage, slowly releasing them as U.S. weapons were provided to Iran, and then taking more hostages who were bartered for more weapons. Hezbollah also bartered Western hostages for Iranian and Hezbollah hostages held by other factions in Lebanon, namely the Christian Phalange forces.[10]

Iranian officials may or may not have been involved in planning, supervising, and carrying out these specific operations, but Iran was supporting Hezbollah with tens of millions of dollars a year while Hezbollah's militia and terrorist arms were carrying out these operations. Moreover, the personal and organizational ties between Hezbollah leaders, many of them Shia clerics, and Iranian clerical leaders are close. Hezbollah declared its loyalty to Khomeini in 1985 and accepted Khamenei as his successor in 1989.[11]

At the same time, Iran continued to want U.S. weapons from 1984 on and was willing to continue to deal with Israel and the United States to get them. Speaker of the Majlis Ali Akbar Hashemi Rafsanjani instructed Ambassador Ali Akbar Mohtashamipour to pressure Hezbollah to release the hostages from Hezbollah's hijacking of TWA Flight 847 in June 1985, and Iran notified the Reagan administration that it was trying to help, but the release of the hostages did not elicit immediate U.S. cooperation with Iran. While it is not entirely clear who initiated these contacts, Ayatollah Hassan Karoubi, a close adviser to Ayatollah Khomeini, did talk to the Israelis in July 1985 about acquiring American weapons and did offer to seek the release of four American hostages held by Hezbollah. After two shipments of American weapons in Israel's arsenal approved by President Reagan, one hostage was released. Karoubi also met with Israelis and Americans in October 1985 in another effort to acquire arms for hostages. And other Iranian clerics who met with Israeli officials in Europe and Israel at this time offered to secure the release of Israeli soldiers held in Lebanon by Hezbollah in return for U.S. arms, although the Israelis later believed that their soldiers had already been dead when these meetings took place.[12]

Moreover, Mohammad Ali Hadi Najafabadi, a close adviser to Rafsanjani, met with Americans in Tehran in May 1986 to discuss arms for hostages. Subsequently, U.S. arms were shipped and American hostages in Lebanon were released. In September 1986, an Iranian associate of Najafabadi met with Americans in Washington, said that Khomeini had been briefed on these discussions, and proposed a meeting of officials to discuss future relations. In October 1986, four senior Iranian officials met in Germany with U.S. officials and agreed to the release of another hostage and another U.S. arms shipment. In November 1986, however, an associate of Ayatollah Ali Montazeri, a personal rival of Rafsanjani, leaked the story of the May 1986 meeting to the press, precipitating a scandal in Washington and in Tehran, and leading the Reagan administration to end the discussions with Iran. Rafsanjani denied that Iran had negotiated with Israel, but indicated that Iran would continue to seek the release of American hostages in return for more American weapons. Khomeini did not permit an investigation into the Iranian contacts with the Israelis.[13]

It should also be noted here that Iran's hostility to the United States and other Western powers, the GCC states, and Israel was not diminished despite the fact that all of them opposed the Soviet invasion of Afghanistan in December 1979 and that all of them were supporting the Afghan *mujahideen,* or peoples' fighters, in their resistance to the Soviet occupation forces during the 1980s.

Although Islamic Iran's leaders rejected communism, resented the history of Soviet interference in Iran, condemned the Soviet invasion of Afghanistan, supported anti-Soviet Afghan forces, and resented Soviet support for Iraq, particularly during the Iran-Iraq War, Khomeini seemed to recognize that he could not directly confront a major superpower on Iran's northern border at a time when Iran was confronting so many other adversaries. Iran maintained correct diplomatic relations with the Soviet Union and engaged in some trade with the Soviets and their eastern European satellite states throughout the 1980s and improved its relations with the Soviet Union before it fell in 1991.[14]

For Iran, the most critical issue during the 1980s was its war with Iraq, and one of the most critical theaters of this war was the Gulf.[15] As the war continued, Iran's economy suffered considerably from a superior Iraqi air force's attacks against Iranian oil facilities, such as at Kharg Island, and against Iranian shipping, particularly oil tankers carrying Iranian oil exports through the Gulf. As during the Shah's time, Islamic Iran depended on the Gulf shipping lanes for its oil exports, which accounted for most of its foreign exchange earnings, because Iran did not have pipelines running through neighboring countries. Thus Iran warned Arab oil producers and their consumers that it would close the Strait of Hormuz if Iran was prevented from exporting its oil through it. Iran also warned the GCC states that it would take action against them if they did not end their support for Iraq. Iran then began searching, seizing, and attacking Kuwaiti shipping and "neutral" commercial shipping in the Gulf and in the Strait of Hormuz on their way to and from Kuwaiti ports, Saudi ports, and ports in the Lower Gulf. This became known as the "tanker war." Iran also laid mines in the Gulf and occasionally attacked UAE offshore oil fields. Iran used its offshore oil platforms as well as islands such as Farsi, Sirri, Abu Musa, and the Tunbs as launching pads for many of these attacks. Iran also fired eight Silkworm antiship missiles from the

Fao peninsula into Kuwait, and one of them hit the U.S. flagged Kuwaiti oil tanker, the *Sea Isle City,* in October 1987.[16]

In 1987, after the U.S. arms for hostages story had been revealed and the U.S.-Iranian discussions had ended, the United States and other major powers and the Soviet Union began to re-flag oil and gas tankers with their own flags and to escort them in convoys through the Gulf, and this became another grievance for Iran.[17] During the next year, there were many more attacks on shipping and numerous confrontations between Iran and the U.S. Navy. Iran's mine-laying led to retaliation by the United States in September 1987 and again in April 1988, when an Iranian mine struck and damaged the USS *Samuel B. Roberts,* a U.S. Navy missile frigate. Iran also fired on U.S. naval forces and re-flagged tankers in October 1987, April 1988, and July 1988, and in each case there was U.S. retaliation. After the war, Iran filed a suit against the United States at the ICJ (International Court of Justice) over the October 1987 and April 1988 retaliatory U.S. attacks against Iranian offshore oil platforms that were used as bases for attacks against shipping.[18]

Iran was outraged that an Iranian civilian aircraft on a flight from Bandar Abbas in Iran to Dubai in the UAE was shot down in July 1988 by the USS *Vincennes,* causing the death of all 290 passengers. Rafsanjani, who had recently been named by Khomeini as Acting Commander in Chief of Iran's armed forces, rejected U.S. expressions of regret and explanations that this was an accident that had occurred in the midst of a naval skirmish and he insisted that it was a deliberate act. This tragedy did contribute to Khomeini's reluctant decision to end this eight-year long war in July 1988, which he said was like drinking poison, in part because Iran was exhausted and some important leaders such as Rafsanjani had already been seeking pragmatic changes like bringing the war to an end, but also because Iranian leaders feared the incident was a deliberate warning that the United States would launch a direct military attack against Iran to topple its regime. Iran has also filed suit at the ICJ seeking reparations for this tragedy. Tehran Radio threatened that "the criminal United States should know that the unlawfully shed blood in the disaster will be avenged in the same blood-spattered sky over the Persian Gulf."[19]

It is not clear whether Iran has actually taken revenge for this tragedy. An unsuccessful attempt was made to kill the wife of the commanding officer of the USS *Vincennes* in San Diego, California. A man calling himself Ahmad Behbahani, who claimed to have coordinated foreign terrorist operations for Iran for a decade, told CBS *Sixty Minutes* while in custody in Turkey that Iran masterminded the bombing of Pan Am Flight 103 over Lockerbie, Scotland in December 1988, a bombing that killed all 259 passengers as well as 11 people on the ground. He claimed that the PFLP-GC (Popular Front for the Liberation of Palestine—General Command) had made the bomb and that Libyan intelligence had put the bomb on the plane. But Iranian officials denied that Behbahani was who he said he was and denied involvement in the bombing and some in the U.S. intelligence world considered this man's credibility to be suspect.[20] A Libyan intelligence operative was convicted of this terrorist act by Scottish judges in a special court in The Hague in 2001, despite the defense's argument that Iran may have financed the bombing, and that it may have been carried out by the PFLP-GC, in revenge for the downing of the Iranian commercial airliner over the Gulf. Libya subsequently took responsibility "for the actions of its officials" in 2003 and agreed to pay financial compensation for the victims. In June 2007, however, the Scottish Criminal Cases Review Commission concluded that the 2001 conviction may have been a "miscarriage of justice" and recommended to the Scottish Court of Appeal that an appeal of the conviction should be heard.[21]

As the war ended, Iran was also resentful about the role that the United Nations Security Council had played. The Security Council had not condemned Iraq's 1980 invasion of Iran or any of Iraq's actions during the war, including Iraqi chemical weapons attacks against Iranian forces and against Iranian cities. Iran did have some small satisfaction, however, in the next few years. Security Council Resolution 620, which was passed in August 1988, did express "dismay" about Iraq's use of chemical weapons against Iranian civilians. And Security Council 598 had called for an impartial body to investigate who was responsible for the war. The Secretary General eventually reported in December 1991 that Iraq's invasion of Iran was unjustified and was a violation of the UN Charter. Moreover, Saddam Hussein did recognize the 1975 Algiers Accord in August 1990, when he needed to turn his attention to his invasion of Kuwait. Nevertheless, the conclusion drawn by most Iranians was that Iran could not count on the United Nations Security Council to be impartial in its deliberations about Iran.[22]

THE POST-KHOMEINI YEARS

The end of the Iran-Iraq War in 1988 and Khomeini's death on June 3, 1989 allowed an emerging group of pragmatists and reformists within the ruling clerical elite to compete more effectively with hard-line conservative followers of Khomeini in the shaping of Iran's domestic and foreign policies. Ali Khamenei, a hard-line follower of Khomeini, succeeded Khomeini as Supreme Leader, but the support of Rafsanjani, a pragmatist who would be elected president in August, was crucial in Khamenei's selection. Although he is a hard-liner, Khamenei has given some room to pragmatists and reformists to try their foreign policy approaches. For Rafsanjani, pragmatism in foreign policy has been necessary for the postwar economic and military reconstruction of Iran. In areas where Iran's policy had already been relatively pragmatic, this pragmatism continued. In areas where Iran's policy had been driven by hard-line ideological imperatives, however, there was some change in the direction of a new pragmatic effort to forge co-operative economic and political ties. Yet hard-line conservative forces continued to compete with pragmatic and reformist forces, these hard-liners still promoted a foreign policy based on revolutionary ideology, they have sometimes prevailed over or at least undermined reformists and pragmatists, and pragmatists and reformers have sometimes agreed with hard-liners. One thing that reformers, pragmatists, and hard-liners have all shared is a concern that the United States is opposed to Iran because of its Islamic character and may therefore seek "regime change."[23]

Islamic Iran's pragmatic relations with the Soviet Union improved after the end of the Iran-Iraq War in 1988 and the death of Khomeini in early June 1989. Rafsanjani, the leader of the pragmatists, visited Soviet Premier Mikhail Gorbachev, who was also improving Soviet relations with the United States and other Western powers, for example, by withdrawing from Afghanistan, and also improving Soviet relations with eastern European states within the Soviet orbit, in Moscow in late June 1989, and signed numerous economic agreements, as well as agreements for the Soviets to supply Iran with sophisticated fighter aircraft. This thaw with the reforming Soviet Union, and Iran's pragmatic policy toward the Russian Federation and the newly independent Muslim republics of Central Asia which emerged after the fall of the Soviet Union in late 1991, can be attributed in part to Iran's many grievances against the West and its desire for a strategic partner to help counterbalance the power of the West. Even after the emergence of the United States as the world's only superpower, Iran has seen post-Soviet Russia as an indispensable source of military hardware, technical assistance, diplomatic support, and critical help in the reconstruction of Iran's economy and in the development of Iran's nuclear industry. Iran has therefore not sought to promote its ideological vision among the Muslim populations of Azerbaijan, Turkmenistan, Uzbekistan, Kazakhstan, Tajikistan, and Kyrgyzstan, despite efforts by Saudi Arabia and Turkey to promote their influence there. It has also not sought to interfere with Russia's policies in Transcaucasia, including Russia's repression of an Islamic insurgency in Chechnya.[24]

Iran has concentrated instead on promoting economic development in these states through bilateral ties and through the Economic Cooperation Organization, a grouping of these states with Iran, Pakistan, Afghanistan, and Turkey. Indeed, Iran saw its own banking system, roads, railways, and gas pipelines as potentially important in linking the economies of the Caucasus and Central Asia to the Persian Gulf and the economies of the Gulf Arab states. Iran hoped to be a transit route for bringing the oil and gas of Central Asia to Persian Gulf terminals, in part through new pipelines planned under the Caspian Sea, for bringing Western goods and services to Central Asia and the Caucasus, and for facilitating GCC investment in these states to Iran's north. Iran also hoped that bilateral ties with these states and with Armenia, Georgia, and the Ukraine would result in new pipelines that would enable Iran to export its oil and gas through these states into Europe.[25]

Moreover, Iran was pragmatic in its policy toward Afghanistan during and after the withdrawal of the Soviets in 1988 and 1989, the subsequent fall of Afghanistan's communist government, and the rise of the Taliban, a Sunni fundamentalist group, in the mid-1990s. As the Soviet withdrawal was followed by tribal warfare, Iran helped bring numerous Afghan Shia guerrilla groups together into a single Hizb-i Wahdat (Unity Party) in 1988 and unsuccessfully sought an alliance between them and the Afghan Sunni mujahedeen.[26] Iran was also cautious in its policy toward Pakistan, even when Iran suspected that a Sunni fundamentalist group based in Pakistan, and possibly linked to al-Qaeda, bombed the shrine of the seventh Imam, Reza, in Iran's northeastern city of Mashhad, in 1994, killing twenty-six people.[27] Iran reacted carefully as Pakistan supported the Taliban in the mid-1990s as a means of building Pakistan's own bridge to Central Asia. Iran provided financial and military support to Afghan Shiites and to the Northern Alliance, primarily Tajiks led by Ahmad Shah Massud, in the northwest of Afghanistan against the Taliban after their rise to power, their assaults against Afghan Shiites, and their support for Sunni radicals inside Iran.[28] Iran even reacted cautiously when eleven Iranian diplomats, or possibly members of the Revolutionary Guards, were killed in northern Afghanistan, in Mazar-e Sharif, by the Taliban in 1998. Iran initially mobilized its armed forces, but did not take other military action.[29] In its cautious resistance to the Taliban and to Pakistan, which alarmed Iran with its successful test of a nuclear weapon in 1998, and in its cautious support for the Northern Alliance, Iran was joined by Russia and India. Iran was also pragmatic in its relations with Turkey, realizing that Turkey could be an economic partner but could also conceivably join its NATO allies in possible military actions against Iran.

On the other hand, Iran and Britain experienced a cultural and diplomatic crisis that began while Khomeini was alive and continued after his death. In September 1988, Salman Rushdie's novel *The Satanic Verses* was published. This work of fiction proved to be offensive to Muslims, who considered it a blasphemous assault on the Prophet Mohammad and on Islam itself. British Muslims protested in January 1989, Pakistani Muslims rioted in February 1989, and later in February Khomeini called upon Muslims to kill Rushdie. British officials acknowledged that the book was offensive to Muslims, but also protested the death warrant, which had forced Rushdie to live under British protection. In March 1989, Iran broke diplomatic relations with Britain. While the book was offensive to Muslims, it seems that Khomeini also calculated that his death warrant against Rushdie could be a way to rally the Iranian public and to reassert Iran's Islamic credentials and status after the costly and unsuccessful 1980–88 Iran-Iraq War, and to restrain the pragmatists and reformers within Iran, in much the same way as Khomeini had exploited the 1979–81 hostage crisis to consolidate his political power. Even after Khomeini's death, Iran's more pragmatic leaders could not reverse this policy.[30]

Iran's relations with other western European states were also jeopardized by the assassinations of opponents of the Iranian regime residing in Europe. Iranian intelligence agents and Hezbollah may have been responsible for the assassination of Shahpour Bakhtiar, the Shah's last prime minister, in Paris in August 1991, and for the assassination of Iranian Kurdish opposition figures in Germany in September 1992, although the Iranian government has denied any involvement.[31] Despite these assassinations, however, President Rafsanjani's pragmatic efforts to develop trade with and to attract loans and investment from western European states were largely successful in the 1990s, as were his efforts to forge economic ties with Japan, the PRC, eastern Europe, and newly industrializing countries such as South Korea and India.

In addition to the pragmatism in Islamic Iran's relations with the Soviet Union and its successor Russia and the Caucasus and Central Asia and Afghanistan and Pakistan and Turkey, Iran also adopted a more pragmatic policy toward the Gulf and even toward the United States with the end of the Iran-Iraq War in 1988, Ayatollah Khomeini's death in the summer of 1989, and the inauguration of President George H. W. Bush earlier in 1989. Despite its many grievances against these states, Iran was exhausted from the 1980–88 war, saw economic relations with these states as beneficial, and saw political ties with these states as important in containing Iraqi power.

Iran began repairing its relations with GCC states during the two years after the Iran-Iraq War ended in 1988. Iran condemned Iraq's invasion of Kuwait in August 1990, as did Kuwait's GCC neighbors, and supported the UNSC resolutions calling for Iraq's withdrawal and ultimately for the use of force to eject Iraqi forces. Iran rejected Iraq's appeal for help and heeded Kuwait's appeal for cooperation during the war. Iran provided support to its Iraqi Shia allies and allowed the Iraqi Shia SCIRIs Badr Brigade to enter Iraq from Iran as an international coalition was preparing to eject Iraq from Kuwait. Rafsanjani met with Saudi Arabia's Crown Prince Abdullah in December 1990, Iran and Saudi Arabia restored diplomatic relations in March 1991, and Rafsanjani traveled to Saudi Arabia for a meeting with King Fahd in April 1991. Iran maintained neutrality during the successful 1990–91 campaign by a U.S.-led coalition to eject Iraq's forces from Kuwait, not contributing any Iranian forces, although it did allow the U.S. Air Force to fly in Iranian airspace. Naturally, Iran saw benefit in the weakening of its adversary Iraq. Iran also did not interfere or permit the Iraqi Shia SCIRI to interfere when these foreign powers watched Saddam Hussein crush a postwar Shia uprising in the south of Iraq, as this would have alienated these powers, particularly the GCC states. Iran also entered into negotiations with Qatar in 1991 and 1992 to resolve their disagreements over the large offshore gas field that straddles their maritime border, known in Iran as the South Pars field and known in Qatar as the North Dome field.[32]

Rafsanjani also initially minimized Iran's involvement in Arab-Israeli affairs. After the Palestinian intifada (i.e., "shaking off" or uprising) against Israeli occupation broke out in December 1987, Iran, which was still at war with Iraq and still ruled by Khomeini, had reportedly provided some limited support to PIJ (Palestinian Islamic Jihad), and even more limited support to Hamas, the largest Palestinian Islamic resistance movement, and to the secular leftist PFLP-GC. Both the PIJ and Hamas are Sunni Islamic movements that received most of their support from the Sunni Arab world. After Khomeini's death, however, Rafsanjani's pragmatic efforts to reach out to the West reportedly included a willingness to accept whatever the Palestinians chose to accept, including a two-state solution, although Iran would not admit this publicly and did not change its anti-Israeli rhetoric. Moreover, between 1989 and 1991, Rafsanjani convinced Hezbollah to release Americans and Britons still held hostage in Lebanon in the context of indirect contacts with the United States through the United Nations. Then, even Ayatollah Khamenei supported the Taif Accord brokered by Saudi Arabia and Syria late in 1989 to end Lebanon's civil war, which demanded that Hezbollah limit its military operations against Israel in order to minimize Israeli retaliations. Khamenei also supported Hezbollah's decision to participate in Lebanon's parliamentary elections in 1992.[33]

When the Bush administration did not invite Iran to attend the Madrid summit conference on Arab-Israeli peace and regional economic and security issues in October 1991, however, Iranian pragmatists and hard-liners alike saw this as an effort to deny Iran its rightful role in the Levant and in the region at large and as an effort to expand Israel's role and influence in the region, and Iran convened an alternate conference of Islamic and secular rejectionist parties in an effort to reassert its role in the Arab world. Iran criticized the Arab governments that participated at Madrid, particularly Syria, fearing that Syria could limit Iran's access to the Levant. Iran also criticized the Oslo Accord between the PLO and Israel in August 1993, the PLO-Israeli Declaration of Principles signed in September 1993 at the White House, the PLO-Israeli negotiations that followed, the peace agreement between Israel and Jordan in 1994, and the Syrian-Israeli negotiations. After the Oslo Accord, Iran reportedly increased its support for rejectionist Palestinian groups, particularly Islamic Jihad, and Iran has been blamed for terrorist attacks against Israelis by these groups in 1994 and thereafter, although Iran has denied involvement. Iranian leaders criticized this peace process for not specifying Palestinian rights to Jerusalem, for not assuring the return of Palestinian refugees who had fled in 1948 and 1967, and for not stopping Israel from building Israeli settlements in the West Bank. They argued that the United States was not a neutral mediator, pointing to numerous occasions when the United States vetoed UN Security Council resolutions critical of Israel. They argued that all Palestinian refugees and their descendants should be allowed to return to their homeland and to participate along with Jewish Israelis in elections about a future government, which would presumably produce a single democratic Palestine in which Palestinians would be the majority and Jews would be the minority, in effect ending the state of Israel as a Jewish state or "Zionist entity."[34]

Iran also continued to support Hezbollah, which it saw as a legitimate resistance movement to Israeli occupation of southern Lebanon. Iran supported Hezbollah's increasingly successful guerilla operations against Israeli and Israeli-backed Lebanese Christian forces in southern Lebanon, and possibly supported Hezbollah's rocket attacks against northern Israel, despite Israeli counterattacks, during the 1990s. In fact, Iran's financial support continued to allow Hezbollah to extend social services to Shia Lebanese communities, particularly after Israeli counterattacks in 1993 and 1996 devastated Shia villages and infrastructure in southern Lebanon, killing Shia and Palestinian civilians and forcing hundreds of thousands of them to flee north to Beirut, and after Israeli counterattacks destroyed infrastructure in Beirut as well in 1996. Iran also helped arrange the cease fire in 1996 that ended this fighting. And Iran may have been involved in Hezbollah's attack on the Israeli Embassy in Argentina in March 1992, killing 29, an attack that was explained as retaliation for an Israeli air strike that killed a Hezbollah leader and his family. Iran and Hezbollah may also have bombed the Argentine-Israel Mutual Association in Buenos Aires in July 1994, killing 86, again possibly in retaliation for an Israeli bombing of a Hezbollah base in Lebanon that killed about 100. Iran has energetically denied involvement.[35]

Closer to home, Iran believed that the United States had deliberately taken advantage of Iraq's invasion of Kuwait in 1990 and deliberately left Saddam Hussein's regime and most of his Republican Guards intact after ejecting them from Kuwait in 1991 in order to increase U.S. forces in the region for the primary purpose of containing and threatening and potentially attacking Iran. Iran appealed to the GCC states to join Iran in collective security agreements that would exclude foreign powers, and Iran protested vigorously when Kuwait signed a defense cooperation agreement with the United States in September 1991. Iran continued rebuilding its military forces and engaged in numerous military exercises to show its defensive and offensive capabilities against Iraq and in the Gulf. In April and May 1992, for example, Iran engaged in naval exercises that included training for blocking the Strait of Hormuz. It subsequently increased its Revolutionary Guard presence and its military assets, including antiship missiles, on its coast and possibly on islands as well, and Rafsanjani stridently warned the UAE and other GCC states against attempting to claim or retake Abu Musa and the Tunbs.[36]

During these years, Iran repeatedly criticized the GCC states for permitting U.S. and other foreign powers to maintain and increase their military forces in the Gulf and appealed to these states to curb these ties. Iran criticized the GCC's financing of this presence, including the large U.S. presence in Saudi Arabia during the 1990s, the developing of bilateral security ties with the United States,

France, Britain, and Germany, and the purchasing of tens of billions of dollars of conventional weapons from the United States and other major powers. Moreover, Iran expressed resentment that the United States did not acknowledge Iran's legitimate defensive concerns and instead portrayed Iran's conventional military forces and exercises, as well as its nuclear programs, as a threat to the GCC states and that the United States promoted arms sales to these states. Iran argued that this undermined its continuing efforts to persuade the GCC states that they should enter into a Gulf security system that would include Iran and exclude foreign powers.

In a September 1994 interview with the author, only months after the UAE had also signed a defense cooperation agreement with the United States, Iran's Ambassador to the United Nations Kamal Kharrazi, a pragmatist, expressed most of these views. "It is a danger to Iran's national security and is not in the interest of the region to have so many foreign forces here," he said. He explained Iran's defensive considerations by saying "We are surrounded by turmoil," pointing to Iraq to the west, Afghanistan to the east, foreign forces to the south, in the Gulf, and conflicts among republics to the north, particularly fighting between Azerbaijan and Armenia. He said, "It is very easy to make the case that we need to keep our military capacity and buy some arms for defensive purposes. If Americans claim that this military expenditure is to threaten the states in the Persian Gulf, that is a baseless accusation. I think they make this claim to sell more arms to other states, and so far they have been successful." Later in the interview, he said, "We have tried our best to convince these southern states of the Persian Gulf that eventually we have to get together and come up with a security plan. But it seems that they are under pressure from outside powers, especially the United States."[37]

Only one month after this interview, Iran objected to the deployment of more U.S. forces to the Gulf to deter another challenge by Iraq to Kuwait in October 1994. Iran increased its forces on its coast and on the islands in response and continued these deployments into 1995 even after the crisis abated and U.S. forces were reduced.

It should be noted here that Iran had by this time developed a military that gave it both defensive and offensive capabilities. Iran had now acquired Russian-made Sukhoi and MiG fighter aircraft and Tupolev bombers; Russian-made surface-to-air defensive missiles that could shoot down aircraft flying in Iraqi and GCC airspace; Chinese and North Korean-made ballistic missiles with ranges sufficient to hit cities in Iraq and GCC states; Chinese and Russian-made surface-to-surface antiship cruise missiles capable of hitting shipping in the narrow Strait of Hormuz; Chinese-supplied fast attack naval craft armed with these antiship missiles; amphibious craft capable of transporting tanks and troops across the Gulf; and mine-laying vessels. Iran had also started taking delivery from Russia in 1992 of three diesel electric powered *Kilo*-class submarines equipped with torpedoes, mines, and SAMs. There were also reports that Iran may have developed chemical weapons and may have been attempting to develop biological and nuclear weapons, although Iran denied this.[38]

It is still not clear whether Iran's nuclear programs in the 1990s were designed for peaceful commercial energy, or whether Iran was seeking the capability to produce nuclear weapons. But a brief review of Iran's programs can be pieced together from what was known in the 1990s and what has since become known. In 1991, Iran imported from the PRC uranium hexafluoride and other fuels that can be enriched for use in the process of producing civilian nuclear energy or nuclear weapons, and Iran did not report this to the IAEA (International Atomic Energy Agency). Iran also secretly experimented with the conversion of imported uranium "yellowcake" into uranium hexafluoride and obtained engineering designs from the PRC that enabled Iran to later build its own uranium conversion facility in Isfahan. In 1993, Iran secured a public agreement whereby Russia would complete two 1,200 megawatt light water nuclear reactors in Bushire that had been started by the German firm Siemens during the Shah's rule but abandoned after the revolution in 1979 and the Iran-Iraq War that followed. These reactors would eventually use LEU (low enriched uranium) to produce electricity, and would not likely yield enough plutonium by-product to be part of a weapons program. Moreover, Iran also agreed to return the spent fuel by-product from these reactors to Russia. Russia agreed to build a uranium enrichment facility in Iran, but this was blocked by the Clinton administration, which also blocked a number of Iranian-PRC agreements. In 1994 or 1995, Iran secretly procured centrifuges and their components from the black market operated by Abdul Qadeer Khan, the Pakistani nuclear scientist who headed Pakistan's nuclear weapons program. Centrifuges like these are used in an enrichment facility to produce LEU for civilian nuclear energy or HEU (high enriched uranium) for nuclear weapons.[39] It is possible that Iran believed that this secrecy was necessary in order to avoid foreign interference with its development of peaceful nuclear energy. If that was *not* the case, however, and Iran was pursuing nuclear weapons, then despite these and other secret activities, Iran was many years away from the capability of producing the HEU—or the plutonium fuel—necessary for nuclear weapons.

In general, throughout the 1990s, Iran resented the U.S. policy of containment of Iran, which was practiced by the Bush administration and was then part of the "dual containment" of Iraq and Iran throughout the Clinton administration's tenure in office from 1993 through 2001. This included U.S. economic sanctions on Iran and U.S. efforts to persuade other states to impose sanctions. Iran has seen this as an effort to cripple Iran's oil and gas industry, stifle Iran's nuclear industry, reduce Iran's exports and foreign earnings, thwart Iran's economic development, and perpetuate Iran's political isolation.[40] Furthermore, Iran has blamed Israel and the pro-Israeli lobby in the United States for advocating the containment policy and thwarting any rapprochement between Iran and the United States. Even pragmatic Iranian officials have argued to the author that Israel sabotages Iran's relations with the United States because Israel sees Iran as a natural strategic partner of the United States and fears that this partnership would make Israel less important to the United States.[41]

Indeed, early in 1995, Iran offered the American oil company Conoco a deal to drill for offshore Iranian oil and gas. In the midst of intense disagreements about the Persian Gulf and the Arab-Israeli peace agreement, Rafsanjani was seeking some way of restoring some level of interaction with the United States and he had secured the approval of Khamenei. The Clinton administration reacted with a March 1995 Executive Order banning such oil and gas deals and President Clinton's May 8, 1995 Executive Order banning other trade with and investment in Iran. When asked about this, Rafsanjani explained in a July interview with CNN that the offer to Conoco was intended to show that Iran was open to economic and technical relations with the United States and said that a rapprochement with the United States was difficult because Americans "have situated themselves within a framework of Zionist propaganda and hence their minds are poisoned with such propaganda and they are pulled by such propaganda to make decisions that are not wise." In this same interview, Rafsanjani also specifically denied U.S. accusations that Iran sought nuclear weapons and tried to turn the focus to U.S. behavior, saying, "We really hate the atomic bomb and its purpose. The crimes committed by the U.S. in Nagasaki, Hiroshima are all sufficient to create a hatred of the atomic bomb. The Iranian people are kind people, and Islam has prevented us from doing such adventurism."[42]

Given these many grievances, and others that will be mentioned later, it is possible that Iran has been involved in attacks against U.S. forces in the Gulf. The 1995 bombing of the U.S.-supported Saudi Arabian National Guard headquarters in Riyadh, Saudi Arabia seems to have been the work of al-Qaeda, which extolled the bombing. The June 1996 bombing of the Khobar Towers housing complex for U.S. military personnel in Dhahran, Saudi Arabia seems to have been carried out by Saudi Shia Hezbollah dissidents, possibly with some involvement by Lebanese Hezbollah and Iran's Revolutionary Guards, which provided some training to them, although U.S. authorities were dissatisfied with the cooperation they received from Saudi authorities in investigating this and were never able to make a definitive judgment about Iranian involvement. Iran evidently reduced its support for Shia movements in the Gulf after the Khobar Towers bombing, fearing that it could provoke U.S. political, economic, or even military action against them, but Iran did not reply to a letter from President Bill Clinton in 1999 asking for Iran's cooperation in investigating the bombing.[43]

Iran had been very tentative and ambivalent about any dialogue with the United States during the 1990s. Khamenei rebuffed overtures from intermediaries for the Clinton administration in 1993, and the Clinton administration rebuffed overtures from Iranian intermediaries linked to Rafsanjani in 1994. Iran was also suspicious about periodic U.S. offers for an "authoritative dialogue" with recognized Iranian officials. Rafsanjani said in the July 1995 CNN interview, after the U.S. sanctions had been imposed against Iran, that "if in the future a situation were to emerge that would be better than the current state of affairs, the Americans would have to demonstrate their goodwill in advance. At present, we have no trust in [the] American administration. Of course, we have no problem with [the] American people."[44]

In December 1997, President Mohammad Khatami, the reformist cleric who had been elected to succeed Rafsanjani in June 1997, called for a "thoughtful dialogue" with the United States. This signaled an effort to improve relations with the United States. In a January 1998 interview with CNN, he said that Iran was not ready for talks with the U.S. government, but he expressed respect for American civilization, expressed regret for the hostage crisis of 1979, and called for an exchange of American and Iranian intellectuals, artists, and tourists, which was, in fact, already taking place and would continue.[45] Khamenei supported this overture, but also made it clear it would not include talks with the U.S. government, and Iran did not reply to Clinton administration overtures in 1998, 1999, and 2000. Indeed, Khatami visited the United States in September 1998, meeting with journalists and others, but not with U.S. government officials.[46] But Khatami and Khamenei were prepared to forge better relations with European governments. Iran assured Britain in the fall of 1998 that it would not seek to carry out Khomeini's death warrant against Salman Rushdie and would not encourage or assist any other actor to do so.[47]

During his January 1998 CNN interview, Khatami also condemned terror and suggested that Iran would accept any agreement the Palestinians found acceptable, which was then apparently a two-state solution of Israel and a Palestinian state. This also seemed designed to improve relations with the United States, where support for Israel was and is extraordinarily high, and where pro-Israeli concerns about Iran had contributed to the economic sanctions that had been imposed on Iran. It also seemed designed to ally Israeli concerns, which had also led to calls for U.S. and European sanctions against Iran. Nevertheless, Khatami did criticize the peace process as flawed and did criticize Israeli policies in the occupied territories.[48] Moreover, Prime Minister Benjamin Netanyahu, elected in May 1996, was an opponent of this peace process and had essentially frozen it. When Netanyahu lost the election in May 1999, and new Prime Minister Ehud Barak withdrew Israeli forces from south Lebanon in June 2000, Khatami urged Syria and Hezbollah to do nothing to jeopardize this victory. But Iran may have supported Hezbollah's support for Palestinian resistance movements when Barak's negotiations with Arafat and Clinton faltered in July 2000, when the second intifada erupted after Ariel Sharon's visit to the Temple Mount/Haram al-Sharif in Jerusalem in September 2000, when Barak, Arafat, and Clinton still did not produce a two-state solution by the end of Clinton's term in office in early 2001, and when Ariel Sharon became Israel's prime minister in 2001.[49]

After President Khatami's election in 1997, Iran also called for improved relations with the Arab world and there was some renewal of the "thaw" in Iran's relations with Saudi Arabia and some of the other GCC states. When Tehran hosted the summit meeting of the Organization of Islamic Conference in December 1997, Khamenei again supported Khatami's initiative, declaring that Iran was not a threat to its neighbors and joining Khatami in calling for closer relations with the Arab world, and these calls were generally received favorably. Iran cooperated with Saudi appeals that both states cut their oil production in early 1999 in an effort to curb a surplus supply of oil on world markets and to stabilize falling prices and revenues. During a visit to Iran by Saudi Defense Minister Sultan in May 1999, Iranian Defense Minister Ali Shamkhani called for discussions on a regional security arrangement and Khatami even called for a military alliance with Saudi Arabia. Khatami also visited Saudi Arabia and Qatar and met with Bahrani and Omani officials during this time. In April 2000, Iran signed a bilateral agreement with Saudi Arabia to fight crime, drug trafficking, and terror, and Iran secured similar agreements with Oman. Iran enjoyed growing trade relations in the Gulf region, particularly with Dubai. But Khatami, Khamenei, and others also continued to denounce the U.S. military presence in the Gulf and the security partnerships between GCC states and the United States, Iran continued to modernize its armed forces, Iran continued to engage in military and naval exercises that included practicing closing the Strait of Hormuz, and Iran continued to reject GCC and Arab League claims that Abu Musa and the Tunbs were legitimately the UAE's. It seemed that Iran, even under a reformist president, saw itself as the rightful hegemon in the Gulf, and this limited the willingness of the GCC states to accept Iran's overtures.[50]

Despite its grievances against them, Iran has at times been willing to cooperate with the United States and other major powers. When al-Qaeda attacked New York and Washington on September 11, 2001, Iran denounced the attacks and expressed its sympathy for the United States. Supreme Leader Khamenei and President Khatami, who had been reelected in 2001, deplored the attacks and thousands of Iranians held candlelight vigils for the American victims. The *9/11 Commission Report,* while noting that Iran had allowed al-Qaeda figures including some of the future hijackers to travel through Iran, wrote that "We have found no evidence that Iran or Hezbollah was aware of the planning for what later became the 9/11 attack."[51] When the Bush administration, which had come to power in 2001, undertook a military campaign with its coalition partners to topple the Taliban government of Afghanistan and their clients al-Qaeda in October, Iranian officials met with Bush administration officials in Paris and Geneva to discuss Iranian cooperation. Iran was very helpful in encouraging the Northern Alliance forces to cooperate with the U.S. forces during the military campaign. Indeed, Iran armed and paid these forces during the fighting. Iran also offered the United States the use of Iranian air fields and offered to assist the United States in search and rescue operations for any U.S. pilots shot down during the fighting. Iran apprehended hundreds of al-Qaeda fighters fleeing across Iran and killed some of them. During the Bonn Conference, which was held in December to determine the future of Afghanistan, Iran's delegation, led by Mohammad Javad Zarif, was very helpful in drafting the interim constitution and in persuading the Northern Alliance to scale back its demands for dominating the new cabinet, thus allowing the new government led by President Hamid Karzai to be established. Iran's delegation also proposed, successfully, that there be future democratic elections in Afghanistan. This cooperation with the United States was based on Iran's calculation that there was a convergence of interests as both sought to defeat their mutual enemies. It was also based on the idea that this might lead to improved relations with the United States and discussions on additional issues.[52]

Iran may, however, have been involved in the *Karine-A* incident in January 2002, when a ship loaded with Iranian arms was intercepted by Israel in the Red Sea. Israel charged that Iran had shipped these weapons from Kish Island to Palestinian Authority President Arafat and the Bush administration accepted this argument. Iran strenuously denied that this had been authorized by the government and unsuccessfully requested to see the evidence in order to conduct its own investigation. Iran did concede that it might have been the work of a rogue unit within the Revolutionary Guards, but reportedly suspected that it had been framed by another state, presumably Israel. Iran also resented the Bush administration's charge in January that it was sheltering al-Qaeda operatives fleeing Afghanistan, given the cooperation Iran had rendered in Afghanistan. Indeed, the Bush administration was referring to only a few very high value al-Qaeda operatives that Iran had hoped to trade in future bargaining with the administration. Iran's leaders resented President Bush's reference to Iran as part of an "axis of evil" of terrorists and their state sponsors later that month.[53]

In Iran, the pragmatic and reformist leaders who had argued in favor of cooperation with the United States were criticized by hard-liners who argued that cooperation was futile. It is even possible that hard-liners had sent the *Karine-A* through the Red Sea, which is well known to be patrolled by Israel, in the hope that it would be captured and thus blow up the diplomatic cooperation, although the real story of the incident is still not known. Despite the setback for pragmatists and reformers, when the Tokyo Conference was held in January 2002 to raise financial assistance for the new Afghan government, Iran pledged $500 million. Iran also photographed and fingerprinted hundreds of captured al-Qaeda fighters in January and shared this information with the UN Secretary General in early February. Iran then turned most of these al-Qaeda fighters and new ones subsequently apprehended over to their countries of origin during the following months. Iran and Israel traded angry rhetoric during these months, but in March 2002, when Saudi Arabia's Crown Prince Abdullah orchestrated an Arab League proposal to grant recognition to Israel in exchange for a Palestinian state in the West Bank and the Gaza Strip, with East Jerusalem as its capital, and with a fair and just resolution of the Palestinian refugee problem, Khatami made the most explicit statement yet that "We will honor what the Palestinian people accept."[54] Moreover, Iran continued to engage in periodic talks with the United States in Geneva in 2002 and offered in March to pay the bill for 20,000 new recruits for the Afghan army.[55]

In August, however, the MEK reported that Iran had been secretly constructing two nuclear facilities. One of them was a uranium enrichment facility near Natanz. The other was a heavy water plant in Arak, which would be part of a heavy water reactor complex that could potentially produce plutonium, another fissile material that can be used in a nuclear weapon. It was now clear that Iran was preparing to develop the eventual indigenous capability to produce the fuel that would be necessary to run the reactors that would generate electricity— and perhaps the fuel that would be necessary in a nuclear weapon. Iran argued that it was entitled to build these facilities as a signatory of the NPT (Nuclear Non-Proliferation Treaty). Iran also claimed that it was not required to notify the IAEA of the existence of these facilities until six months before introducing nuclear materials such as uranium hexafluoride into them. This was an interpretation of the NPT that was no longer observed by most signatories, which notify the IAEA when construction of such facilities begins.[56]

During talks with a U.S. delegation in Geneva in early 2003, Iran offered cooperation on the U.S. invasion of Iraq. In particular, Iran again offered to help in search and rescue missions and encouraged its Iraqi Shia allies not to resist U.S. forces. Iran welcomed the demise of its enemy Saddam Hussein and his Sunni Arab Baath regime, but Iran was concerned that a U.S. invasion and occupation of Iraq could be followed by an attack against Iran, or the establishment of a hostile Iraqi government, or the fragmentation of Iraq. Thus, Iran was willing to cooperate enough to prevent these outcomes from occurring.[57]

Furthermore, in early May 2003, soon after the United States had invaded Iraq and toppled the Saddam Hussein regime, Iran offered to negotiate with the United States over the range of issues at dispute, including Iran's nuclear programs, its relations with Islamic Jihad, Hamas, and Hezbollah, its policy toward Israel, the stability of Iraq, and al-Qaeda. The proposal, which was endorsed by Khamenei, Khatami, Kharrazi, and Zarif, became known as the "grand bargain" proposal. The proposal suggested that Iran was prepared to agree to "full cooperation" with the IAEA, including the acceptance of additional protocols for more intrusive IAEA inspections, to show that Iran did not seek WMD (weapons of mass destruction). It also suggested "full cooperation" against terrorists, particularly al-Qaeda; help in stabilizing Iraq and establishing democratic institutions and "a non-religious government"; an end to "material support from Iranian territory" for Hamas and Islamic Jihad and pressure on them to stop violence against Israeli civilians "within [the] borders of 1967"; action to make Hezbollah "a mere political organization within Lebanon"; and "acceptance of the Arab League declaration (Saudi initiative, two-states-approach)."[58] Many clarifications of this language and guarantees of compliance would have been necessary, but this was a far-reaching and noteworthy overture by Iran.

In return, Iran wanted security assurances, particularly that the United States end "interference in [Iran's] internal or external relations" and abandon the "axis of evil" language and the designation of Iran as terrorist. Iran also sought the "abolishment of all sanctions." Moreover, Iran wanted recognition of its national and religious interests in a democratic and fully representative Iraq, recognition of Iran's "legitimate security interests in the region with according defense capacity," and acceptance of Iran's "full access to peaceful nuclear technology, biotechnology, and chemical technology." Finally, Iran sought decisive action against all anti-Iranian terrorists, particularly the MEK or "MKO," and their repatriation to Iran from Iraq.[59] In discussions, Iran reportedly offered to turn over the remaining high-value al-Qaeda operatives under house arrest in Iran, including Osama bin Laden's son, in exchange for MEK operatives who were based in Iraq and could operate against Iran from this base. The assurances Iran sought in this proposal seem to have been motivated by a fear that the United States would attack Iran after Iraq or ratchet up sanctions or build an Iraq hostile to Iran.[60]

Iran's proposal was rejected by the Bush administration, which also broke off the talks in Geneva when an al-Qaeda attack in Saudi Arabia on May 12 killed eight Americans and two dozen Saudis, and the Bush administration blamed Iran for sheltering an al-Qaeda operative said to have been involved. While the evidence does not prove that he was involved, or that Iran was involved, Iran had not met a U.S. request on May 3 to gather information from these al-Qaeda operatives about what U.S. intelligence correctly suspected was an impending attack. Iran was perhaps not aware that this attack was imminent, and may even have been waiting for the Bush administration's reply to its "grand bargain" proposal before committing to help. Once again, however, pragmatists and reformers who advocated negotiation with the United States were discredited by the rejection of their overture.[61]

Despite the Bush administration's rejection of the "grand bargain' offer and subsequent termination of the Geneva talks in May 2003, Iran, which had sent some Revolutionary Guards and intelligence agents into Iraq, continued to urge its Iraqi Shia Arab allies to concentrate on the economic reconstruction of Iraq and not to oppose the U.S. occupation. Iran provided refined fuel and electricity to southern Iraq. Iran urged its Shia Arab allies to participate in the election for

Iraq's parliament in January 2005, in the government established in April 2005, and in the drafting of the constitution that was finished in October 2005, and then in the new elections for parliament in December 2005, believing that this was the best way for Iran to ensure that it would enjoy some influence in Iraq, ensure that another hostile Sunni Arab regime did not emerge, and ensure that there would be a U.S. withdrawal from Iraq. At the same time, Iran has supported Iraqi Shia Arab militias that operate both inside and outside Iraq's official security forces. In Afghanistan, Iran also funded reconstruction, education, health, and religious projects in western Afghanistan and Kabul, including roads, electrical power lines, fiber optic cable lines, schools, hospitals, and mosques. Once again, it has viewed this as the best means of ensuring Iranian influence, particularly in the west, ensuring that a hostile Taliban does not reestablish control in Afghanistan, and ensuring an eventual withdrawal of U.S. forces. At the same time, Iran has reportedly engaged in surveillance and in planning for possible defensive or offensive operations against U.S. and NATO forces.[62]

On the nuclear front, in response to numerous concerns of the IAEA, Iran agreed in October 2003 to cooperate with the IAEA, to sign an Additional Protocol to the Safeguards Agreement of the NPT, which would give the IAEA expanded power to aggressively monitor Iran's declared nuclear sites as well as undeclared but suspected sites, and to suspend all uranium enrichment and reprocessing activities. It continued some activities that concerned the IAEA, such as uranium conversion and the assembly and testing of centrifuges, until it agreed in November 2004 to completely suspend all conversion and enrichment processes while it negotiated with Britain, France, Germany, and the European Union (the EU-3). Iran proposed a solution in March 2005 that would have permitted Iran to continue low uranium enrichment for commercial purposes at Natanz under an intense IAEA inspection regime, but it was rejected by the EU-3 and strongly opposed by the Bush administration. Moreover, in 2004 Iran began production of its own indigenous Shahab-3 intermediate range ballistic missile, based on the North Korean No-Dong model, with a range of 1,300 kilometers (840 miles), after testing it successfully in 2002 and 2003. Iran also began construction of a heavy water nuclear research reactor in June 2004. In May 2005, Iran successfully tested a solid-fueled motor for its Shahab-3 missiles and said that this would improve their accuracy.[63]

In late June 2005, Mahmoud Ahmadinejad was elected President of Iran, defeating much better known candidates such as Rafsanjani and Mohsin Rezai, the former commander of the Revolutionary Guards. The election of Ahmadinejad, a hard-line former mayor of Tehran, may have been due in part to the promises of economic relief and social justice he made to the electorate. But his election may also have been due to a perception that Iran was being subjected to numerous pressures from the United States and other Western powers and that a hard-liner was better able to respond than a pragmatist or reformist.

There was a perception in Iran, expressed even by Rafsanjani, that the election had been rigged. The new president did seem to have the support of Khamenei. Moreover, the new president, who took office in August but who of course did not have the constitutional power to make foreign policy decisions or command the armed forces, did confront the West, at least with his rhetoric. Within months, in October, he began making statements that were widely reported, calling for the end of the State of Israel, questioning whether the Holocaust had really taken the lives of six million Jews, and arguing that the killing of Jews in Europe should not justify the establishment of Israel in Palestine. The first statement was widely translated as calling for Israel to be "wiped off the map," and this was usually interpreted as a call for the military destruction of Israel, perhaps even meaning genocide against the Jewish citizens. But a more accurate translation is "The Imam [Khomeini] said this regime occupying Jerusalem must vanish from the page of time." This was perhaps a call for "regime change" rather than war and genocide, particularly given the fact that Ahmadinejad called in this same speech and in a subsequent interview with *Time* magazine for a referendum in which all Palestinian exiles would be able to participate and which would thus give Palestinians a majority voice. It was certainly a rejection of the idea of accepting a two-state agreement between the Palestinians and Israel. Khamenei responded to Ahmadinejad's remark by saying that Iran would not attack any nation. Other powerful Iranian leaders, particularly Ali Larijani, the secretary of the Supreme National Security Council, also responded by saying that this issue remained one for the Palestinians to decide.[64]

Later in the year, when the EU-3 finally proposed a promised package of incentives to Iran, including possible membership in the World Trade Organization and access to U.S. aircraft spare parts, Iran declared that it was insufficient and said it would end its voluntary suspension of uranium enrichment activities.[65] Moreover, Iran signed contracts late in 2005 to acquire Russian-made TOR-M1 surface-to-surface missiles and the Russian-made SA 15 (Gauntlet) SAMs in order to better defend its skies either during defensive or during offensive military engagements. The contracts also called upon Russia to modernize Iran's fighters, bombers, and military helicopters.[66]

Ahmadinejad's election, Iran's rejection of the EU-3 offer, Iran's growing influence in Iraq at a time when U.S. plans seemed to be unraveling there, and Ahmadinejad's belligerent remarks about Israel set the stage for a very tense 2006 and 2007, a subject that will be addressed in chapters 5 and 6.

NOTES

    1. Hamid Algar, translator and annotator, *Islam and Revolution: Writings and Declarations of Imam Khomeini* (Berkeley: Mizan Press, 1981), 258.

    2. Takeyh, *Hidden Iran*, 195–99.

    3. Parsi, *Treacherous Alliance*, 83–84.

4. Takeyh, *Hidden Iran*, 24–26, 95–101. See also Nikkie Keddie, *Modern Iran: Roots and Results of Revolution* (New Haven: Yale University Press, 2003), 248–49. See also Lenczowski, *American Presidents*, 199–203.

5. Takeyh, *Hidden Iran*, 167–72; Twinam, *The Gulf*, 131–44. See Anthony H. Cordesman and Abraham R. Wagner, *The Lessons of Modern War, Volume II: The Iran-Iraq War* (Boulder: Westview Press, 1990), for a comprehensive account of the war. See R. K. Ramazani, *Revolutionary Iran: Challenge and Response in the Middle East* (Baltimore: The Johns Hopkins University Press, 1986), for a detailed study of Iran in the early years of revolution and war.

6. Daniel Byman, *Deadly Connections: States that Sponsor Terrorism* (Cambridge, UK: Cambridge University Press, 2005), 37, 39, 46.

7. Lenczowski, *American Presidents*, 243–54; Byman, *Deadly Connections*, 39. Former U.S. Ambassador to Bahrain Joseph Twinam cites the figure of $50 billion in *The Gulf, Cooperation and the Council*, 133. See also Anoushiravan Ehteshami, *After Khomeini: The Iranian Second Republic* (London and New York: Routledge, 1995), 204–5, 210–11.

8. Parsi, *Treacherous Alliance*, 97–109.

9. Nasr, *The Shia Revival*, 85, 141–42; Robert A. Pape, *Dying to Win: The Strategic Logic of Suicide Terrorism* (New York: Random House, 2005), 130–33, 188. Byman, *Deadly Connections*, 80–84.

10. Byman, *Deadly Connections*, 84–89; Pape, *Dying to Win*, 129–39, 189–91, stresses that these suicide operations were motivated primarily by the desire to drive foreign occupiers from Lebanon.

11. Byman, *Deadly Connections*, 79–91, argues that these operations were supervised by Iranian officials such as Iran's Ambassador to Syria Ali Akbar Mohtashamipour.

12. Parsi, *Treacherous Alliance*, 114–21. See also David Menashri, *Iran: A Decade of War and Revolution* (New York: Holmes and Meier, 1990), 377.

13. Ibid., 121–28.

14. Takeyh, *Hidden Iran*, 76–77.

15. For detailed studies of this war in the Gulf, see Mattair, *Three Occupied UAE Islands*, and Martin S. Navias and E. R. Hooton, *Tanker Wars: The Assault on Merchant Shipping During the Iran-Iraq Crisis, 1980–1988* (London: I.B. Tauris and Company, Ltd., 1996).

16. Mattair, *Three Occupied UAE Islands*, 213–14; Navias and Hooton, *Tanker Wars*, 8, 64, 122, 154.

17. R. K. Ramazani, "Iran's Resistance to the US Intervention in the Persian Gulf," in *Neither East Nor West: Iran, the Soviet Union, and the United States*, ed. Nikkie R. Keddie and Mark J. Gasiorowski (New Haven and London: Yale University Press, 1990), 38.

18. Mattair, *Three Occupied UAE Islands*, 409–12; Navias and Hooton, *Tanker Wars*, 141, 143–46, 153–56, 169, 170–71, 173–74; Lenczowski, *American Presidents*, 244–48.

19. Cordesman and Wagner, *Iran-Iraq War*, 394, provide this quote.

20. William Samii, Iran Report, Radio Free Europe/Radio Liberty, Vol. 3, no. 3, June 12, 2000, at www.rferl.org.

21. *New York Times*, June 28, 2007.

22. A number of Iranian officials expressed this to the author in Tehran in December 1994.

23. For an excellent study drawing the distinctions between hard-liners, pragmatists, and reformers, see Takeyh, *Hidden Iran*. For a statement by a pragmatic leader about U.S. opposition to the Islamic character of Iran's regime, see Thomas R. Mattair, "Interview with U.N. Ambassador Kamal Kharazi of Iran," *Middle East Policy* 3, no. 3 (Fall 1994): 125.

24. Takeyh, *Hidden Iran*, 76–79.

25. Mattair, "Interview with Kamal Kharazi," 128; Ehteshami, *After Khomeini*, 158.

26. Byman, *Deadly Connections*, 63.

27. *Financial Times*, July 6, 2007.

28. Byman, *Deadly Connections*, 193, 213.

29. Takeyh, *Hidden Iran*, 80.

30. Ehteshami, *After Khomeini*, 139.

31. Byman, *Deadly Connections*, 94, 108.

32. Mattair, *Three Occupied UAE Islands*, 289–90; Parsi, *Treacherous Alliance*, 141–42; Byman, *Deadly Connections*, 51.

33. Parsi, *Treacherous Alliance*, 132–34.

34. Ibid., 151–56; Mattair, "Interview with Kamal Kharazi," 130–31.

35. Parsi, *Treacherous Alliance*, 176–78; Mattair, "Interview with Kamal Kharazi," 130–33, for Kharazi's extended denial of Iranian involvement in the bombing in Argentina in 1994. Byman, *Deadly Connections*, 85, 87–88, argues that Iran was involved in both bombings in Argentina. See also Thomas R. Mattair, "The Peace Process: Can It Bridge Water *This* Troubled?" *Middle East Policy* 1, no. 2 (1996): 76, for a statement by the Islamic Jihad unit of Hezbollah claiming credit for the 1992 bombing in Argentina.

36. Mattair, *Three Occupied UAE Islands*, 136–39, 218.

37. Mattair, "Interview with Kamal Kharazi," 127–29. Courtesy *Middle East Policy.*

38. Mattair, *Three Occupied UAE Islands*, 220–24.

39. Paul Kerr, "The Iran Nuclear Crisis: A Chronology," Arms Control Association, at www.armscontrol.org.

40. R. K. Ramazani, "The Shifting Premise of Iran's Foreign Policy: Towards a Democratic Peace?" *Middle East Journal* 52 (Spring 1998): 179.

41. Author's discussions with pragmatic officials of Iran's Foreign Ministry, Tehran, December 1994.

42. Text of the Live Interview by President Akbar Hashemi Rafsanjani with CNN, Tehran, July 2, 1995, courtesy of the Islamic Republic of Iran Permanent Mission to the United Nations. See also coverage by the *Associated Press* on July 2, 1995.

43. Richard A. Clarke, *Against All Enemies: Inside America's War on Terror* (New York: Free Press, 2004), 112–21, 134; Byman, *Deadly Connections*, 85, 261; Barbara Slavin, *Bitter Friends, Bosom Enemies: Iran, the U.S., and the Twisted Path to Confrontation* (New York: St. Martin's Press, 2007), 188–89.

44. CNN interview with Rafsanjani; *Associated Press*, July 2, 1995.

45. See www.cnn.com/WORLD/9801/07/iran/interview.html for the transcript of the interview with Iranian President Mohammad Khatami on January 7, 1998. The author had already been invited to lecture at a conference sponsored by the Foreign Ministry in Tehran in 1994 and had met many Iranian officials, academics, and journalists.

46. Takeyh, *Hidden Iran*, 113–15; Slavin, *Bitter Friends, Bosom Enemies*, 186–89.

47. Parsi, *Treacherous Alliance*, 204.

48. www.cnn.com/WORLD/9801/07/iran/interview.html.

49. Parsi, *Treacherous Alliance*, 210–14, 219; Byman, *Deadly Connections*, 86.

50. Mattair, *Three Occupied UAE Islands*, 216–17, 302–25.

51. *The 9/11 Commission Report: Final Report of the National Commission on Terrorist Attacks Upon the United States*, Authorized Edition (New York and London: W.W. Norton and Company, 2004), 240–41.

52. This story has been told by a number of U.S. officials who were involved. Ambassador James Dobbins spoke about this at the New America Foundation on August 24, 2006 and at the Middle East Institute annual conference in November 2006 at www.mei.org. See also Flynt Leverett, "Dealing with Tehran: Assessing U.S. Diplomat Options Toward Iran," A Century Foundation Report, 2006, at www.tcf.org. See also Takeyh, *Hidden Iran*, 122–24. See also Parsi, *Treacherous Alliance*, chap. 18, for a comprehensive review.

53. Leverett, "Dealing with Tehran"; Parsi, *Treacherous Alliance*, 233–37; Byman, *Deadly Connections*, 86, argues that Iran and Hezbollah were involved in the *Karine-A* incident.

54. Takeyh, *Hidden Iran*, 211, quotes from the *Islamic Republic News Agency* (IRNA), March 13, 2002.

55. Leverett, "Dealing with Tehran"; Gareth Porter, "How Neocons Sabotaged Iran's Help on al-Qaeda," *Inter Press Service News Agency*, February 23, 2006.

56. Kerr, "Iran Nuclear Crisis," at www.armscontrol.org.

57. Leverett, "Dealing with Tehran"; Parsi, *Treacherous Alliance*, chap. 18.

58. The text of this proposal can be found at the Arms Control Association Web site, www.armscontrol.org.

59. Ibid.

60. Leverett, "Dealing with Tehran"; see Parsi, *Treacherous Alliance*, chap. 19, for a comprehensive review of the story, and Appendix, for the text.

61. Parsi, *Treacherous Alliance*, chap. 19; Slavin, *Bitter Friends, Bosom Enemies*, 203–4.

62. *New York Times*, January 2007.

63. Kerr, "Iran Nuclear Crisis."

64. Takeyh, *Hidden Iran*, 212–13; Scott MacLeod interview with Mahmoud Ahmadinejad, *Time*, September 25, 2006, 35; Agence France Press, "Supreme Leader Vows Iran Will Not Attack Any Countries," November 4, 2005.

65. Kerr, "Iran Nuclear Crisis."

66. *New York Times*, July 7, 2006; Lionel Beehner, "Russian-Iranian Arms Trade," Council on Foreign Relations, January 1, 2006, at www.cfr.org.

CHAPTER 4

The World and the Islamic Republic of Iran

THE WORLD AND THE NEW REGIME

The policy of the United States and its allies of relying upon a well-armed and pro-Western Iran to play an important role in protecting Western interests in the Gulf and in the larger Middle East came to an end after the revolution of 1978–79 overthrew the Shah and brought the Islamic Republic of Iran into being. Indeed, the United States has had no official diplomatic relations with Iran since U.S. Embassy officials were taken hostage in November 1979 and has been committed to the containment of Iran throughout the following decades. Soon after the United States had lost its strategic ally the Shah and suffered the hostage taking, in December 1979, the Soviet Union invaded Afghanistan to support the communist regime that had come to power there in 1978 against religious and tribal opposition, arousing Western concerns that Soviet military forces had moved closer to the oil resources and strategic waterways of the Gulf. This led President Jimmy Carter to warn in January 1980 that "An attempt by any outside force to gain control of the Persian Gulf region will be regarded as an assault on the vital interests of the United States. It will be repelled by use of any means necessary, including military force." This was a statement of general policy that became known as the Carter Doctrine. To implement this doctrine, the United States developed a RDF (Rapid Deployment Force) for possible military intervention in the region, reached agreement with Oman that allowed the U.S. military to use Omani air bases and naval ports, continued its significant military sales to Saudi Arabia, and began to provide arms supplies to the anti-Soviet mujahideen in Afghanistan, using Pakistan as a conduit.[1]

The U.S. concern about Iran escalated sharply when Iranian students took U.S. Embassy personnel hostage in November 1979 and held them in captivity, with Ayatollah Khomeini's approval, for 444 days. The Carter administration initially attempted to secure their release through economic sanctions and diplomacy. Indeed, the administration froze $12 billion of Iranian assets in U.S. banks at this time and refused delivery of U.S. weapons for which the Shah's regime had already paid. Carter himself was concerned that any military effort to rescue the hostages could lead to the murder of the hostages by the Iranian students and others who held them. But when diplomacy did not produce results, Carter authorized a rescue mission which was launched in the spring of 1980 and quickly was aborted when U.S. aircraft flew into a sandstorm over the Iranian desert and could not continue on to Tehran. Two aircraft then collided and killed eight crewmen as they were leaving their staging ground in the desert of Iran. The Carter administration then resumed diplomatic efforts, and Deputy Secretary of State Warren Christopher negotiated the release of the hostages later in 1980 near the end of Carter's term. This agreement called for the release of the hostages, the unfreezing of Iranian assets in the United States, Iranian claims on the Shah's assets to be resolved in U.S. courts, Iranian claims and U.S. counterclaims concerning other corporate and financial disputes to be adjudicated by the ICJ, and no U.S. direct or indirect intervention in Iran's internal affairs. Iran did not sign the agreement until January 19, 1981 and did not physically release the hostages until after Ronald Reagan was inaugurated as president on January 20, 1981. Much of Iran's frozen assets were then released although many claims and counterclaims were yet to be resolved.[2]

Western interests were challenged again when the Iran-Iraq War began in September 1980. Saddam Hussein, reacting to Iranian appeals to Iraqis to overthrow him, and taking the opportunity presented by postrevolutionary instability in Iran to reject the political and territorial concessions made to Iran in the 1975 Algiers Accord, as well as to assert Iraqi territorial claims in Iranian Khuzistan, ordered his forces to invade Iran. The United States was officially neutral, but, as previously noted, its general policy was to provide critical support to Iraq and its Gulf Arab supporters as a means of containing Iran. It was joined in this effort by others, including Britain and France. The Carter administration demonstrated its commitment to support Saudi Arabia against any potential threat from Iran when the administration deployed U.S. AWACS (airborne warning and control systems) aircraft to the oil-rich Eastern Province of Saudi Arabia in the fall of 1980 and promised to sell the Saudis sixty-two F-15 fighter aircraft. The Reagan administration approved the sale of AWACS and the F-15s to Saudi Arabia in 1981, and also made some military sales to the other members of the newly established GCC during the war. The Reagan administration also provided financial support, weapons, and intelligence to Iraq, including critical satellite intelligence about Iranian positions on the battlefield, particularly after

March 1982, when Iran pushed Iraqi forces out of Iran, although the administration also provided some secret support to Iran, as did Israel.[3]

The story of secret Israeli and U.S. arms supplies to Iran during this war was started in the previous chapter and will be resumed here. Israeli supplies began in 1980 and were motivated largely by the calculation of the governing Likud leaders that Iraq was a greater immediate threat to Israel and that relations with Iran could help Israel check any threat from the Arab world, which had rejected Egypt's peace agreement with Israel. These arms transfers precipitated angry recriminations by President Carter, whose administration sought to embargo Iran while it held U.S. hostages. It is not entirely clear whether Israeli Prime Minister Begin stopped these supplies after Carter's protests, but it is clear that Israeli supplies flowed to Iran as soon as the Reagan administration took office and seemed to give a "green light." The Israeli Air Force also bombed Iraq's Osirak nuclear research reactor in June 1981, thus thwarting any possible medium-term Iraqi ability to develop nuclear weapons. Israeli arms supplies flowed to Iran even when Islamic Iran was organizing Shia Hezbollah and supporting its resistance to Israeli forces in Lebanon after Israel's June 1982 invasion. U.S. supplies were later made available to Iran even though Hezbollah's Islamic Jihad unit, which professed loyalty to Khomeini, was considered responsible for the bombing of the U.S. Embassy in Beirut in April 1983, when Hezbollah was also considered responsible for bombing the U.S. Marine barracks in Beirut in October 1983, and the Iranian-supported al-Dawa was considered responsible for the bombing of the U.S. Embassy in Kuwait in December 1983. France's embassies in Beirut and Kuwait were also bombed in 1983. Indeed, one explanation for these arms sales to Iran is that the Israelis and the Reagan administration hoped they could appeal to pragmatists in Iran.[4]

In 1983 and 1984, however, the Reagan administration sought to prevent its U.S. allies from providing U.S. military supplies to Iran. In 1984, Iran was added to the U.S. State Department's list of state sponsors of terror, which mandated the denial of U.S. arms to Iran. In 1985, however, Israel, now governed by a national unity government of Likud and Labor, informed the Reagan administration that Iranian officials had told Israel of their interest in a dialogue with the United States and that these Iranian officials were willing to influence Hezbollah to release Americans taken hostage in Beirut earlier that year. An emissary from Prime Minister Shimon Peres, after meeting with Ayatollah Karoubi, then informed the Reagan administration that Iran was willing to do this in exchange for 100 TOW antitank missiles. The Israelis wanted to promote this primarily because they continued to view Iran as an important counterweight to Iraq and thought there was a possibility of cultivating pragmatic Iranian officials to reorient Iran's policy toward Israel and the West and also because they were led to believe by Iranian emissaries that Iran would help secure the release of Israeli soldiers held by Hezbollah in Lebanon. The Reagan administration primarily wanted to elicit the assistance of Iranian pragmatists in obtaining the release of the U.S. hostages in Lebanon, and also hoped that Iranian pragmatists would reorient Iran toward the West and resist any Soviet pressures against Iran. Beginning in August 1985, therefore, Reagan agreed to Israel supplying hundreds of its U.S.-made TOW antitank missiles (as well as hundreds of Hawk SAMs and spare parts) to Iran. One hostage was released in September but for months afterward no others were released.[5]

Nevertheless, in May 1986, after hearing that Iran was ready for a high-level dialogue, Reagan sent his former National Security Adviser Robert McFarlane and a small team of U.S. officials on a secret visit to Tehran to discuss the release of more hostages and the transfer of more weapons, as well as to probe the possibility of ending the Iran-Iraq War and improving U.S.-Iranian relations. The U.S. team, which was accompanied by an Israeli, was not met by high-ranking Iranians and did not strike a successful bargain, but McFarlane's discussions with Rafsanjani's associate Najafabadi led him to think that Rafsanjani was serious about negotiating. Over the course of the next few months, the United States shipped its own arms to Iran, with an occasional release of a hostage but also with the taking of additional hostages. There were also official U.S.-Iranian meetings in Germany in October and in Switzerland in November. These arms sales and official meetings did not come to an end until domestic rivals of the pragmatic Rafsanjani made the story public, precipitating the Iran-Contra scandal in the United States and denials by Rafsanjani. President Reagan explained to the American people that his administration had sold arms to Iran, despite the arms embargo it had imposed and was encouraging other states to observe, in an effort to establish better relations with a state of strategic importance as well as importance in the Islamic world, and Israeli officials explained their behavior in similar terms, although they claimed that it had been the United States and not Israel that initiated the idea. The results of this U.S. effort were poor, with most of the hostages remaining in captivity. Moreover, Saudi Arabia and the other GCC states were appalled when they learned that the Reagan administration had cooperated with Israel to aid Iran, which they considered a threat, and particularly because Israel had successfully opposed many of the arms supplies they had sought from the Reagan administration. Indeed, one of the observations of the *Report of the President's Special Review Board,* also known as the *Tower Commission Report,* was that "elements in Israel undoubtedly wanted the United States involved for its own sake so as to distance the United States from the Arab world and ultimately establish Israel as the only real strategic partner of the United States in the region."[6]

Nevertheless, the Reagan administration tilted toward Iraq during this war, particularly after March 1982. Ironically, this placed the United States on the side of a radical pan-Arab regime that was not only vehemently opposed to the 1979 Egypt-Israel peace treaty mediated by the Carter administration, but also a Soviet client state. Indeed, the Soviet Union also supplied weapons to its client Iraq during this war and voted along with the other permanent members of the UN Security Council for the numerous resolutions implicitly critical of Iran. For the United States, Iraq was essentially a bulwark against potential Iranian advances toward the GCC states, a threat that seemed to grow in the spring of 1982. For the Soviet Union, Saddam Hussein's regime was seen as a foothold for wider Soviet influence in the Middle East. The Soviet Union did, however, maintain diplomatic and trade relations with Iran throughout the war.

A major concern for the United States and major European powers during the Iran-Iraq War was expressed in their numerous warnings that freedom of navigation in the Gulf as well as to and from the Gulf must not be violated by the parties to this war. The United States had been strengthening the RDF since its establishment in 1980 and had established the Central Command in December 1982 to command all U.S. forces in the region. The United States, Britain, and France all increased their naval forces in and near the Gulf. In October 1983, however, after Iraqi air force attacks against Iranian oil installations and shipping in the Gulf, Iran threatened to block the Strait of Hormuz. President Reagan then warned, "I do not believe the free world could stand by and allow anyone to close the Straits of Hormuz in the Persian Gulf to oil traffic through those waterways." The UN Security Council also passed Resolution 540 on October 31, calling for adherence to the principle of freedom of navigation.[7]

After intensified Iraqi air attacks against Iranian oil installations and shipping, Iran responded in the spring of 1984 with its own attacks on shipping. Iran attacked "neutral" shipping going to and from Kuwaiti and Saudi ports, primarily in the northern Gulf, inasmuch as Kuwait and Saudi Arabia were supporting Iraq. These neutral ships were not owned by or flying the flag of Kuwait or Saudi Arabia. The UN Security Council now passed Resolution 552 on June 1, insisting on freedom of navigation and condemning all attacks against neutral shipping. The UN Security Council also passed cease-fire resolutions during 1986 and 1987, including UNSC Resolution 582 of February 24, 1986, which again insisted on freedom of navigation. Nevertheless, Iran continued to attack neutral shipping in the Gulf as well as in the Strait of Hormuz and by 1986 Iran also began to attack Kuwaiti and Saudi shipping, even in the Lower Gulf. In 1986, therefore, the U.S. Navy began to escort U.S.-flagged merchant vessels in the Gulf.[8]

In March 1987, the Reagan administration also agreed to meet Kuwait's request for the United States to re-flag and escort Kuwaiti vessels. Later, the administration viewed the May 17, 1987 Iraqi Mirage jet and Exocet missile attack on the USS *Stark* as an accident, but thought that it increased the possibility that Iran would harass U.S. naval convoys in the Gulf. Nevertheless, Reagan publicly explained this decision to carry out what would be called Operation Earnest Will on May 19, 1987, saying: "The use of the sea lanes will not be dictated by the Iranians."[9] To make this point, U.S. warships in the Gulf were now increased to forty and a U.S. aircraft carrier was stationed in the Gulf of Oman.[10] Moreover, the United States warned Iran that it would destroy Iranian Silkworms in the area of the Strait of Hormuz if they were fired against U.S.-escorted convoys.[11]

There were other reasons for undertaking this mission. First, Secretary of Defense Caspar Weinberger, Secretary of State George Shultz, and National Security Advisor Frank Carlucci were concerned that Kuwait already had a tentative agreement from the Soviet Union to do this and they did not want the Soviets to play this important role. For Chairman of the JCS (Joint Chiefs of Staff) Admiral William Crowe, another reason was to improve political relations with Kuwait, Saudi Arabia, the UAE, Oman, and Jordan, particularly because Saudi Arabia was angered that the U.S. Congress had rejected Saudi requests to purchase U.S. arms.[12] Kuwait was angered by similar refusals. As a matter of fact, these countries were also questioning the reliability of the United States after learning from the November 1986 "Iran-Contra" revelations that since August 1985 the United States had worked with Israel to supply weapons to Iran in an attempt to secure the release of the U.S. hostages held in Lebanon, and also after seeing the United States withdraw from Lebanon in 1983.[13]

The United States and Britain also secured UNSC Resolution 598 on July 20, 1987, which demanded an end to the fighting on land, sea, and in the air, and called for the UN Secretary General to mediate peace. The resolution invoked Articles 39 and 40 of Chapter VII of the UN Charter, which authorizes the use of force, and called for future meetings if necessary to insure compliance, which suggested the potential future use of force against either party refusing to accept the resolution. UN Secretary General Javier Perez de Cuellar visited Tehran in September 1987, but did not obtain Iranian agreement to the resolution. In the aftermath of this visit, the United States and its Western allies made an unsuccessful effort to obtain UN sanctions prohibiting arms supplies to Iran. The Soviet Union, however, insisted on an international naval force, which would include Soviet naval vessels, to enforce such an embargo, thus formally legitimizing a Soviet naval presence in the Gulf at a time when Soviet frigates and minesweepers were already operating in the Gulf. The PRC was intent on supplying arms to Iran, including the Silkworm antiship missiles Iran would soon employ.[14]

The "tanker war" and "Operation Earnest Will" led to limited but still serious U.S.-Iranian military confrontations.[15] On July 24, 1987, as the U.S. Navy was escorting its first re-flagged convoy through the Gulf, the *Bridgeton* tanker was hit by a mine in international waters west of the island of Farsi, where Revolutionary Guards were based. This came only days after UNSC Resolution 598. The United States then stated it would attack anyone laying mines in international waterways.[16] Britain and other Western allies now deployed naval vessels to escort their own convoys in the Gulf and also sent minesweepers to help clear mines. Then, on the night of September 20, the United States attacked and captured the *Iran Ajr* while it was laying mines.[17] Two weeks later, on October 8, U.S. helicopters spotted small Revolutionary Guard boats in international waters southwest of Farsi. When the Iranians opened fire, the helicopters sank one boat and captured two others.[18]

Soon thereafter, on October 16, the U.S.-flagged Kuwaiti oil tanker *Sea Isle City,* while anchored at port in Kuwait, was hit by a Silkworm missile fired by the Iranian Revolutionary Guards from Iraq's Fao peninsula, which Iran had captured in 1986. This was an escalation, but after strong arguments by the State Department, it was decided to limit the U.S. response to shelling two Iranian offshore oil platforms, which were bases for the Revolutionary Guard units that had fired at the U.S. helicopters a week earlier. These were Iranian property, but were in international waters, so this did not constitute an attack against Iranian land territory, as would an attack against Farsi Island, and did not constitute an attack against Iranian forces inside Iraq, which would end the official U.S. position of neutrality.[19] On October 28, the United States banned oil imports from and other trade with Iran and began its unsuccessful effort to promote an international embargo of Iran, as noted earlier.[20]

For Israel, which still viewed Iraq as the greater threat and still viewed Iran as a potential partner, these naval confrontations were disturbing developments. Then-Defense Minister Yitzhak Rabin complained in October 1987 that Iraq had manipulated the United States into attacking Iran and stated that "Iran is Israel's best friend and we do not intend to change our position in relation to Tehran, because Khomeini's regime will not last forever."[21]

During the following year, the confrontations came to a head. On April 14, 1988, a mine laid by Revolutionary Guards one day earlier badly damaged the USS *Samuel B. Roberts,* a missile frigate, in international waters between Kuwait and Bahrain. Reagan himself now authorized attacks against offshore oil platforms used by the Revolutionary Guards as well as any approaching Iranian vessel.[22] Days later, on April 18, the United States attacked two more Iranian offshore oil platforms and sank an Iranian patrol boat after it fired a missile at the USS *Wainwright.* Then, when Iranian Boghammer patrol boats from Abu Musa fired on a U.S. helicopter, a U.S. supply ship, a British tanker, and an oil platform offshore of Abu Musa, U.S. Navy A-6s from the aircraft carrier USS *Enterprise* sank two of the Boghammers as well as the *Zahan* frigate.[23] U.S. A-6s and A-7s also attacked the Iranian frigate *Zabalon* after it fired a missile at the frigate USS *Jack Williams* and another missile at U.S. Navy jets.[24] Nevertheless, five missiles were fired at the USS *Jack Williams* later that day. They all missed their target, but if one had struck the frigate, and if it had been found to be a Silkworm, the U.S. threat to attack those Silkworm batteries on Iranian territory would have been tested.[25]

As noted earlier, the USS *Vincennes* shot down an Iranian commercial aircraft on July 3, killing its 290 civilian passengers. The *Vincennes* was involved in an engagement with Iranian speedboats to the west of the Strait of Hormuz when it mistook the commercial aircraft for an Iranian F-14 fighter aircraft. The speedboats had reportedly fired on a helicopter sent by the *Vincennes* to investigate Iranian harassment of a Pakistani merchant vessel.[26] The United States expressed "deep regret" for this tragic accident and offered to pay compensation for the passengers who had died, but Iran considered this an intentional attack against civilians and feared that the United States would attack Iran itself. Iran then accepted UNSC Resolution 598 in July 1988 and by August 1988 the UN Secretary General negotiated the terms of the cease-fire. By January 1989, U.S. naval forces in the Gulf were being reduced substantially as the Reagan administration was leaving office and the administration of George H. W. Bush, the father of the current president, was entering office.[27]

THE WORLD AND POSTWAR IRAN

While the war left Iran in a state of military, economic, and political exhaustion, major Western powers continued to see Iran as a threat. Indeed, from 1989 until 1999, there was a rupture in diplomatic relations between Britain and Iran over Salman Rushdie's 1988 novel *The Satanic Verses* and Khomeini's 1989 religious order condemning Rushdie to death and appealing to Muslims worldwide to carry out this verdict. The British government acknowledged that the book was offensive to Muslims but protested Khomeini's order and Iran then broke diplomatic relations with Britain. Iran was widely viewed as a sponsor of terror and assassination worldwide and Iran evidently did carry out the assassinations of political figures abroad, such as the August 6, 1991 assassination near Paris of the Shah's last prime minister, Shahpour Bakhtiar, and the September 1992 assassinations of Iranian Kurdish leaders in Germany.[28]

The new Bush administration's original hope for its relations with Iran was expressed by President Bush in his inaugural address in 1989 when he signaled to Iran that "good will begets good will." Nevertheless, the Bush administration saw Iraq as a counterweight to Iran during 1989 and into 1990 and did not respond very positively when Iran helped secure the release of Americans held hostage in Lebanon. Israel on the other hand was concerned about the possibility of Iraq turning its military power against Israel, wanted Iran to continue absorbing Iraq's attention, did not at that time view Iran as providing significant support to Islamic Jihad and Hamas after the intifada (i.e., uprising) that had broken out in the West Bank and Gaza Strip in December 1987, and still thought Iran was a potential partner. Israel did agree to purchase Iranian oil in November 1989 in a deal whereby Iran would help secure the release of Israeli soldiers captive in Lebanon.[29]

But the Western powers were then confronted with Iraq's invasion of Kuwait in August 1990 and the requirements of building a coalition to force Iraqi troops from Kuwait. This entailed a major deployment of U.S. ground, sea, and air forces to the Gulf, as well as similar forces from Britain, France, Italy, Canada, Australia, the GCC states, and others, but not Israelis, who were unacceptable to the Arab members of the coalition. Once that was accomplished, the Bush administration led the coalition in the successful ejection of Iraq from Kuwait in February 1991. The Bush administration did this pursuant to a UN Security Council resolution, although the administration indicated that a selective coalition would have the right to engage in "collective self-defense" with Kuwait in ejecting Iraqi forces even without such a resolution. Even the Soviet Union under Gorbachev, facing the economic crisis that would lead to its collapse at the end of 1991, and seeking to bolster its growing détente with the United States, finally and reluctantly supported this resolution against its longtime client Iraq, although it did not commit any military forces to the effort. The United States and its co-alition partners did not encounter any serious challenge from Iran—and actually received some cooperation from Iran—while they were carrying out this war, while they were passively allowing Saddam Hussein to crush the postwar Shia uprising in the south, while they were subsequently prohibiting Iraqi air force flights over "no fly zones" in the Shia south of Iraq and over the Kurdish north of Iraq, and while they were enforcing UN economic and military sanctions against Iraq, although U.S. naval forces did monitor some Iranian smuggling of Iraqi oil. After all, the West was now containing Iran's principal regional adversary and attempting to dismantle its WMD programs. Nevertheless, the Bush administration did not invite Iran to participate in the October 1991 Madrid summit conference to discuss Arab-Israeli issues and regional economic and security issues. It was not prepared to include Iran in discussions of a new regional order. The Bush administration did endorse the UN Secretary General report in December 1991 concluding that Iraq's invasion of Iran was not justified and expressing deep regret for Iraqi chemical weapon attacks against Iranian civilians, but this must have been cold comfort to Iran.[30]

With Saddam Hussein's Iraq remaining in power but effectively defeated and contained, and with the bulk of U.S. and coalition forces withdrawn in the year following the war, Iran now had the potential to become the strongest power in the Gulf. Indeed, a Pentagon study conducted under the supervision of Paul Wolfowitz, a noted neoconservative, and then leaked to the press in March 1992 expressed a concern that Iran posed a potential offensive military threat to the Gulf Arab states. The study, which was still in draft form and called the "Draft Defense Planning Guidance," and which argued that the United States should maintain its status as the world's only superpower after the fall of the Soviet Union, designated the Persian Gulf as a key region for U.S. dominance. It argued that it was important for the United States to develop a greater sealift and airlift capability, and to obtain permission to pre-position heavy support equipment and spare parts in the region, and to engage in temporary deployments for training and joint exercises, but that these steps were not sufficient. The study argued, therefore, that increased U.S. arms sales to these Gulf Arab states would be necessary, a conclusion that dismayed Israel as well as Iran. Secretary of Defense Richard Cheney thus promised to continue to support Israel's qualitative military edge over all potential enemies, but told Israel's Defense Minister Moshe Arens that these Gulf Arab states were not likely to be military enemies of Israel. Notably, this study stressed the need to control the proliferation of nuclear weapons and other WMD in Iraq and North Korea, but did not name Iran as a problem in these areas.[31] In the following months, the administration began to push for increased arms sales to the Gulf Arab states. In September 1992, the administration proposed the sale of seventy-two advanced F-15 aircraft to Saudi Arabia, and in October the Congress approved it.[32]

In late 1991, when the Soviet Union finally collapsed, the Russian Federation emerged from its ashes. The Soviet superpower passed into history and was replaced by a Russia that was rapidly losing influence in the Caucases and in Muslim Central Asian states and that was in economic crisis. Despite the fact that the new Russia sought economic assistance from the United States, this new state and its leader, President Boris Yeltsin, had a new policy toward Iran. The Soviet Union's former client Iraq was subjected to military and economic sanctions that effectively removed it as a reliable and profitable client. Russia now saw Iran as a regional power that was not challenging Russia's interests in the Caucases and Central Asia and as a major oil exporter attempting to rebuild a shattered military and capable of purchasing Russian arms exports. Russia therefore began to provide Iran with many of the major conventional weapons systems that Iran is now fielding. Moreover, Russia agreed to assist in the development of Iran's nuclear programs, including completing the building of the two light water nuclear reactors at Bushire that had been started under the Shah, bombed and neglected during the Iran-Iraq War, and then resumed by Germany until it stopped under U.S. pressure. Furthermore, Russia has provided Iran with critical diplomatic support in the face of Western containment efforts.[33]

As all of these developments were occurring in 1991 and 1992, Israeli strategists were beginning to articulate a dramatic change in their regional strategy, which had argued that Iran was a partner against Iraq. Indeed, Iraq was now defeated and contained. The Soviet Union and its support for radical pan-Arabs and for the Palestinian cause crumbled. The conventional military threat to Israel was diminished. On the other hand, the United States was forging closer relations with a wider number of Arab states. Israel was now facing international pressure to make territorial and political compromises with the Palestinians and the Arab world. Israel was concerned that its strategic significance to the United States and its political influence with the United States were diminishing. Moreover, Russia was forging ties with Iran. Israel now made the argument that Iran was the greatest potential strategic threat to Israel, the Arab world, and the West. When the Labor Alignment won Israel's parliamentary election in May 1992, new Prime Minister Yitzhak Rabin and new Foreign Minister Peres actively pressed this argument on the Bush administration and then on the team around Bill Clinton immediately after his victory in the November 1992 U.S. presidential election. The Pentagon report leaked in March 1992 had not named Iran as a potential nuclear threat, but Rabin and Peres argued that Iran was seeking nuclear weapons and would have them by 1999 and that Iran's brand of fundamentalist Islam made this a grave threat to the world.[34]

Soon after taking office in January 1993, the Clinton administration announced a policy of "dual containment" of Iraq and Iran. Iraq was being contained because of its 1990 invasion of Kuwait. The "dual containment policy" meant that the Clinton administration intended to contain Iran as well. Administration officials such as Anthony Lake, the National Security Adviser, and Martin Indyk, the Director for Near East Affairs on the National Security Council, who had worked for major pro-Israeli organizations in Washington and was widely viewed as a chief architect of the administration's Middle East policies, articulated this policy. They argued that Iran's conventional arms purchases threatened the Gulf Arab states, that Iran was promoting terror and assassination around the world, including support for Islamist movements seeking to overthrow the governments of Egypt and Algeria, and including support for movements opposed to Israel, and even that Iran was attempting to develop WMD. After the administration embraced the Oslo agreement reached between Israel and the PLO in August 1993 and held the signing ceremony for the Declaration of Principles on September 13, 1993, Israeli and Clinton administration officials saw Iran as expressing opposition to this peace process through support for terror. The Department of State's annual reports on *Patterns of Global Terrorism* regularly described Iran as, for example, "the world's most active and dangerous state sponsor of terrorism," and numerous officials, including Secretary of State Warren Christopher, who had negotiated the release of American hostages held in Iran in 1980, frequently made this case in public.[35]

One early and essential element of the dual containment policy was the maintenance of a significant U.S. military presence in the region, including the U.S. forces in Saudi Arabia and in the Gulf. Secretary of Defense William J. Perry noted in 1994 that the United States did not have a significant military presence in the region when Iraq had invaded Kuwait in 1990, that the United States and the Gulf Arab states did not have a strategy for responding to that crisis, and that it had taken months to rectify those issues. He noted that the Clinton administration had based a larger number of forces in and near the Gulf, prepared to deploy forces to the Gulf more rapidly, trained for a similar crisis, developed a strategy with its Gulf Arab allies, and assisted in the improved training of Gulf Arab military forces, which is essentially what the Bush administration had been doing before it lost power. The Clinton administration had developed what Perry called "a credible, ready-to-fight force" capable of backing up a policy of "coercive diplomacy" and noted that when Iraq challenged Kuwait again in October 1994, these U.S. and GCC capabilities deterred Iraq.[36] The primary immediate focus of this military strategy was to deter Iraq, but it was certainly also intended to deter Iran.

By early 1995, the Clinton administration was concerned that Iranian military activities on Iran's Persian Gulf coast and on and around islands near the Strait of Hormuz were a potential threat. Chairman of the JCS General John Shalikashvili said in late February that one possible explanation for this was that Iran wanted the capability to close the Strait of Hormuz to shipping. He and other Pentagon officials observed that Iran had increased its troops on Abu Musa and the Tunbs to 4,000, had deployed tanks, SAMs, and 155-millimeter artillery on the islands, and noted that these deployments, along with Chinese-made Seersucker antiship missiles on the Iranian mainland and on other islands in the area, brought the waterways of the Strait within Iran's range of fire.[37] Other Pentagon officials were less concerned, noting that the Iranian deployments seemed to be a "defensive" response to the increased U.S. deployments when Iraq challenged Kuwait in October 1994.[38]

When Secretary of Defense Perry visited the six GCC states later in March, however, he argued that the Iranian deployments were beyond what was necessary for Iran's defense and had to be regarded as a threat to shipping. Some officials thought that Perry was emphasizing these deployments in order to persuade the GCC states to increase their military cooperation with the United States, including increasing their purchases of U.S. equipment and permitting more pre-positioning of U.S. equipment. Others who had originally thought these Iranian deployments were a defensive reaction to the U.S. deployments to the Gulf in October 1994 were now reevaluating this, however, as they noted that the Iranian deployments were still continuing and increasing.[39]

Thus, in the summer of 1995, the U.S. Navy reactivated the Fifth Fleet as part of the Central Command, basing the fleet in Bahrain and giving it responsibility for the Gulf and the Indian Ocean. Over the course of the next few years, Pentagon officials continued to take note of Iranian military assets and exercises in the Gulf, including tests of ship-launched and air-launched antiship missiles in the Gulf, and warned Iran that the United States would not allow Iran to close the Strait or intimidate its neighbors. Nevertheless, numerous interviews with Defense and State Department officials and a former Centcom commander at this time revealed that the United States had no intention of initiating military force against the Iranian military on these islands or along its coast, in part because the United States did not want to precipitate action that could escalate and then disrupt shipping, and that the United States would not consider military action unless Iran actually attacked shipping or a GCC state, in which case the United States would have the capability to neutralize Iranian military assets on the islands quickly by aerial and sea bombardment.[40] Moreover, the United States supported the UAE and GCC efforts to persuade Iran to agree to bilateral negotiation with the UAE or adjudication by the ICJ in order to resolve the issue of sovereignty over Abu Musa and the Tunbs and they received support for this position from Britain, Germany, the European Union, the PRC, and other states during this time.[41]

As the U.S. concern with Iranian opposition to the peace process and Iranian military activities in the Gulf was growing in late 1994 and early 1995, the United States was still engaging in considerable economic trade with Iran. Israel and AIPAC, however, were pressing for U.S. economic sanctions against Iran and AIPAC was preparing a comprehensive set of recommendations for the U.S. Congress and the Clinton administration. When the American oil company Conoco announced a deal with Iran in which the company would develop two Iranian oil and gas fields in the Gulf offshore of the island of Sirri, the Israeli and AIPAC pressure intensified. In response, President Clinton issued an Executive Order prohibiting oil and gas development deals with Iran on March 14, 1995. On April 30, President Clinton told the World Jewish Conference of additional steps he would take, and on May 6, 1995 he signed an Executive Order prohibiting all U.S. trade, trade financing, loans, and financial services to Iran. In 1996, the Anti-Terrorism and Effective Death Penalty Act prohibited financial relations with Iran and prohibited U.S. assistance to foreign countries that supplied Iran with military assistance. In August 1996, the Iran and Libya Sanctions Act, legislation that had been advocated by Israel and written in part by AIPAC, authorized the President to impose sanctions on foreign firms investing more than $20 million in the development of Iran's oil and gas resources. The United States also sought to stop the construction of an oil pipeline across Iran, blocked World Bank and IMF funding for Iran, and blocked Iran's candidacy for admission to the World Trade Organization.[42]

The U.S. Congress and the Clinton administration were now committed to economic sanctions. In addition to Iranian ambitions in the Gulf, Iran's opposition to the Arab-Israeli peace process known as "the Oslo process," indeed Iran's opposition to Israel itself, and Iran's support for Hezbollah, Islamic Jihad, and to a lesser extent Hamas, aggravated the administration, the Congress, AIPAC, and Israel. Indeed, Israel under Labor leaders Rabin and Peres hoped that a successful peace process would neutralize Iran's influence and the threat they now saw in Iran. Administration and congressional figures also suspected that Iran was involved with Hezbollah in the terrorist bombing of the Israeli Embassy in Buenos Aires, Argentina in 1992 and an Israeli-Argentinian cultural center in Buenos Aires in 1994, although they acknowledged that they had no "smoking gun."[43] Moreover, there were continuing Israeli and U.S. government assessments, which later proved to be too pessimistic, that Iran might develop nuclear weapons within a few years, and that this would jeopardize the security of Israel and the Gulf Arab states.[44] The sanctions were intended in part to prevent Iran from maintaining and developing its oil and gas resources so that its export revenues would be restricted and its ability to finance its support for anti-Israeli forces and its nuclear programs would be restricted. There were objections to the economic sanctions by some officials in the Defense, Commerce, Energy, and Treasury Departments who were concerned about the loss of American trade opportunities and jobs, but these concerns were subordinated to the policy of containment.[45]

The other major world powers did not want to cooperate with the United States on these economic sanctions. The Clinton administration had asked Europe and Japan not to reschedule Iran's debt payments, not to issue new loans to Iran, and not to invest in Iran in 1994. The G-7 countries did reschedule Iran's repayment of about $14 billion in loans in 1994 and 1995, however, and were concerned that any embargo of Iranian oil would make it difficult or impossible for Iran to repay this debt. They continued to engage in trade with Iran, and to issue new loans to Iran so it could finance imports, and to invest in Iran, particularly in its oil and gas sector, and argued that their policy of "constructive engagement" and "critical dialogue" would be more likely to produce change in Iranian policies than the U.S. policy of containment. This included Britain, which had no diplomatic relations with Iran after the 1989 Salman Rushdie affair, but which sent a Charge d'Affaires to Tehran in 1997 and then resumed diplomatic relations with Iran in 1999.[46] Some GCC officials were also not convinced that U.S. economic sanctions, which slowed Iran's oil and gas development, was a good strategy, worrying that U.S. sanctions might motivate Iran to intimidate and pressure them into investing in Iran's troubled oil and gas industry.[48]

Russia and the PRC, which have both valued their commercial and diplomatic relations with Iran very highly, also resisted U.S. efforts. As noted in a previous chapter, Russia and China both engaged in lucrative arms exports to Iran. Moreover, China, undergoing rapid economic growth, was becoming a larger importer of Iran's oil, as was India. More importantly, Russia was unwilling to cancel its contract to build light-water nuclear reactors in Bushire, and both Russia and China were interested in developing and expanding their nuclear contracts with Iran. Clinton administration efforts to dissuade them had mixed results at that time. Russia did agree to various safeguards, particularly that it would return spent fuel from Iran's nuclear reactors to Russia. And in December 1995, Vice President Al Gore negotiated an agreement with Russian Prime Minister Victor Chernomyrdin whereby Russia reluctantly agreed to restrain its conventional arms sales to Iran and work on only one of the two reactors at Bushire. In the meantime, the IAEA carried out intrusive inspections.[47]

In the spring of 1996, when a series of terrorist bombings in Israel claimed fifty-nine lives, Israel blamed Iran. Peres, who was now prime minister after the assassination of Rabin, said that Israel had evidence that Iran had pressed Islamic Jihad and other groups to engage in terror to abort the peace process and topple the Labor government. Hamas, which did not receive much support from Iran, claimed responsibility, and Israel did not present the evidence Peres had referenced. In the aftermath of these bombings, the Likud Bloc and its leader Benjamin Netanyahu, an opponent of the Oslo peace process, defeated Peres and Labor in Israel's May 1996 parliamentary election. Netanyahu reportedly worried more about Iraq after his election in late May 1996, but by early 1997 he was more worried about Iran.[49]

Moreover, in June 1996, when a truck bomb exploded at the Khobar Towers complex housing U.S. Air Force personnel near Dhahran, Saudi Arabia, killing nineteen Americans and wounding three hundred and seventy-two more, the Clinton administration strongly suspected that Iran had been involved. The attack was evidently carried out by Saudi Hezbollah with some assistance from Lebanese Hezbollah, and U.S. intelligence assessments pointed to Iranian Revolutionary Guard involvement, although the FBI did not get the kind of cooperation from Saudi authorities they wanted, and could not prove an Iranian connection. Saudi authorities reportedly feared that U.S. retaliation would damage Saudi relations with Iran and bring additional U.S. troops to the Kingdom. They reportedly reached an agreement with Iran that Iran would not sponsor terror in Saudi Arabia and Saudi Arabia would not allow the United States to launch an attack against Iran from Saudi territory. In fact, the Clinton administration drew up a contingency plan to attack Iranian military facilities, but did not carry it out because they could not prove Iran's involvement. The administration did, however, launch a campaign that identified Iranian intelligence operatives around the world and led to their expulsion from numerous countries in 1997.[50] In June 2006, Louis Freeh, who was the FBI Director in 1996, argued in the *Wall Street Journal* that Iran was responsible for the bombing and also argued, incorrectly it seems, that the Clinton administration had not been aggressive in investigating the bombing. It should also be noted that in June 2007, William Perry, who was the Defense Secretary in 1996, told a Council on Foreign Relations audience that he had since come to believe that the attack had been masterminded by al-Qaeda's Osama bin Laden rather than by Iran.[51]

It should also be noted that there were some tentative efforts to have a dialogue between the United States and Iran during the first term of the Clinton administration. Clinton officials used intermediaries to make discreet contacts in the fall of 1993 but were rebuffed by the hard-line Khamenei. When representatives of the pragmatic Rafsanjani sought discreet contacts late in 1994 and early in 1995, Clinton administration officials remembered being rebuffed in 1993, were blaming Iran for opposing the Arab-Israeli peace process through support for terror, and had no confidence in private overtures. The Clinton administration insisted that it would only enter into a dialogue with authoritative Iranian officials, and privately doubted that any pragmatic Iranian official could be an authoritative spokesperson for the Iranian regime.[52] As the second term of the Clinton administration began in 1997, some prominent Americans were calling publicly for improving relations and a dialogue with Iran. Perhaps the most important example of this was an article entitled "Differentiated Containment" by former Carter administration National Security Adviser Zbigniew Brzezinski, former Reagan administration Assistant Secretary of State Richard Murphy, and former Bush administration National Security Adviser Brent Scowcroft in the May/June 1997 issue of *Foreign Affairs*.[53]

When a reformist, Mohammad Khatami, was elected to Iran's presidency in June 1997, the possibility for improving U.S.-Iranian relations increased. The Clinton administration removed Iran from its list of states engaged in narcotics trafficking. The Clinton administration also placed the MEK, the Iranian opposition movement that had become popular with some in AIPAC and in the Congress, on the State Department's list of terrorist organizations.[54] In December 1997, when President Khatami called for a "thoughtful dialogue" with the United States, President Clinton answered by saying "I would like nothing better than to have a dialogue with Iran."[55] Clinton was ready for a dialogue, but Khamenei quickly ruled it out, as previously noted, and his position did not change. The author's interviews with Clinton administration officials during this period indicated that most were not hopeful about such a dialogue, noting that Iran was not willing and that there was no significant change in Iranian policies after Khatami's election. Some even argued that there was no real difference between hard-liners and pragmatists in Iran. Others argued that the administration's ability to negotiate with Iran was constrained by the U.S. Congress.[56]

Nevertheless, in 1998 the Clinton administration issued a waiver to the Iran Libya Sanctions Act and allowed Total, the French oil company, to invest in Iran's oil and gas industry. Moreover, the Clinton administration made several private overtures to Iran. In 1998, Saudi Crown Prince Abdullah relayed a message from Clinton and Gore to Khatami proposing direct talks, and the Swiss Embassy in Tehran also delivered a proposal for direct talks from the Clinton administration. Iran did not reply to either message. In 1999, Oman's foreign minister delivered a letter from Clinton to Khatami requesting Iran's cooperation in investigating the Khobar Towers bombing and proposing wider cooperation against common threats. Iran replied only that it was not responsible for and knew nothing about the Khobar Towers bombing. In 1999, U.S. food and medicine exports to Iran were permitted. After reformists also won Iran's parliamentary elections early in 2000, U.S. Secretary of State Madeleine Albright announced the end of the U.S. ban on importing Iranian carpets, caviar, and pistachios, Iran's most important exports after oil and gas. Albright also acknowledged Iran's grievances against the United States for restoring the Shah in 1953 and supporting him thereafter and for supporting Iraq during the Iran-Iraq War. She stopped short of an apology, but said that these U.S. policies had been shortsighted, and she called for a new relationship with Iran, although she offended the regime with a reference to Iran's "unelected" leaders. But again, Iran did not respond to these overtures, the U.S. Congress continued to have concerns, and the Clinton administration left office in January 2001.[57] In the final months of the Clinton administration, in October 2000, Russia's new President Vladimir Putin made a bid to improve relations with Iran by abrogating the secret Gore-Chernomyrdin agreement. Russia now increased its conventional arms exports to Iran and accelerated its work on Iran's nuclear plant at Bushire.[58]

The new administration of President George W. Bush, the son of former President George H. W. Bush, was committed to U.S. dominance in world affairs as the world's sole superpower. Important neoconservatives in the administration, such as Deputy Secretary of Defense Paul Wolfowitz, had argued after the fall of the Soviet Union that the United States must "prevent any hostile power from dominating a region whose resources would, under consolidated control, be sufficient to generate global power," continuing that "We must maintain the mechanisms for deterring potential competitors from even aspiring to a larger regional or global role."[59] In 1998, he and other neoconservatives who would later enter the Bush administration in 2001 had been joined by the future Secretary of Defense Donald Rumsfeld in sending a letter to President Clinton urging his administration to undertake a policy of "regime change" in Iraq through political, economic, and military action. In September 2000, many of these neoconservatives had contributed to a report that made recommendations on rebuilding America's defenses, including an enhanced military presence in the Persian Gulf. This report termed Iraq and Iran "deeply hostile to America," noted that Iran was developing ballistic missiles, and expressed concern that projecting American conventional military power and political influence would be complicated "when the American homeland and the territory of our allies is subject to attack by otherwise weak rogue regimes capable of cobbling together a miniscule ballistic missile force."[60] There were "realists" in the administration, notably Secretary of State Colin Powell and some officials around him, who thought that containment and negotiation could be worthwhile, but they were soon eclipsed.

In the aftermath of the al-Qaeda terrorist attacks on New York and Washington DC on September 11, 2001, the Bush administration publicly expressed a willingness to engage in unilateral "preemptive" military action against terrorists and their state sponsors. Preemptive military action has normally meant action to thwart an imminent attack, but the administration was also arguing for action to prevent a growing potential threat, or "preventive" action. Indeed, the Bush administration invaded Afghanistan in October, toppling the Taliban government and driving al-Qaeda from its sanctuaries in Afghanistan. In the process of doing so, the Bush administration received Iran's cooperation in defeating the Taliban, routing al-Qaeda, and establishing a post-Taliban government.

A U.S. delegation met with Iranian officials in Paris and Geneva in October and November to coordinate this cooperation in the actual fighting. These delegations met again in December at the Bonn Conference, where Iran's Ambassador Mohammed Javad Zarif helped U.S. Ambassador James Dobbins and others arrange the agreement to establish the Hamid Karzai government in Kabul.[61]

State Department and CIA officials proposed exploring wider cooperation with Iran, including intelligence-sharing and joint operations against al-Qaeda along the long Iran-Afghan border as well as discussions about Iran's nuclear programs. Neoconservatives in the Defense Department and the White House, as well as Israel, now led by Prime Minister Ariel Sharon of the Likud Bloc, were concerned that these U.S. discussions with Iran and any larger cooperation between the United States and Iran would leave a strong Iran intact and not address its challenge to Israel, and Rumsfeld and Vice President Cheney seemed to agree. In December, therefore, the proposal was rejected.[62] At the same time, the Defense Department was beginning to plan for military action against Iraq, with the full support of the neoconservatives. When Israeli officials learned of this planning, they warned the administration that Iran was a greater threat than Iraq, that a war against Iraq should not distract the United States from focusing on Iran, and that an occupation of Iraq would be unwise.[63]

It was later reported that in December, while State Department officials were meeting with Iranians in Bonn and gaining Iranian cooperation on Afghanistan, neoconservatives in the Defense Department had met in Rome with Iranian arms dealer Manucher Ghorbanifar and other Iranian exiles and dissidents, reportedly including MEK members, and including someone introduced as a former member of the Revolutionary Guards who claimed to have information about dissidents in Iran's security services, and with high-ranking Italian defense and intelligence officials. The purpose of the meeting was reportedly to gather intelligence on Iran and to consider the prospects for regime change in Iran. The individuals involved were Michael Ledeen, a consultant to Undersecretary of Defense Douglas Feith, and Larry Franklin and Harold Rhode, who were working with Feith. Ledeen and Ghorbanifar had been involved in the arms for hostages affair in the mid-1980s. As the meetings were ending, Rhode sent a cable to the Pentagon saying that his group had "made contact with Iranian intelligence officers who anticipate possible regime change in Iran and want to establish contact with the United States government," adding that "A sizable financial interest is required."[64] Evidently, the Iranians wanted to be paid. The meeting had been held without the required CIA authorization, and when the CIA and the State Department learned of the meeting, they protested. Deputy National Security Adviser Stephen Hadley warned Ledeen and the officials in Feith's office not to have future meetings. But Ledeen and Rhode reportedly arranged for an unnamed Defense Department official to hold another meeting with

Ghorbanifar associates in Rome in June 2002, and Rhode reportedly held other meetings with Ghorbanifar and his associates in Paris in June 2003.[65]

Then, on January 3, 2002, Israel captured a vessel called the *Karine-A* in the Red Sea. This vessel was loaded with Iranian arms. Israel charged that Iran was shipping these arms from Iran's Kish Island to Palestinian Authority President Arafat, and the Bush administration accepted this argument despite Iranian insistence that the shipment had not been authorized by the government and despite the fact that Iran had traditionally supported the Palestinian Islamist opponents of Arafat's secular national movement. On January 11, Defense Department officials also accused Iran of providing "safe-haven" to al-Qaeda terrorists fleeing from U.S. military operations in Afghanistan. The Bush administration had already decided not to share any intelligence about al-Qaeda with Iran, but Iran was already apprehending hundreds of al-Qaeda members fleeing into Iran. Thus, when President Bush said in his *State of the Union* speech in late January that Iran, along with Iraq and North Korea, was part of an "axis of evil" of terrorists and their state sponsors, it seemed to be a warning that his administration might engage in preventive military action not only against Iraq but also against Iran, despite Iran's cooperation with U.S. efforts in Afghanistan.[66]

Nevertheless, the administration remained focused primarily on military action against Iraq. When Israel's Prime Minister Sharon was convinced of this during a meeting with Bush in February, Israel did then quietly support this action against Iraq, even providing intelligence that supported the assessments that Iraq had WMD, intelligence that later proved to be erroneous. At the same time, Israel argued that Iran should be the next target of U.S. military action after the defeat of Iraq.[67]

In early February, after Bush's "axis of evil speech," Iran provided the United Nations with the photographs and fingerprints of 290 al-Qaeda members it had apprehended, and subsequently turned them over to their countries of origin. Bush administration officials then charged that Iran was shipping arms to its allies in western Afghanistan and that this would destabilize the new Afghan government. In March, however, Dobbins was told in Geneva by the Iranian general who had armed the Northern Alliance during their collaboration with U.S. forces against the Taliban that Iran would provide assistance to twenty thousand new recruits for the Afghan army under U.S. supervision. At this point, Dobbins met in Washington with Secretary Powell, National Security Adviser Condoleezza Rice, and Secretary Rumsfeld and told them that he thought Iran was interested in a larger dialogue, but Rumsfeld was not interested.[68]

In May 2002, the United States and Israel noted with concern that Iran successfully test-launched the intermediate range Shahab-3 ballistic missile. In July, Bush warned Iran to abandon its "uncompromising and destructive" policies and to embrace reform. In August, it was reported by the NCRI

(National Council of Resistance of Iran), i.e., the MEK, that Iran had been secretly constructing two nuclear facilities, a heavy water plant near Arak and a uranium enrichment facility at Natanz, which Iran then acknowledged. Israel had reportedly provided this information to the NCRI/MEK. Under the terms of the NPT, which Iran had signed, Iran was legally entitled to build these facilities and to indigenously produce the fuel necessary to produce electricity, but was not permitted to use these facilities to produce fuel for nuclear weapons. The fact that Iran was building these facilities without notifying the IAEA, coupled with their test of their intermediate range ballistic missile in 2002 and again in 2003, strengthened the conviction of many in the Bush administration and Israel that Iran was seeking nuclear weapons and delivery vehicles for these weapons in violation of the NPT.[69]

In September, the Bush administration officially articulated the doctrine of "preemptive" military action, really "preventive" military action, in *The National Security Strategy of the United States of America* and warned that it was prepared to apply this doctrine against Saddam Hussein's Iraq, as it later did in March 2003, despite an assessment by the IAEA that there was no evidence that Iraq was rebuilding a nuclear weapons program and despite the opposition of the other permanent members of the UN Security Council. The administration's arguments about Iraqi WMD and Iraqi cooperation with al-Qaeda were later found to be erroneous.[70]

It was reported at the time that the Bush administration abandoned any effort to engage in dialogue with Iran in July 2002, but in fact the administration, represented by Ryan Crocker and later by Zalmay Khalilzad, did continue to meet periodically and in relative secrecy with Iranian officials in Geneva from May 2002 until May 2003 and discussed Iraq, the MEK, al-Qaeda, the Taliban, and Afghanistan, as well as other issues. Cheney and Rumsfeld and neoconservatives on their staffs opposed these meetings and Khalilzad, a neoconservative, was reportedly not as hopeful about Iranian cooperation as Dobbins. The Bush administration did, however, receive more cooperation from Iran after U.S. forces toppled Saddam Hussein's regime, when Iran called on Iraqi Shias not to resist U.S. forces.[71]

On May 4, 2003, while these talks were being conducted, the administration received through another channel an Iranian proposal to negotiate a comprehensive resolution of every issue at dispute between the two countries, namely, Iran's nuclear programs, Iran's support for Hezbollah, Islamic Jihad, and Hamas, Iran's policy toward Israel, efforts against al-Qaeda, and how to stabilize Iraq. This has been called the "grand bargain" proposal. It was sent to the State Department on May 4 by the Swiss Ambassador to Iran, Tim Guldiman, who days later briefed State Department officials in person in Washington, when it was also provided to Congressman Robert Ney, who provided it to Karl Rove in the White House. Powell and other State Department officials such as his Chief of Staff Lawrence

Wilkerson and his Deputy Secretary Richard Armitage wanted to explore this opening but Cheney and Rumsfeld rejected the proposal. They reportedly believed that the rapid initial U.S. success in toppling Saddam Hussein's regime in Iraq in March and April would be followed by other U.S. successes in Iraq and that these would enable the administration to actually overthrow the Iranian regime, perhaps with another preventive military operation, or at the very least to negotiate with a weak and frightened Iran from a position of even greater strength at a later date. Condoleezza Rice, who was then the National Security Adviser in the White House, subsequently claimed that she did not remember ever seeing the proposal. Israel was also urging the Bush administration to make sure that Iran did not benefit from the toppling of Saddam and reportedly objected to the United States entering into talks with Iran about a "grand bargain."[72] Neither the Bush administration nor the Sharon government in Israel wanted to give Iran the security assurances it sought. Neither government seemed impressed with the Iranian suggestion that it could accept the Arab League's 2002 proposal for a two-state resolution of the Israeli-Palestinian conflict, and in fact Israel rejected the key elements of this proposal, namely withdrawal to the 1967 boundaries, acknowledging East Jerusalem as the capital of Palestine, and allowing the return of Palestinian refugees.[73]

Indeed, the Bush administration terminated the talks in Geneva after al-Qaeda carried out attacks in Riyadh, Saudi Arabia on May 12, 2003 that killed eight Americans and twenty-six Saudis. Rumsfeld and others in the Pentagon argued that Iran had some responsibility for this as it was allegedly providing "safe haven" to several senior al-Qaeda operatives in Iran who allegedly had "planned and directed" the attacks in Riyadh. Indeed, Iran had captured several high-ranking al-Qaeda figures in Iran in 2002 and had placed them under house arrest. On May 3, Khalilzad had asked Iran for help in gathering information from these individuals about an attack that the Pentagon suspected was coming and Iran had not responded, evidently not realizing that the attack was imminent and also waiting for the Bush administration's answer to Iran's "grand bargain" proposal, which was being sent on May 4. In the "grand bargain" proposal, however, Iran offered to exchange these al-Qaeda operatives under house arrest in exchange for MEK operatives in Iraq, but the administration rejected the entire bargain and this particular aspect of it. Cheney and Rumsfeld and the neoconservatives on their staffs reportedly thought that they could use the MEK in operations against Iran from Iraqi territory. Concerning the May 12 attack itself, electronic intercepts indicated that there was some communication between one of these al-Qaeda detainees, Saif al-Adel, an Egyptian and an al-Qaeda military planner, and someone involved in the attack in Riyadh, although proof of al-Adel's involvement was not actually established by those intercepts and proof of Iranian involvement was not actually established either.[74]

Dismissing this Iranian "grand bargain" proposal may have been a missed opportunity with sad consequences, as the next chapters will discuss. Indeed, in January 2003, the NIC (National Intelligence Council) produced a classified study called "Regional Consequences of Regime Change in Iraq," a study that reflected the thinking of the sixteen intelligence agencies of the U.S. government, and it provided many accurate predictions for the administration. It acknowledged that some elements of the Iranian regime could work against the United States in Iraq by using their Iraqi Shia and Kurdish contacts or by themselves targeting U.S. forces, but it argued that Iran would likely cooperate with the occupation authority in Iraq, or at least not undermine it, if its interests were given due regard and if it did not think U.S. interests there challenged or threatened Iran's interests. Indeed, the study argued that including Iran in negotiations about a post-Saddam Hussein Iraq, as it had been included in the Bonn conference negotiations about Afghanistan, would encourage Iran to contribute to its success. The study did argue that all regional states, including Iran, would view an invasion to rid Iraq of alleged WMD as an argument in favor of their own development of nuclear weapons as a deterrent to any future attack on them, particularly by Israel. The study also argued that Iran would continue to support Hezbollah and Palestinian rejectionism. On these two points, nuclear weapons and opposition to Israel, the study did not anticipate the Iranian offer of a "grand bargain" made several months later. The study did argue that quick success in Iraq might strengthen reformists in Iran, who would argue that reform and diplomacy were the best means to avoid attacks against Iran, but any State Department officials who may have believed that this was a real possibility were trumped by Cheney, Rumsfeld, and their staffs. But the report also argued that a long occupation would convince Iran that the United States was attempting to encircle Iran and undertake military operations against Iran, just the kind of challenge that could strengthen hard-liners in Iran and lead them to work against the United States.[75]

When the Bush administration rejected Iran's suggestion of a "grand bargain" in May 2003, and when the initial success in toppling the Saddam Hussein regime was later followed by a growing Sunni Arab insurgency, Shia Arab resistance, Iranian support for their Shia Arab allies, and a prolonged U.S. occupation of Iraq, the stage was set for some of the NIC's predictions to come true. Indeed, when the administration reportedly began to use Iraq as a platform for operations against Iran, the opportunity for Iranian cooperation may have been lost. U.S. military and intelligence forces and Israeli forces reportedly began conducting covert operations against Iran in 2004, in part from bases in Iraq, working with Kurdish, Azeri, Baluchi, and possibly Arab ethnic forces, and possibly with some forces from the MEK, to identify targets, to destabilize the Iranian regime in those areas, and to prepare the ground for changing the regime after a military strike against Iran.[76] At approximately the same time, the Council on Foreign

Relations released a study entitled "Iran: Time for a New Approach." It was authored by former Carter administration National Security Adviser Brzezinski and former CIA Director Robert Gates, and it advocated a new approach based on a "compartmentalized process of dialogue, confidence building, and incremental engagement."[77] This was not the approach the Bush administration was choosing.

In 2005, the Bush administration accused Iran of working against U.S. forces in Iraq. General Vines, who commanded U.S. forces in Iraq in 2005, blamed former Sunni Baath regime elements for making the IEDs (improvised explosive devices) that were used as roadside bombs and that killed so many U.S. forces. The Bush administration argued publicly in August 2005, however, that IEDs were being shipped from Iran into northeast Iraq to Iraqi Shia militias, and argued that this was probably being done by Revolutionary Guards with the knowledge of the Iranian government. Iraqi Shiites tend to live in the south and in Baghdad, not in the northeast. In fact, the United States sent a diplomatic protest to Iran about this on July 19, 2005, and Iran denied it in a response in August 2005. Ambassador Khalilzad was then authorized to hold talks about Iraq with Iranian officials in the fall of 2005, but these talks did not take place, reportedly because Iran wanted to discuss a wider range of issues and the Bush administration did not.[78]

Meanwhile, after IAEA Director General El-Baradei visited the uranium enrichment facility at Natanz in February 2003 and after other IAEA inspectors visited other facilities, El-Baradei issued a report in June 2003 expressing concern about a number of nuclear activities Iran had not reported. In particular, the IAEA had learned that Iran had imported uranium hexafluoride and other fuels that could be enriched for use in producing civilian nuclear energy or nuclear weapons. In August, he reported that the IAEA had found particles of highly enriched uranium in some environmental samples at Natanz. This raised fears that Iran might be closer than previously thought to enriching uranium fuel to the high level necessary for nuclear weapons. The IAEA had not yet been able to verify Iran's claim that these particles must have been on centrifuge components Iran had imported. In October 2003, however, the foreign ministers of Britain, France, Germany, and the European Union (the EU-3) elicited an Iranian agreement to cooperate with the IAEA to resolve all outstanding issues, to accept an Additional Protocol to the NPT allowing IAEA inspectors to visit Iranian nuclear facilities without prior notification, and to suspend all uranium and reprocessing activities. Iran signed this in December 2003 but its parliament did not ratify it. In 2004, the IAEA noted that Iran had separated very small amounts of plutonium, in the milligram range, from the spent fuel at a research reactor in Tehran. The IAEA also noted that Iran had suspended enrichment activities at Natanz, but also noted that Iran had not reported importing used centrifuges from Pakistan in 1994 or 1995, and had not reported research and development on more advanced centrifuges (the P-2), and was converting raw uranium into uranium hexafluoride for the subsequent enrichment process. However, the IAEA did report that it appeared "plausible" that the particles of highly enriched uranium previously found at Natanz and another site "may not have resulted from enrichment of uranium by Iran."[79] This would suggest that Iran did not yet have the capability to enrich uranium fuel to the high level necessary for weapons.

After Iran's mixed record of compliance with the October 2003 agreement, the EU-3 reached another agreement with Iran in November 2004. Iran now agreed to the voluntary suspension of all uranium enrichment activities for the duration of negotiations, including the import, manufacture, assembly, testing, and operation of centrifuges. Iran also agreed to suspend testing and production at uranium conversion facilities and agreed not to separate plutonium or build a facility for separating plutonium. The EU-3 and Iran agreed to negotiate long-term arrangements to "provide objective guarantees that Iran's nuclear program is exclusively for peaceful purposes" and to provide "firm guarantees on nuclear, technological, and economic cooperation" as well as "firm commitments on security issues."[80] El-Baradei subsequently reported that all of Iran's known nuclear material "has been accounted for and . . . is not diverted to prohibited activities," but that the IAEA could "not yet . . . conclude that there are no unde-clared nuclear materials or activities in Iran." He now reported that environmental sampling "tends, on balance, to support" Iran's contention that particles of highly enriched uranium previously found came from imported machinery.[81] He also reported, however, that the IAEA remained concerned about Iran's P-2 centrifuge project and about activities at sites that Iran had demolished before IAEA inspections or which the IAEA had not yet inspected. He did report that Iran had implemented the suspension called for in the November agreement.[82]

The EU-3 clearly hoped to draw the Bush administration into these talks, but the administration would not join them. In February 2005, French President Jacques Chirac and other European leaders also called on the Bush administration to offer some incentives to Iran. In the same month, Russia gained Iran's agreement that Russia would supply nuclear fuel for use in the nuclear reactor at Bushire and that Russia would take back the spent fuel from this process so that Iran could not separate plutonium from this spent fuel. In March, the Bush administration agreed to minor incentives for Iran, namely that the United States would not object to Iran's application to the WTO and that the United States would consider the licensing of spare parts for Iran's commercial aircraft from the EU to Iran. In March 2005, however, when Iran submitted a proposal that it would enrich uranium only to low levels for industrial purposes at its Natanz facility, and allowing a continuous on-site presence of IAEA inspectors at its uranium conversion and enrichment facilities, and rejecting both highly enriched uranium production and plutonium production, the Bush administration pressured the EU-3 to reject Iran's proposal. The Bush administration and Israel opposed *any* uranium enrichment in Iran because they sought to deny Iranian scientists the knowledge and expertise to do this themselves, fearing that Iranian knowledge about the nuclear fuel cycle would enable them to understand the process necessary to produce fuel for nuclear weapons. A month later, Iran resumed uranium conversion but agreed in June to continue its voluntary suspension of enrichment until the EU-3 offered a package of economic incentives.[83]

At about the same time, in mid-2005, U.S. intelligence provided the IAEA with the contents of a laptop computer that had reportedly been spirited out of Iran. This material included designs for configuring the reentry vehicles, or warheads, on Iran's ballistic missiles, possibly to carry a nuclear weapon, drawings of subterranean testing of high explosives, and research on uranium tetrafluoride, or "green salt," which is used during uranium enrichment. IAEA officials were suspicious about the authenticity of the material on this laptop, which included relatively crude drawings and notes that were reportedly in English rather than Farsi, particularly because the IAEA had been presented with forged "evidence" of an Iraqi nuclear program in 2002.[84] Nevertheless, a NIE prepared by the sixteen U.S. intelligence agencies in May 2005 reported that the intelligence agencies "assess with high confidence that Iran currently is determined to develop nuclear weapons despite its international obligations and international pressure, but we do not assess that Iran is immovable" and asserted "with moderate confidence" that Iranian production of a nuclear weapon "is unlikely before early-to-mid next decade." This assessment appeared to have been based in part on the contents of the laptop computer.

In August, the EU-3 finally offered a very modest package that included European cooperation with Iran in the field of civil nuclear energy, economic and technological cooperation, and political and security cooperation, in return for Iranian suspension of uranium enrichment for ten years, and Iran rejected the package as insufficient. Later that month, Iran began to enrich uranium in small amounts to low levels of purity, far short of the quantity necessary for industrial use and far short of the quality necessary for nuclear weapons. In November, IAEA officials found a document showing how to form highly enriched uranium into the hemispherical configuration used in the core of a nuclear bomb, but Iran claimed the document came from Pakistan and did not allow the IAEA to have a copy of the document for analysis. Later in 2005, the Bush administration proposed that Iranian nuclear reactors should import enriched uranium from Russia, but AIPAC opposed even this and Iran rejected it.[85]

Meanwhile, there had been tension between the Bush administration and the IAEA General Director Mohammed El-Baradei for several years, ever since he had disputed the administration's erroneous claims in 2002 and 2003 that Iraq had WMD. The Bush administration attempted unsuccessfully to block the reappointment of El-Baradei to a third term in 2005. Several months afterward, El-Baradei won the Nobel Peace Prize.

It is possible that the Bush administration's unwillingness to negotiate with Iran after May 2003 may have contributed to the election of the hard-line Mahmoud Ahmadinejad as Iran's president in late June 2005, inasmuch as Iranian pragmatists and reformists seemed discredited in Iran. U.S., Israeli, and European officials have naturally condemned the many verbal provocations Ahmadinejad has subsequently hurled forth, particularly about Israel, but these states seem to have overestimated his importance in Iran. How these states have dealt with Iran in 2006 and 2007 is the subject of the next chapter.

NOTES

1. Lenczowski, *American Presidents,* 203–8; Twinam, *The Gulf,* 73, 98.

2. Lenczowski, *American Presidents,* 199–203.

3. Twinam, *The Gulf,* 145–47, 159–62. For a comprehensive study of the war, see Cordesman and Wagner, *Iran-Iraq War.*

4. Parsi, *Treacherous Alliance,* 95–109. Lenczowski, *American Presidents,* 233–42. See also the Tower Commission Report, called *Report of the President's Special Review Board,* Washington DC, February 26, 1987. See also *Report of the Congressional Committees Investigating the Iran-Contra Affair, With the Minority Views,* edited and with an introduction by Joel Brinkley and Stephen Engelberg (New York: Random House, 1988). The story of Israel's early arms supplies to Iran is also covered in Gary Sick, *October Surprise* (New York: Random House, 1991).

5. See Lenczowski, *American Presidents,* 233–42; the Tower Commission Report; the *Report of the Congressional Committees;* and Parsi, *Treacherous Alliance,* 112–26, particularly for his detailed account of the secret Israeli-Iranian meetings and secret U.S.-Iranian meetings.

6. Lenczowski, *American Presidents,* 233–42, provides the quotation on 237; the Tower Commission Report; the *Report of the Congressional Committees Investigating the Iran-Contra Affair;* and Parsi, *Treacherous Alliance,* 112–26.

7. For a much more detailed account of U.S.-Iranian confrontations in the Gulf and the U.S. political and legal reasoning behind them, see Mattair, *Three Occupied UAE Islands,* esp. 408–14, and also Navias and Hooton, *Tanker Wars,* 39–40, 62–63, 68–69. See Lenczowski, *American Presidents,* 246, for Reagan's statement.

8. Navias and Hooton, *Tanker Wars,* 77–79, 92–96, 123–25.

9. See Mattair, *Three Occupied UAE Islands,* 409, for Reagan's statement and for author's interview with Frank Carlucci, Washington DC, October 1997. See also Lenczowski, *American Presidents,* 246, and Navias and Hooton, *Tanker Wars,* 140.

10. Lenczowski, *American Presidents,* 246.

11. Cordesman and Wagner, *Iran-Iraq War,* 379; Navias and Hooton, *Tanker Wars,* 143, 173.

12. See Caspar Weinberger, *"Fighting for Peace": Seven Critical Years in the Pentagon* (New York: Warner Books, 1990), 397; George Shultz, *Turmoil and Triumph: My Years as Secretary of State* (New York: Charles Scribner's Sons, 1993), 925; Admiral William J. Crowe, Jr., with David Chanoff, *The Line of Fire* (New York: Simon and Schuster, 1993), 181–82.

13. Lenczowski, *American Presidents,* 233–42.

14. Twinam, *The Gulf*, 140–42; Lenczowski, *American Presidents*, 247.

15. For substantially more detailed accounts of both the "tanker war" and Operation Earnest Will, see Mattair, *Three Occupied UAE Islands*, 409–10; Navias and Hooton, *Tanker Wars*, 31, 112–15, 121, 135–38, 141, 170, 183; and Cordesman and Wagner, *Iran-Iraq War*, 298 and 563.

16. Navias and Hooton, *Tanker Wars*, 143–44.

17. Crowe, *Line of Fire*, 197–99. See also Navias and Hooton, *Tanker Wars*, 141, 143–46, 155–56, 169, 173–74. The United States later destroyed the *Iran Ajr* and returned its crew to Iran.

18. Navias and Hooton, *Tanker Wars*, 153.

19. See Mattair *Three Occupied UAE Islands*, 411; Navias and Hooton, *Tanker Wars*, 154.

20. Navias and Hooton, *Tanker Wars*, 155.

21. Parsi, *Treacherous Alliance*, 128.

22. Crowe, *Line of Fire*, 200–201; Cordesman and Wagner, *Iran-Iraq War*, 375–76; Navias and Hooton, *Tanker Wars*, 170–71.

23. Crowe, *Line of Fire*, 201–2; Cordesman and Wagner, *Iran-Iraq War*, 378; Navias and Hooton, *Tanker Wars*, 171.

24. Crowe, *Line of Fire*, 202–3; Cordesman and Wagner, *Iran-Iraq War*, 378; Navias and Hooton, *Tanker Wars*, 170–73. Author's interview with Frank Carlucci, October 1997.

25. Cordesman and Wagner, *Iran-Iraq War*, 379; Navias and Hooton, *Tanker Wars*, 143, 173.

26. Navias and Hooton, *Tanker Wars*, 174–75.

27. Ibid., 177–81.

28. Byman, *Deadly Connections*, 94.

29. Parsi, *Treacherous Alliance*, 131.

30. Twinam, *The Gulf*, 177–89.

31. Excerpts from the Defense Department's classified 1992 Draft Defense Planning Guidance were quoted in the *New York Times*, March 8, 1992. The finished version is classified and not available to the public.

32. Twinam, *The Gulf*, 256.

33. Robert V. Barylski, "The Collapse of the Soviet Union and Gulf Security," in *Gulf Security in the Twenty-First Century*, ed. David E. Long and Christian Koch (Abu Dhabi: The Emirates Center for Strategic Studies and Research, 1997), 97–98. See also Takeyh, *Hidden Iran*, 76–79.

34. Parsi, *Treacherous Alliance*, 147–51, 157–71.

35. See Anthony Lake, "Confronting Backlash States," *Foreign Affairs*, March/April 1994. See also "Symposium on Dual Containment: U.S. Policy Toward Iran and Iraq," featuring Martin Indyk, Graham Fuller, Anthony Cordesman, Phebe Marr, George McGovern, and Thomas R. Mattair, *Middle East Policy* 3 (Spring 1994). See also Thomas R. Mattair, "Horizons for Cooperation in the [Persian] Gulf: The View from Washington," *Iranian Journal of International Affairs* 7 (Fall 1995): 576–84. Iran was suspected of supporting training camps in the Sudan, the Islamic Group in Egypt and the Armed Islamic Group in Algeria, and may have trained some al-Qaeda figures. Indyk had worked for the American Israeli Public Affairs Committee and for the Washington Institute for Near East Policy. See also U.S. Department of State, *Patterns of Global Terrorism 1993*, April 1994, 1, and successive years.

36. See "Symposium: U.S. Secretary of Defense on Gulf Security and U.S. Policy," *Middle East Policy* 3 (April 1995), based on a December 1994 event in Washington DC organized by the author.

37. Mattair, *Three Occupied UAE Islands,* 417–18, cites the *New York Times,* March 1, 1995, A11, and the *Washington Post,* March 1, 1995, for these statements.

38. Ibid., 417–18, cites the *Washington Post,* March 3, 1995 for this statement.

39. Ibid., 419. See *New York Times,* March 23, 1995, A9; *Christian Science Monitor,* March 23, 1995, 1 and 8.

40. Ibid. cites author's interviews, U.S. Department of State, Washington DC, and U.S. Department of Defense, Arlington, Virginia, 1997.

41. Ibid., 416–17, 420–22.

42. See Neal M. Sher, "Comprehensive U.S. Sanctions Against Iran: A Plan for Action," American Israel Public Affairs Committee, April 2, 1995. See also Executive Order #12957 Prohibiting Certain Transactions With Respect to the Development of Iranian Petroleum Resources, March 15, 1995. See also Executive Order #12959 Prohibiting Certain Transactions With Respect To Iran, May 6, 1995. See also "U.S. Policy Toward Iran: From Containment to Relentless Pursuit?" a panel discussion featuring Ellen Laipson, Gary Sick, Richard Cottam, and Thomas R. Mattair, *Middle East Policy* 4, nos. 1 and 2 (1995), for a discussion about these executive orders. See also Meghan L. O'Sullivan, *Shrewd Sanctions: Statecraft and State Sponsors of Terrorism* (Washington DC: Brookings Press, 2003), for a comprehensive study of these sanctions.

43. Author interview with Martin Indyk, Old Executive Office Building, Washington DC, November 1994.

44. The author attended a small meeting in the spring of 1995 at which then-Israeli Foreign Minister Shimon Peres and future Prime Minister Ehud Barak warned that Iran could have nuclear weapons within a few years, i.e., by about 1998 or 1999.

45. Thomas R. Mattair, "Containment or Collision?" *Middle East Insight* 11, no. 5 (1995): 26.

46. Ibid.

47. Ibid. See also Barylski, "Collapse of the Soviet Union and Gulf Security," esp. 106–17.

48. Mattair, *Three Occupied UAE Islands,* based on author's interviews with GCC officials in Abu Dhabi, 1997 and 1998, and author's interview at the Crescent Oil Company, Sharjah, December 1997.

49. Parsi, *Treacherous Alliance,* 193.

50. Clark, *Against All Enemies,* 112–21; *9/11 Commission Report,* 60 and note on 148; Byman, *Deadly Connections,* 106, 108.

51. *Wall Street Journal,* June 25, 2006; *United Press International,* June 6, 2007.

52. Mattair, "Containment or Collision," 29, based on numerous discussions with U.S. officials.

53. Zbigniew Brzezinski, Brent Scowcroft, and Richard Murphy, "Differentiated Containment," *Foreign Affairs* 76 (May/June 1997).

54. Byman, *Deadly Connections,* 109.

55. *Wall Street Journal,* December 16, 1997.

56. Author's interviews, U.S. Department of State, Washington DC, and U.S. Department of Defense, Arlington, Virginia, 1997. One State Department official said to the author that "We do not make our policy toward Iran based on our national interests. We make our policy toward Iran based on our domestic politics."

57. Byman, *Deadly Connections,* 109; Mattair, *Three Occupied UAE Islands,* 429; and see Slavin, *Bitter Friends, Bosom Enemies,* 188–89, for details on the Clinton proposals for talks with Iran.

58. Bulent Aras and Fatih Ozbay, "Dances with Wolves: Russia, Iran and the Nuclear Issue," *Middle East Policy,* Winter 2006.

59. See the 1992 Draft Defense Planning Guidance, Department of Defense, 1992.

60. Some of these neoconservatives had also prepared a study for an Israeli think tank called the Institute for Advanced Strategic and Political Studies. This study, "A Clean Break: A New Strategy for Securing the Realm," advised Netanyahu to abandon the Oslo peace process and to "contain, destabilize, and 'roll back'" Israel's adversaries, particularly Syria. The January 1998 letter to Clinton was sent by the Project for the New American Century. The September 2000 study was also done under the auspices of this same group and called "Rebuilding America's Defenses: Strategies, Forces, and Resources for a New Century." See www.newamericancentury.org.

61. James Dobbins has discussed this in spellbinding speeches at the New America Foundation on August 24, 2006 and at the Middle East Institute annual conference on November 13–14, 2006. See also James Dobbins, "How to Talk to Iran," *Washington Post,* July 22, 2007. See also Leverett, "Dealing with Tehran," at www.tcf.org. See also Parsi, *Treacherous Alliance,* chap. 18, for a comprehensive account.

62. Porter, "How Neocons Sabotaged Iran's Help."

63. Gareth Porter, "Israel Warned US Not to Invade Iraq after 9/11," *Inter Press Service,* August 28, 2007.

64. Laura Rozen, "Three Days in Rome," *Mother Jones,* July/August 2006, provides this quotation. See also Joshua Micah Marshall, Laura Rozen, and Paul Glastris, "Iran Contra II: Fresh Scrutiny on a Rogue Pentagon Operation," *Washington Monthly,* September 2004.

65. Marshall, Rozen, and Glastris, "Iran Contra II," and Rozen, "Three Days in Rome." Ledeen and Ghorbanifar had both been involved in the shipments of Israeli and U.S. weapons to Iran in the 1980s. The CIA had since then reportedly issued notices that Ghorbanifar was a "fabricator" and had instructed its officials not to meet with him. The meeting in December 2001 required CIA authorization because it included members of a foreign intelligence agency, and that CIA authorization had reportedly not been obtained. Members of Feith's staff were later prominent in arguing that Iraq's Saddam Hussein regime had working relations with al-Qaeda and that Iraq had WMD, both arguments later shown to be mistaken. Franklin was later convicted for passing classified intelligence about Iran to Israel, with the involvement of AIPAC officials, who were forced to resign. The Pentagon Inspector General later issued a report concluding that Feith's office had been involved in "inappropriate" intelligence operations.

66. Leverett, "Dealing with Tehran." See also Porter, "How Neocons Sabotaged Iran's Help."

67. Porter, "Israel Warned US."

68. Porter, "How Neocons Sabotaged Iran's Help."

69. For a brief review of these developments, see *Jane's Sentinel Security Assessment: The Gulf States, 2003,* at www4.janes.com.

70. *The National Security Strategy of the United States of America,* Washington DC: the White House, September 2002, at www.whitehouse.gov.

71. Leverett, "Dealing with Tehran," and Parsi, *Treacherous Alliance,* 241–43. Author's discussions with former State Department officials, 2006.

72. Parsi, *Treacherous Alliance,* provides by far the most comprehensive account of all this material in his chapter 19, which draws on interviews with U.S. and Iranian officials involved in the story. For early reporting, see, for example, Guy Dinmore, "U.S. Rejects Iran's Offer for

Talks on Nuclear Programme," *Financial Times,* June 15, 2003, and "Washington Hardliners Wary of Engaging with Iran," *Financial Times,* March 16, 2004. See also Gareth Porter, "Burnt Offering," *American Prospect,* May 21, 2006, and "Cheney-Led 'Cabal' Blocked 2003 Nuclear Talks with Iran," *Inter Press Service,* May 28, 2006. See also Leverett, "Dealing with Tehran." The author verified some details in several brief discussions with former U.S. officials in 2006.

73. See William Quandt, *Peace Process: American Diplomacy and the Arab-Israeli Conflict since 1967,* 3rd ed. (Washington DC and Berkeley: Brookings Institution and University of California Press, 2005), for Israel's positions on these issues.

74. Porter, "Burnt Offering"; Leverett, "Dealing with Tehran"; Parsi, *Treacherous Alliance,* chap. 19.

75. "Regional Consequences of Regime Change in Iraq," a study of the NIC, CIA, January 2003. A partially redacted declassified version of this study was released in May 2007 by the Senate Intelligence Committee. See http://intelligence.senate.gov/prewar.pdf.

76. Seymour M. Hersh, "The Iran Plans," *New Yorker,* April 17, 2006; and Seymour M. Hersh, "The Next Act," *New Yorker,* November 20, 2006. These forces reportedly work with unmanned aerial vehicles (UAVs), or drones, to identify potential nuclear sites, and then plant equipment such as sensors designed to detect radioactivity from such sites.

77. Zbigniew Brzezinski and Robert Gates, "Iran: Time for a New Approach," Council on Foreign Relations, 2004, at www.cfr.org.

78. Gareth Porter, "Bush's New Iran Policy—No Evidence for IED Charges," *Inter Press New Service,* January 16, 2007; Slavin, *Bitter Friends, Bosom Enemies,* 216.

79. For a brief review of the following developments, see Kerr, "Iran Nuclear Crisis," at www.armscontrol.org.

80. Ibid.

81. Ibid.

82. Ibid.

83. Ibid. See also Leverett, "Dealing with Tehran."

84. Julian Borger, "US Iran Intelligence Is Incorrect," *Guardian,* February 22, 2007; *New York Times,* February 22, 2007; Bob Drogin and Kim Murphy, "UN Calls US Data on Iran's Nuclear Programs Unreliable," *Los Angeles Times,* February 25, 2007.

85. Borger, *Guardian,* February 22, 2007; *New York Times,* February 22, 2007; Drogin and Murphy, *Los Angeles Times,* February 25, 2007.

CHAPTER 5

Current Crises Between Iran and Major Powers

From 2006 through early 2008 the questions on the minds of analysts of Iran have been: Do recent developments increase or decrease the possibility of U.S. or Israeli military strikes against Iran? Would strikes be necessary or successful? Are sanctions or diplomacy reasonable alternatives for promoting U.S. national interests in the Middle East? Throughout these years, there were numerous developments in Iran's nuclear programs, Iran's policies on Arab-Israeli issues, Iran's involvement in Iraq, and Iran's policies in the Gulf. There were also numerous developments in U.S. policies on all of these issues. This chapter is an empirical effort to weave all of these developments together and an analytical effort to understand how the involved states may have been reacting to each other.

WAR DRUMS

The Bush administration was taken by surprise in January 2006 when Israeli Prime Minister Sharon had a stroke that left him unable to govern and when the U.S. demand for Palestinian legislative elections resulted in a victory for Hamas. The United States and Israel, now led by Ehud Olmert, regarded the Palestinian legislature as unacceptable because it was dominated by Hamas, and they regarded the cabinet named by Mahmoud Abbas as unacceptable because he was compelled to name Hamas officials to it. The Bush administration and Israel were unwilling to provide funds to or negotiate with the Hamas-dominated Palestinian Authority unless it recognized Israel, accepted previous agreements between Israel and the Palestinian Authority, and renounced terror. Hamas was not willing to meet these conditions, but did offer a ten-year truce to Israel and had abided by a one-year cease-fire. Shia Iran now reportedly attempted to build stronger relations with Sunni Hamas by increasing its funds to Hamas, which also received funds from Sunni Arabs across the region.

In January 2006, Iran ended its voluntary suspension of work on uranium enrichment and resumed these efforts at its underground facility at Natanz. In February, Iran indicated that it would no longer comply with the Additional Protocol to the NPT that it had accepted in 2003. It would no longer permit the IAEA to conduct aggressive inspections of Iran's declared nuclear sites and suspected undeclared sites. Iran would not permit any visits to undeclared sites after February, so the IAEA would not be able to determine if undeclared nuclear activity was occurring at such sites. Nevertheless, then Director of National Intelligence John Negroponte said in March 2006 that Iran would need about five or ten more years before it could develop a nuclear weapon, which was the assessment made in the May 2005 NIE report. But Israeli intelligence believed Iran was closer to such a weapon and many in the White House and the Pentagon accepted this Israeli assessment. In April, Iran announced that it had successfully enriched a small amount of uranium in its underground facility at Natanz.[1]

In March, one month after the bombing of a Shia mosque in Iraq ignited a Shia retaliation against Sunnis, Bush repeated his assertion that some of the most powerful IEDs U.S. forces were encountering in Iraq came from Iran. Chairman of the JCS Peter Pace said the following day, however, that there was no firm evidence of this. British government officials had also acknowledged that they had no firm evidence that the IEDs killing their troops in the south of Iraq, where their conflicts were normally with Shia factions, came from Iran, although they suspected that Iran and/or Hezbollah had a hand in this. The borders are long, rugged, and porous along the northeast and southeast of Iraq, and even without concrete evidence, it is possible that IEDs and EFPs (explosively formed penetrators)—or components for them, such as spherical copper discs—could cross the many smuggling routes across them, with or without the official sanction of the Iranian government. The technology is also known well enough that IEDs and EFPs and their components could be coming from Lebanon or from other states or from the "black market," and that they could be easily manufactured or assembled in Iraq, by both Shia militias and Sunni insurgents.[2]

The concerns about Iran led to arguments for U.S. or Israeli military strikes against Iran.[3] In its March 2006 "National Security Strategy," the Bush administration continued to argue that "preemptive" military action to prevent any "rogue state" from attacking the United States or its friends with WMD was justifiable if other strategies were failing, and it named Iran as potentially the greatest threat in this respect. This argument was also made in the September 2002 "National Security Strategy" and was applied in Iraq in 2003, although the assertions that Iraq had WMD and ties to al-Qaeda were inaccurate. Again, although the administration used the term "preemptive" action, which means action to cope with an imminent attack, the policy the administration was explaining could more accurately be termed "preventive" action, which means action to cope with a growing potential threat.[4] President Bush specifically asserted in March 2006 that the United States would use military means if necessary to protect Israel against Iranian threats, and this was meant to reassure Israel and to dissuade Israel from implementing its own contingency plans too quickly. When asked in April if his statement that all options were on the table included a possible nuclear strike on Iran, Bush replied by repeating all options were on the table, implying the answer is yes. At this time, the Pentagon had reportedly, at Bush's direction, developed operational plans for air strikes against Iran and had reportedly, at Cheney's direction, developed plans for the use of nuclear "bunker-busting" weapons in such strikes. Opposition from Air Force officers and from the JCS in late April 2006 to the nuclear option, and the willingness of some officers to resign if it were ordered, reportedly led to the shelving of the nuclear option, but that may be only temporary. In the meantime, U.S. military forces were reportedly inside Iran, developing knowledge about potential targets, and providing funds and encouragement to Azeri, Kurdish, and Baluchi ethnic minorities opposed to the Iranian regime.[5]

The possibility of war with Iran led to some energetic counterarguments. Strong counterarguments were advanced that conventional or even nuclear "bunker-busting," earth-penetrating weapons may not destroy Iran's hardened underground nuclear facilities, that the location of all of these facilities may not even be known, that nuclear weapons would cause enough radioactive fallout to cause large civilian casualties, that military measures might have to be repeated several years later if nuclear facilities are reestablished, and that Iran has many retaliatory capabilities. It was also argued that military strikes may even enable the regime to consolidate its power and embark on a crash program to develop nuclear weapons by using unknown facilities or the black market or even by extracting plutonium from spent fuel rods if the Bushire reactor were operating when bombed and Russian technicians fled.[6]

Nevertheless, some in the National Security Council, the Vice President's office, the Pentagon, and even in the State Department reportedly thought that setbacks in Iraq and Afghanistan made it even more necessary to strike Iran, even with nuclear weapons, in order to overthrow its regime and prevent it from exploiting these problems and expanding its power and influence.[7]

While Saudi Arabia and the other GCC states shared these concerns about Iran's nuclear programs and Iran's growing influence in Iraq and in the Levant, as well as Iran's influence in the Gulf, and while they were committed to their ongoing security partnerships with the United States, they were very wary of military strikes. While they may have allowed U.S. surveillance aircraft to use their airfields for flights over Iran, they nevertheless said at their GCC summit in Riyadh in May 2006, and they have frequently said in private for years, that they want their problems with Iran resolved through diplomacy rather than force. They fear that if Iran is attacked, they would be targets of Iranian retaliation.[8]

The Bush administration also launched other efforts that could substitute for war or complement war. In March 2006, a high-level interagency group called the ISOG (Iran Syria Policy and Operations Group) was established to coordinate efforts against Iran and Syria. This group was initially cochaired by Deputy Assistant Secretary of State Elizabeth Cheney, the Vice President's daughter, until she took maternity leave, and then by Deputy National Security Adviser Elliott Abrams and Deputy Assistant Secretary of State for Near Eastern Affairs James Jeffries, and reportedly coordinated with representatives from the Treasury Department, the Pentagon, and the CIA. The ISOG was initially described in April 2006 as being established to coordinate democracy promotion activities in the two states, such as through broadcasting programs, which were intended to promote "regime change." It was later reported, however, that ISOG was also coordinating covert financial assistance to Iranian dissidents and democracy advocates; military sales and assistance to and joint exercises with Saudi Arabia, the UAE and Bahrain, and others; restricting cooperation between international banks and Iranian banks; and "building international outrage against Iran" by publicizing Iran's alleged role in the 1994 terrorist attack in Argentina.[9] This latter effort may also have entailed publicizing alleged activities of Iranians in Iraq and Afghanistan and alleged Iranian nuclear weapons programs. The group was modeled after a group that had been established to coordinate actions against Iraq prior to the 2003 invasion of Iraq.

Soon afterwards, the administration also agreed to the efforts of Secretary Rice's State Department to revive the diplomatic track concerning Iran's nuclear programs. In June 2006, the United States and the other permanent members of the UN Security Council plus Germany (the P5+1) made an offer to resume British, French, and German (E3/EU) talks with Iran about Iran's nuclear programs, and that the United States would now join these talks, on the precondition that Iran first suspend uranium enrichment and reprocessing of spent nuclear fuel. The incentives held out as possible outcomes of these negotiations were a less detailed version of the incentives that Iran had found unsatisfactory in August 2005.[10] Moreover, the Bush administration did not offer the security assurances Iran had been seeking. Even if Iran had accepted this precondition, it was not likely to accept the objective of some U.S. officials for the outcome of negotiations, namely, that Iran suspend these processes for many years and resume them only with permission from the UN Security Council, where the United States has a veto. Some in the Bush administration would intend this as a virtually permanent suspension.[11]

Iran rejected the P5+1 precondition that it suspend enrichment and reprocessing before the United States would join new multilateral talks. Iran also rejected

UNSC Resolution 1696, which demanded that it suspend enrichment and reprocessing by August 31, 2006. Iran's initial answer to the P5+1 offer came in August and hinted that Iran might accept suspension for one or two months *after* negotiations began, but Iran's chief negotiator, Ali Larijani, later said Iran would not do so. Iran's initial answer also indicated that Iran was willing once again to abide by the Additional Protocol to the NPT, i.e., to resume the permission it withdrew in February for the IAEA to aggressively monitor its declared nuclear sites as well as undeclared sites. Larijani then suggested to EU Foreign Minister Solana in September that Iran would temporarily suspend *the expansion of* its enrichment program during negotiations, presumably meaning that Iran would not continue work on developing industrial-scale enrichment capability at the underground facility at Natanz, but would continue its experimental research activity.[12]

As this diplomatic track was being launched in June, Hamas members participated in capturing an Israeli soldier in the Gaza Strip and then Hezbollah captured two Israeli soldiers in July. The Bush administration and Israel thought that Iran was involved, but it was not clear to U.S. intelligence or the U.S. military that Iran called for these operations or that Iran could have stopped these operations.[13] Hezbollah's leaders, who are close to leaders in Iran's clergy, military, and Revolutionary Guards, may have informed Iran about the impending kidnappings of the Israeli soldiers and Iran may have given a "green light." Shia Iran supports Shia Hezbollah and Sunni Islamic Jihad and Sunni Hamas because it sympathizes with their grievances, and to generate popular support at home and abroad for its desire for Islamic leadership throughout the Arab and Islamic world, and to pressure Sunni Arab regimes, or to promote at least a Shia crescent, but it would not likely want to provoke Israel or the United States to attack Iran or Syria. Iran would more likely give a "green light" to limited actions against Israel to make Israel and the United States see Iran can pressure them if there are no negotiated solutions, or to show that Iran has some deterrent to Israeli and/or American military action against Iran. But Hezbollah's leader Shaikh Nasrallah said Hezbollah did not anticipate Israel's furious reaction and it is not likely that Iran did.[14]

The outcome of the subsequent summer 2006 war between Israel and Hezbollah was not the decisive victory expected by Israel and the United States, which backed Israel, and which reportedly hoped to learn lessons applicable to a strike against Iran and to eliminate the rockets and missiles that Hezbollah could use against Israel during a war with Iran. Hezbollah demonstrated surprising capabilities against Israeli ground and naval forces attacking their positions in Lebanon. Israel could not locate and destroy all of Hezbollah's rockets and missiles, many of them previously supplied by Syria and Iran, so even after firing four thousand of these weapons during the fighting, Hezbollah still retained fifteen to twenty thousand rockets and missiles when the fighting ended.[15] In August, UNSC

Resolution 1701 ended the fighting, but did not solve the conflict. Fifteen thousand Lebanese Army forces and a UN force of fifteen thousand were deployed in southern Lebanon, but they could not disarm and disband Hezbollah, drive it from southern Lebanon, or indefinitely prevent it from striking Israel from southern Lebanon, and especially not from positions north of these forces, although more than a year later Hezbollah had not launched strikes against Israel. Lebanese and international monitoring of the Beirut airport and the Lebanese seacoast could diminish the ability of Iran and Syria to send new arms to Hezbollah. But Syria appeared unwilling to accept any international presence along its land border with Lebanon, and Syria's own reinforced border forces could not be expected to stop any flow of arms sanctioned by the government.[16] Israel continued scrutinizing Iran and Syria and was willing to take military action against supply movements, but in time Hezbollah's patrons would be able to resume arms transfers in defiance of the UNSC call for an arms embargo on Hezbollah. In the meantime, Iran quickly began to finance reconstruction and social services in the Shia south of Lebanon after the war, thus increasing its influence and popularity there.

At the same time as this Israeli-Hezbollah war was occurring, and as civil war was raging in Iraq, U.S. Ambassador Khalilzad argued that Iran supported rocket and mortar attacks by Shia militias then considered to be part of Moqtada al-Sadr's Mahdi Army against the "Green Zone" housing Iraqi and American government officials in Baghdad. But there were already two dozen Shia militias in Baghdad alone, and many of them were rogue cells that were not loyal to al-Sadr, who is an Arab nationalist and known to be very suspicious of Iran.

It was later reported that Bush signed a secret presidential finding in 2006 authorizing the CIA to carry out nonlethal covert operations against Iran. These operations had reportedly been proposed by the CIA to the administration and were reportedly designed to spread propaganda and disinformation about Iran, to manipulate Iran's currency, to interfere with Iran's financial transactions, and particularly to interfere with efforts by the Revolutionary Guards to purchase technology or equipment for Iran's nuclear and missile programs. Elliott Abrams was among the administration officials who approved this CIA proposal.[17] Indeed, the ISOG may have been involved in overseeing these CIA operations. The revelation that one element of the CIA plan was a propaganda and disinformation campaign against Iran, along with the revelation that one element of the ISOG mandate was to generate international outrage against Iran, raises unavoidable questions about the truthfulness of what the Bush administration was telling the media and the American people about Iran's nuclear programs and Iran's involvement in Iraq and Afghanistan and the Levant. It should be noted here that nonlethal operations means that CIA officers cannot use deadly force in carrying out these particular operations, but there are other presidential findings authorizing lethal force in counterterrorism and in nonproliferation efforts, which could possibly apply to Iran. Moreover, covert operations carried out by the U.S. military do not require a presidential finding, and so may possibly use deadly force without a presidential authorization. Iran accused the United States and Britain of supporting attacks by Sunnis Arabs in Iran's province of Khuzistan in the summer of 2006.[18]

In addition, senior administration and counterterrorism officials later reported that U.S. military forces had been authorized since the fall of 2006 not only to capture but also to kill Iranian Revolutionary Guards and intelligence operatives inside Iraq and that this kind of pressure was meant not only to curtail Iranian influence in Iraq but also to pressure Iran to make concessions on its nuclear programs. Bush's senior aides, including Rice, reportedly approved this decision, as did Elliott Abrams and others on his ISOG. Abrams and his colleagues also argued for operations against Iranian influence in Afghanistan, Lebanon, and the Palestinian territories, particularly after the summer war between Israel and Hezbollah.[19] Reportedly, some of these operations would be coordinated with Israel, Egypt, Jordan, Saudi Arabia, and other GCC states.[20] Indeed, the mood of the administration during the fall was reflected when Iran asked the International Assistance Force led by NATO to help stabilize Iran's border with Afghanistan against drug dealers entering Iran from Afghanistan and killing Iranian border police, and at U.S. request NATO refused to help.[21]

By September 2006, some informed observers raised serious concerns that the Bush administration was preparing to carry out military strikes against Iran.[22] In October, overt measures were being taken that stoked these concerns. As expected, in early October 2006, the Eisenhower aircraft carrier strike group, including a destroyer, cruiser, frigate, fast combat support ship, and fast attack submarine, set out for the Persian Gulf. Expeditionary Strike Group 5, including marines and amphibious landing craft, was also sent to the Gulf. Orders to deploy were also issued for other vessels, including submarines, minehunters, minesweepers, and an *Aegis*-class cruiser. Later in October, the United States coordinated multinational military exercises in the Gulf to train for the interception of any vessels carrying components for WMD or their delivery systems to Iran. This training exercise, part of the administration's Proliferation Security Initiative, involved the participation of three Bahraini navy vessels, observers from Kuwait, Qatar, and the UAE, and Australian, British, French, and Italian warships, along with one U.S. Coast Guard vessel. The Eisenhower carrier group then arrived in the Persian Gulf on December 11.[23]

Furthermore, there were Israeli military, intelligence, political, and civilian figures who also argued that U.S. or Israeli military action may be necessary. Israel might want a "green light" from the United States before taking military action, and Cheney had reportedly advised Israel "don't go without us." Bush subsequently told French President Chirac in late October 2006, however, that an Israeli strike on Iran could not be ruled out and that he would understand if

Israel took this course of action, an indication that Israel may have a "green light" if the Bush administration cannot act itself.[24]

An alternative explanation for these overt military activities and public reports, and one that seems correct in retrospect, was that normal contingency planning, routine deployments, and routine exercises were being combined with covert operations and a heavy dose of psychological warfare, and that they were all part of a "coercive diplomacy" campaign designed to confront Iran with credible threats and pressures in an effort to alter its behavior before any resort to war.

When the Democratic Party won control of the House of Representatives and the Senate in early November 2006 and President Bush announced that Secretary of Defense Rumsfeld would be leaving his post, some thought that these developments not only were a reflection of a public demand for a new policy on Iraq, but would undercut any movement toward military action against Iran as well. Even before the November election, Democrats in the House and Senate had voted in favor of the 2006 Iran Freedom Support Act, which Bush signed into law in October. This act insisted on the termination of Iran's enrichment and reprocessing programs, codified and strengthened previous economic sanctions, and authorized $66 million to support democratic transformation through nonmilitary means such as broadcasting to Iran, support for nongovernmental organizations, promoting civil society, democratic reform, human rights, and educational and cultural exchanges, despite prescient warnings from Iranian civil society activists that they would now be repressed as U.S. agents seeking "regime change." This congressional act is consistent with the emphasis on democracy promotion found in the new National Security Strategy issued in March 2006. But the act stipulated that this money cannot be used to support military efforts to bring about regime change.[25] Old and new Democrats could be expected, however, to share U.S. and Israeli security concerns about Iran. Indeed, Democratic National Committee Chair Howard Dean, Senator Hillary Clinton, Senator Barak Obama, and former Senator John Edwards all said that all options must remain on the table. The Democrats were expected to be more cautious about U.S. military action against Iran, not favoring this for regime change, but willing to do it as a last resort.

Moreover, the newly designated Secretary of Defense, Robert M. Gates, was a member of the Iraq Study Group until resigning in order to take over the Pentagon. As widely expected, the Iraq Study Group's recommendations in early December included a call for gradual withdrawal of most U.S. forces from Iraq and strategic redeployment of remaining U.S. forces in Iraq and a call for dialogue with Iran, Syria, and other neighbors of Iraq. Gates had also been a coauthor with former Carter administration National Security Adviser Zbigniew Brzezinski of a 2004 Council on Foreign Relations study that had advocated a new approach to Iran based on a "compartmentalized process of dialogue, confidence building and incremental engagement."[26] In written answers to the Senate Armed Services

Committee later in November, prior to his confirmation hearings, Gates discussed the possibility of multilateral or even bilateral talks with Iran, adding that "even in the worst days of the cold war, the United States maintained a dialogue with the Soviet Union and China."[27] Moreover, in his confirmation hearings before the Senate Armed Services Committee in early December, Gates argued that military action against Iran should be a last resort, only if diplomacy had failed, and he noted, accurately, that Iran would have significant retaliatory capabilities if attacked.[28] Furthermore, it was later reported that the JCS unanimously argued against air strikes against Iran in a meeting with Bush and his top national security advisers at the Pentagon in December, arguing that air strikes would be devastating but would not necessarily destroy all of Iran's nuclear facilities and would unleash devastating Iranian retaliation.[29]

At the same time, in November 2006, when Iraq's President Jalal Talabani had visited Iran, Ahmadinejad claimed that Iran would do anything to support a peaceful and strong Iraq. In the same month, U.S. forces had discovered machine shops in Baghdad where EFPs were being assembled, which meant that it was not necessary to get the finished weapons from Iran. It was still possible that some of the components or even finished weapons were coming from Iran, but there were other possible sources. Larijani and Iran's Foreign Minister Manouchehr Mottaki said in early December 2006 that Iran would cooperate over Iraq if the Bush administration committed to gradual withdrawal of its forces. Larijani also made Iran's often repeated call upon GCC states to eject U.S. military forces from their countries and to enter into a regional security pact with Iran.[30]

By mid-December, however, the Pentagon recommended increasing the size of the U.S. military establishment, particularly the army and marines, over a period of years. This was explained as being necessary in order to sustain a long-term presence in Iraq and to prepare the United States to deal with potential adversaries such as Iran and North Korea, and in particular to discourage any state from aggression based on the United States being bogged down in Iraq.[31] At the same time, new Secretary of Defense Gates met a request from Centcom Commander John Abizaid to deploy a second aircraft carrier strike group—the Stennis aircraft carrier group—in the region by early 2007. This was meant as a show of force to Iran. And Britain was preparing to send two minesweepers to supplement its naval forces in the Gulf.[32] In early January, Gates recommended that retiring General Abizaid's replacement be Admiral William Fallon, the commander of U.S. forces in the Pacific. The recommendation of this experienced naval aviator seemed to indicate that the administration wanted a commander who could easily command warships and naval aircraft, including aircraft carriers and their aircraft. Some thought this signaled an intention to strike Iran, although in retrospect that was not the case, but at least it was another signal to Iran.

These overt and covert U.S. measures and these U.S. decisions and public statements were designed in part to elicit Iranian agreement to suspend its nuclear programs, but they had not worked as the end of 2006 was approaching. The Bush administration then secured unanimous passage of a relatively weak UNSC Resolution 1737 on December 23, 2006. This resolution banned exports to and imports by Iran of materials used in uranium enrichment, reprocessing, and ballistic missiles. It also mandated a halt to financial transactions with and a freeze of the assets of twelve individuals and ten companies involved in these programs. The resolution allowed for the assets to be unfrozen under certain circumstances, and it also excluded any sanctions against the nuclear plant Russia is building at Bushire. It gave Iran sixty days to stop its program or face stronger sanctions.[33] Iran's parliament then passed a bill calling on the government to "revise its cooperation" with the IAEA; the bill was immediately approved by the Guardian Council. Iran then demanded the recall of the IAEA's top inspector in Iran and announced that it would deny entry to thirty-eight IAEA inspectors.

As noted in an earlier chapter, the United States has found it difficult to obtain support from Russia and China, and even from France and Germany, for extremely punitive economic and political sanctions against Iran, although in 2006 several banks in Switzerland and Japan agreed to reduce their involvement in Iran. In part, this difficulty is because Iran, which has the second largest oil reserves in the world as well as the second largest natural gas reserves in the world, is an important trading partner and investment opportunity for them.[34] In addition, Russia and even China are concerned about U.S. military power in the Middle East, the Caucasus, and Central Asia—and globally—and want to maintain strategic alliances with Iran that could limit or balance U.S. power in the region and in the world.[35] On the other hand, both countries want to maintain good political relations with the United States and do not want Iran to be the target of U.S. military strikes. In addition, it appears that both countries have some concerns about Iran developing nuclear weapons.[36] So Russia and China supported a UNSC resolution with moderately punitive sanctions that signaled to Iran that it should compromise. Even so, the EU was slow to implement these sanctions, and this elicited U.S. complaints in January 2007.

After securing this resolution and after renewing accusations that Iran was supplying Shia militias in Iraq with EFPs, and saying that U.S. forces had intercepted weapons with 2006 Iranian factory markings and/or serial numbers on them, the administration aggressively confronted Iran in Iraq. U.S. forces staged two raids in late December 2006, capturing a number of Iranians in Iraq. Several of them detained in one raid, however, turned out to be accredited Iranian diplomats who had had meetings with President Talabani, Prime Minister Nuri Kamal al-Maliki, and SCIRI leader Abdul Aziz al-Hakim. They were released to Iraqi authorities.

The United States claimed that the other raid led to the capture of eight Iraqis and two Iranians who were members of the Qods Force of the Revolutionary Guards, the force responsible for the foreign covert operations of the

Revolutionary Guards, including Mohsin Chizari, reportedly a very high-ranking officer in the Qods Force, and suggested that maps, videos, photos, and documents found in the raid indicated they had been linked to arms shipments to armed Iraqi groups and to planning for attacks against Iraqi civilians, Iraqi security forces, and U.S. and other coalition forces. The documents reportedly included receipts for sniper rifles, maps of Baghdad indicating which neighborhoods are Sunni, Shiite, or mixed, and something referred to as "material relating to sophisticated IEDs." But these two Iranians were captured in a raid in the housing complex of SCIRI leader Hakim, inside the home of the commander of SCIRI's Badr Brigade. He also served as the head of the Iraqi parliament's security committee, and the Badr Brigade has many men inside Iraq's official security forces as well as many men outside the official security forces. It was difficult to know, then, whether these Iranians were supporting the authorized activities of the official Iraqi security forces that were also being supported by the United States, or whether Iran was supporting unauthorized Shia "death squad" attacks on Iraqi Sunnis and U.S. forces by Badr Brigade elements inside or outside the official security forces. Iraqi authorities argued that the evidence was circumstantial and the arrests were intended to subvert relations between the Iraqi government and Iran. U.S. forces released the two Iranians to the Iraqis within days, despite having claimed that one of them was such a high-ranking Qods Force officer, and they were quickly driven into Iran. It did not appear that these raids had been based on very good intelligence or that they had produced very convincing evidence, certainly not EFPs with Iranian factory markings or serial numbers.

A NEW YEAR

On January 10, 2007, President Bush announced his new strategy for Iraq, which was in the throes of a civil war almost four years after the U.S. toppling of Saddam Hussein's regime. It was, as expected, a rejection of the Iraq Study Group's calls for withdrawal and redeployment of U.S. forces and negotiations with Iran and Syria. He said that the administration would surge another 21,500 troops to Baghdad and Anbar province (this later became 30,000), accused Iran and Syria of allowing their territory to be used by "terrorists and insurgents," accused Iran of "providing material support for attacks on American troops," warned that the United States would "destroy the networks providing advanced weaponry and training to our enemies in Iraq," announced that the Stennis aircraft carrier group would be deployed to the Gulf, and announced the deployment of antiballistic missile systems to the states of the GCC. He also warned Iran to "stop killing our soldiers."[37]

Hours after Bush's January 10 speech, U.S. forces raided an Iranian office in Erbil, in the Kurdish region of northern Iraq, detaining six Iranians, saying that five of them were members of Iran's Revolutionary Guards, and accusing them of involvement in planning attacks against U.S. forces. It was later reported that Mohammad Javad Jafari, a former officer in the Revolutionary Guards who was serving as deputy to the secretary of the Supreme National Security Council, had been the target of the attack and that he had escaped. Kurdish regional officials protested the U.S. raid; Iran unsuccessfully sought their release. Iran and Iraq both said they were diplomats carrying on official business in Iraq, although their office had not yet been officially designated a consulate by the Iraqi government or the Kurdish regional government. Iran's ambassador to Iraq, Hassan Kazemi-Qomi, announced defiantly that Iran would continue to offer further training, advisers, and equipment for Iraqi government security forces as well as increased economic assistance, including trade and reconstruction assistance.[38]

When Secretary Rice was asked in Senate Foreign Relations Committee hearings on January 11 if actions against Iranians in Iraq could lead to actions inside Iran, she would not take the option off the table. Committee Chairman Joseph Biden, a Democrat, warned Rice that military actions against Iran without congressional authorization would provoke a constitutional crisis, and committee member Chuck Hagel, a Republican, warned that actions comparable to expanding the Vietnam War into Cambodia in 1970 would be a grave mistake. Chairman of the JCS Pace and Defense Secretary Gates and Undersecretary of State R. Nicholas Burns said there were no plans for this. Indeed, Pace said that there was "zero chance" of war with Iran. But the *New Yorker* reporter Seymour Hersh had previously reported that U.S. military forces were already engaged in covert actions inside Iran and soon reported that U.S. forces in Iraq were crossing over into Iran in pursuit of Iranian agents reportedly fleeing into Iran from Iraq.[39]

On the eve of Rice's January 15 visit to Saudi Arabia, Larijani delivered a letter from Khamenei and Ahmadinejad to Saudi Arabia's King Abdullah reportedly asking him to ease U.S.-Iranian tensions.[40] King Abdullah later said that Saudi Arabia had urged Iran to act with restraint in order to avert war in the Gulf.[41] This probably included Iranian restraint in Iraq; and Iranian restraint in Saudi Arabia, where Saudi officials think Iranian agents have been involved with Saudi Shiites in numerous terrorist acts; Iranian restraint in the Gulf, where Iran's military exercises concern the GCC; Iranian restraint in Lebanon and toward Israel; and Iranian restraint in its nuclear programs. The GCC states had already announced that they would pursue peaceful nuclear technology in a cooperative endeavor, but this was understood as a signal to Iran that they would react if Iran developed nuclear weapons, and most GCC states have the funds to actually purchase their own nuclear weapons from sources such as Pakistan. It was later reported that Prince Bandar had discussed the nuclear issue with senior Iranian officials and that Bandar told Bush administration officials that the Iranian overture to Saudi Arabia in January was based on their concern about U.S. shows of military strength in the region, UN sanctions, and the possibility of expanding Sunni-Shia tensions in the region.[42]

King Abdullah's message to Iran about Iraq may have been reflected by the GCC foreign ministers who, along with the foreign ministers of Egypt and Jordan, issued a statement on January 16 expressing general support for the Bush administration's effort to stabilize Iraq, subdue sectarian violence, promote national reconciliation, and prevent external interference.[43] This GCC position actually understated Saudi Arabia's concern with Iran's influence in Iraq, where Iraqi Shia parties with close ties to Iran were in power, and where Iraqi Sunnis were being marginalized. Indeed, during January, Saudi officials provided Khalilzad with evidence that al-Maliki was working with Iran and al-Sadr, but Khalilzad reportedly viewed the evidence as forged.[44]

In addition, Saudi Arabia was working to limit Iranian influence in other ways. King Abdullah had told Cheney in November 2006 that Saudi Arabia would support Iraqi Sunnis if a hasty U.S. withdrawal from Iraq exposed the Iraqi Sunnis to assaults by Iraqi Shiites, and in January, Saudi Arabia asked the other GCC states to provide funds to the Iraqi Sunnis. In that same month, King Abdullah and other GCC leaders also pledged financial support for Lebanon's Sunni-Druze-Christian government to counter Iran's financial support to Hezbollah. King Abdullah also met with Hezbollah leaders in January and presumably urged caution on them. Bandar also met with Larijani several times to try to coordinate a Saudi and Iranian effort to prevent civil war in Lebanon and Iran reportedly responded by pressing Hezbollah to act with restraint. Bandar reportedly sought Iran's agreement to a Lebanese deal that would increase Hezbollah's representation in the government and that would authorize a UN tribunal to try those suspected of involvement in the assassination of Lebanon's former Prime Minister Rafiq Hariri, with the intent of driving a wedge between Iran and Syria, but Iran did not agree to this. At the same time, Saudi Arabia was also providing financial support to Fatah in an effort to diminish Iranian influence in the Palestinian territories.[45] U.S. officials said in February that both Iran and Syria had resupplied Hezbollah, including long-range missiles that can strike deep within Israel, and Nasrallah later confirmed that Hezbollah has missiles with this range, but Hezbollah did not fire missiles or rockets into Israel in the year after the summer 2006 war.[46]

An Iranian message to the Saudis might have been in line with what Khamenei had said a week earlier: "If some Arab and Islamic governments think that by joining an alliance with Britain and the United States and imposing sanctions on Iran they can earn the satisfaction of the Zionist regime, they should know that they are making a political blunder."[47] This was directed at Qatar, which had voted for UNSC Resolution 1737 in December, and at other GCC and Arab states that might abide by the sanctions. And Iran had reportedly signaled the GCC that if the United States attacks Iran from bases in the GCC states, Iran would retaliate against those GCC states. This could include Iranian ballistic missiles, which could explain why more Patriots were being sent to GCC states.[48]

U.S. military intelligence soon indicated that Iran was suspected in a January 20 attack on a meeting of U.S. and Iraqi forces in Karbala, a Shia city in southern Iraq, in which one American was killed on the spot and another four abducted and later killed, although they did not at that time have evidence to support the suspicion and were basing it on the notion that the operation had simply been too sophisticated for any Iraq group. Iran then accused the United States of involvement in a February 14 bombing by Sunni Baluchis in Iran's south-eastern province of Sistan-Baluchistan, which killed eleven Revolutionary Guards. *ABC News* reported on April 3, 2007 that U.S. and Pakistani intelligence officials said that the United States was supporting the Sunni Baluchi group Jundallah, which had killed the eleven Iranian Revolutionary Guards. The CIA was reportedly providing financial support to the group through Iranian exiles in Europe. The group was reportedly launching attacks inside Iran from bases in Pakistan, with some support, funds, and arms from Pakistani military forces, the government of Pakistan's Baluchistan province, and Pakistan's Inter Services Intelligence agency.[49] Pakistani officials denied this, and the veracity of one of the investigators on the story was later questioned, but it was still somewhat consistent with previous reports that the U.S. military was encouraging and funding such groups.

By early 2007, a special planning group in the Office of the JCS had been charged with developing a contingency plan for bombing Iran that could be implemented within twenty-four hours of the president's command. Hersh reported that this was essentially a continuation of contingency planning that Bush had ordered in early 2006 and that this would now include not only nuclear targets and targets designed to bring about "regime change" but also any targets that might be part of Iranian support for Iraqi militants. A BBC report indicated that virtually all of Iran's military infrastructure would be targeted. It appeared to many observers that the presence of two aircraft carrier strike groups in the Gulf —the Eisenhower and the Stennis—would indicate a possible air war against Iran, although heavy bombers would also be critical. The carriers and the antiballistic missiles in the GCC states could also be designed to deter and counter an Iranian retaliation against U.S. strikes. The Pentagon plan envisioned the possibility of an attack in the spring although senior officers on the Joint Chiefs reportedly hoped the administration would not be "foolish" enough to go forward with an attack.[50] Indeed, British defense and intelligence sources indicated that five U.S. generals and admirals were prepared to resign if Bush ordered an attack against Iran. British Prime Minister Blair also opposed military action.[51] It was later reported that in February, while still under consideration to be the new Centcom Commander, Fallon had rejected the idea of having a third aircraft carrier group in the Persian Gulf, had insisted that there would be no strikes against Iran while he served in this position, and had advocated talks with Iran.[52] Nevertheless, he was appointed to his new post in March.

Details of Israel's contingency plans for air strikes against Iran were also emerging. These contingency plans reportedly involve striking at the underground enrichment facility at Natanz, the uranium conversion facility at Isfahan, and the heavy water plant and heavy water research reactor at Arak. At Natanz, one report suggested that Israel would launch laser-guided conventional weapons to open "tunnels" and then drop low-yield nuclear bombs into the "tunnels" to destroy the facilities built under 70 feet of rock and concrete. Two air force squadrons were reportedly training for this mission and considering three routes to Iran, one of them involving overflight of Turkey, which would not likely allow the use of its airspace.[53] Some Israelis think Israel must be prepared to do it alone because the Bush administration may not do it while struggling with Iraq and Afghanistan. One of them is Ephraim Sneh, the deputy director of defense, who has said that Israel might have to strike Iran's nuclear facilities as a last resort.[54] In extremely frank remarks, Israeli Brigadier General Oded Tira, formerly Israel's chief artillery officer, wrote that "President Bush lacks the political power to attack Iran. As an American strike in Iran is essential for our existence, we must help him pave the way by lobbying the Democratic Party (which is conducting itself foolishly) and US newspaper editors." He argued that Israel must also gain the support of Europe and Saudi Arabia for U.S. strikes on Iran. "For our part," he wrote, "we must prepare an independent military strike by coordinating flights in Iraqi airspace with the US. We should also coordinate with Azerbaijan the use of airbases in its territory and also enlist the support of the Azeri minority in Iran. In addition, we must immediately start preparing for an Iranian response to an attack." He wrote that "The Americans must act. Yet if they don't, we'll do it ourselves...."[55]

In late January 2007, IAEA Director General El-Baradei had proposed a plan to suspend UN sanctions if Iran suspended enrichment, and Iran's top negotiator Larijani said Iran needed time to study it. In the meantime, however, in February 2007, the IAEA suspended twenty-two of its fifty-five technical aid programs to Iran. And Russia delayed work on the Bushire reactor, saying that Iran had not made payment for Russia's work in a month, and saying that third countries were withholding supplies of equipment in observance of UN sanctions imposed in December. Days later, on February 22, the IAEA reported that Iran had not complied with the sixty-day deadline to suspend enrichment and reprocessing and that Iran had in fact expanded its enrichment activities. Larijani told EU Foreign Minister Solana that Iran wanted to have negotiations and Iran circulated a document which repeated the proposal Iran had made in September 2006, namely, that Iran would not install new centrifuge cascades for two months in exchange for the lifting of UN sanctions. But the IAEA noted in its report that Iran had installed as many as four new 164-centrifuge cascades since September and was on the verge of turning them on so it would now be more important to the P5+1 that Iran not begin actually operating these new cascades. The Bush administration then announced that it would seek another UNSC resolution with even stronger sanctions against Iran, as called for in UNSC Resolution 1737.[56]

At the same time, it seemed that the administration was prepared to widen the diplomatic track with Iran. Undersecretary of State Burns said in February that if Iran suspended enrichment, the UN sanctions would be suspended while negotiations on nuclear issues took place. On February 21, 2007, Rice said that if Iran suspended enrichment, "we could begin negotiations on whatever they would like to talk about."[57] Then, even when Iran insisted it would not suspend enrichment, and the United States said that it would seek new UN sanctions against Iran, Rice said that the United States would take part in international talks about Iraq that would include the participation of Iran and Syria. This is essentially what the Iraq Study Group report had recommended in December 2006 and constituted an about-face from the administration's previous rejection of this recommendation unless Iran suspended uranium enrichment and Syria stopped supporting Hezbollah. State Department officials such as Rice, Burns, and Khalilzad said, however, that they were now willing to engage in these talks because the UNSC sanctions, the deployment of additional forces to the Persian Gulf and to Iraq, and the arrest of Iranians in Iraq had worried Iran and provided the administration with the leverage it needed to negotiate from a position of strength. They also said these talks would be only about Iraq and would not involve direct U.S.-Iranian talks.[58]

Indeed, Khamenei was reportedly worried in May 2003 when Iran made the "grand bargain" offer; he was reportedly still worried enough in March 2006, as U.S. forces in Iraq remained at a level of 135,000–145,000 and as stories of operations in Iran by U.S. Special Forces and Israelis were circulating, to want talks with the United States about Iraq; and Prince Bandar had reported that the Iranians were worried in January 2007.[59] Moreover, an unnamed Iranian official told CNN's Christiane Amanpour in early 2007 that Khamenei's thinking was that Iran and the United States should negotiate and offer security assurances to each other and that conflict only benefitted their mutual enemy al-Qaeda.[60] In public, however, Khamenei said he was not worried about sanctions or attacks and Ahmadinejad said Iran could negotiate from a position of strength, so Iran's leaders did not have to appear weak in the eyes of their own public if they entered talks.

A NIE (National Intelligence Estimate) on Iraq released on February 2, 2007 did say in its short declassified version that the involvement of Iraq's neighbors in Iraq "is not likely to be a major driver of violence or the prospect for stability because of the self-sustaining character of Iraq's internal sectarian dynamics. Nevertheless, Iranian lethal support for select groups of Shia militants clearly intensifies the conflict in Iraq."[61] The declassified report did not say that Iran supplied IEDs or EFPs to Iraq. But U.S. officials continued to argue that the consensus of U.S. intelligence agencies as reflected in a classified 2006 study and in evidence gleaned from the recent raids on Iranians in Iraq in December and January was that Iran's Revolutionary Guard Qods Force was, with the consent of Iran's highest leaders, including Khamenei, providing EFPs to Iraqi Shia militias which were using them in roadside bombs that were penetrating U.S. armored humvees and killing U.S. forces. At that point, the administration had not actually provided such evidence from its December and January raids in Iraq.

After several postponements, the administration held a press conference in Baghdad to present publicly its evidence of Iranian arms supplies to Iraqi Shia militias, presenting several RPGs (rocket-propelled grenades) and mortars with serial numbers that U.S. officials who insisted on anonymity said were from Iranian arms factories. They also presented one EFP that they said had a component manufactured in Iran. The anonymous U.S. officials also claimed that Iran's top leadership, including Khamenei, had authorized the supply of these weapons and components by the Revolutionary Guard Qods Force to Iraqi Shia militias that had used them to kill as many as 170 U.S. forces since the U.S. invasion in 2003, although they provided no evidence for this assertion about the involvement of Iran's leadership. Critics were concerned that the administration was attempting to justify a war with Iran based on false "intelligence" as they had done to justify war with Iraq in 2003. They noted that the mortars and rockets could have been provided by Hezbollah or obtained on the black market, and they noted that the component for the EFP could also be obtained on the black market or manufactured in small machine shops in Iraq.[62] It may also be noted here that at this time approximately 3,200 U.S. forces had been killed in Iraq since 2003 and Iran was being blamed for 170 of these killings, which would indicate that even if Iran was providing some of this material, it was not the biggest challenge for U.S. forces in Iraq.

Gates and Pace then indicated that the weapons were from Iran, but Pace said he had no evidence that the top Iranian leaders were involved in this. At a subsequent news conference, Bush said the weapons were from the Qods Force, and said that this made Iran's leadership complicit even if it did not order the provision of the weapons, admitting in effect that he did not know if Iran's top leadership was actually involved.[63] In subsequent weeks, the U.S. military continued to provide weapons and components seized in raids in Iraq that were allegedly of Iranian origin, including infrared sensors, triggering devices, C-4 plastic explosives, and 107-millimeter Strella rockets.[64] And the new DNI, Vice Admiral Michael McConnell, said Iran was actually training Iraqi Shiites to use armor-piercing weapons and that it was "probable" that Iran's top leadership, including Khamenei, was aware that Iran was providing weapons to Iraqi Shiites.[65] While Iran's Qods Force could certainly be involved in providing these weapons or components for them, and while Iran's top leadership certainly could be aware of, or consent to, or authorize this, critics continued to argue that it is possible that these weapons and their components could be manufactured elsewhere, even inside Iraq itself, where assembly factories had already been discovered, or in a third state. Critics also argued that it is possible and somewhat common to counterfeit factory markings and serial numbers.

The position of the House of Representatives, now led by the Democrats, who had been expected to be cautious about military strikes against Iran, seemed to be evolving in February. When they drafted legislation to require the Bush administration to adhere to a timetable for withdrawal from Iraq, a bill that was passed in March 2007, they removed the original language also requiring the president to obtain congressional authorization for war against Iran after intense lobbying by AIPAC. And even before the Democratic-led Senate passed a bill in March attempting to constrain Bush in Iraq, Senator Clinton said as president she would leave some forces in Iraq for various purposes, including containing Iran. President Bush vetoed the bill that was subsequently submitted by the House and Senate and they later submitted a new bill funding the war without setting any timetable for a U.S. withdrawal but calling on the Iraqi government to meet certain "benchmarks" in order to receive further reconstruction aid.

In early March, Ahmadinejad traveled to Saudi Arabia for meetings with King Abdullah and other Saudi officials. Iran had reportedly sought this meeting, presumably because of concerns about U.S. threats and actions. They reportedly discussed ways of curbing the sectarian, ethnic, and political conflicts in Iraq, Lebanon, and the Arab-Israeli arena, and were assumed to have discussed ways of avoiding U.S.-Iranian conflict, which would presumably include Iran's nuclear programs, but they did not announce any specific agreements. Given Saudi concerns about growing Iranian influence in the region, and given Saudi diplomatic and financial efforts and even reported covert efforts to contain this influence, it is not clear how much Iran would be willing to cooperate with Saudi Arabia or heed Saudi Arabia's warnings, or how much Iran may have issued warnings to Saudi Arabia. Nevertheless, the Saudi Press Agency reported that Ahmadinejad expressed support for Abdullah's 2002 Israeli-Palestinian land-for-peace initiative, but while Ahmadinejad said Palestinian issues had been discussed, an Iranian Foreign Ministry official denied that Abdullah's initiative had been discussed.[66]

In February, King Abdullah had persuaded Fatah and Hamas to forge a national unity government and had pledged $1 billion to support it. Later in March, King Abdullah's land-for-peace initiative was endorsed again by an Arab League meeting. In part, these were efforts to contain Iranian influence over Palestinian militants, although Saudi Arabia already had more influence with Hamas than Iran had with Hamas, and although there were reasons to think Iran would accept the terms of this initiative. Moreover, just before the Arab League meeting, Khaled Meshaal, the Hamas leader exiled in Damascus, told King Abdullah that Hamas would not oppose the 2002 Arab League initiative, which would mean that Hamas would not oppose a two-state solution and Arab recognition of Israel, which seems even more forthcoming than the offer of a ten-year truce.[67] Furthermore, Syrian officials had even told former Secretary of State James Baker of the Iraq Study Group "that they do have the ability to convince Hamas to acknowledge Israel's right to exist."[68] Certainly, if Israel returned the Golan Heights to Syria and returned the Sheba Farms to Lebanon, that would motivate Syria, a secular regime that does not tolerate Islamic extremism at home, to urge restraint on these forces in Lebanon and Palestine. It would be extremely difficult for Iran to oppose Arab-Israeli agreements that Hamas, Hezbollah, and Syria considered fair. It should also be noted here that Iran has invested in Syria's economy; the restoration of many Shiite mosques and the opening of an automobile assembly plant partially financed by Iran are among the first of these investments. Iran has also invested heavily in construction and social services in southern Lebanon through Hezbollah.[69] This means that Iran could be in a position to influence Syria and Hezbollah to accept advantageous agreements with Israel if they were advantageous for Iran as well. And this means that Iran would continue to have some influence in Syria and Lebanon even if Arab-Israeli conflicts were resolved.

There had been rumors for months of certain GCC states consenting to U.S. contingency plans to launch attacks against Iran from GCC territory. It was even reported that Saudi Prince Bandar supported this and had assured the Vice President's staff that Saudi Arabia will not oppose and might even support this. One Saudi official in Washington told the author in November 2006 that Saudi Arabia had not consented to U.S. military action.[70] It was also reported that Saudi Prince Turki's abrupt resignation in December 2006 as Ambassador to the United States was based in part on opposition to this option and a desire to return to Saudi Arabia and argue against it.[71] Soon after Ahmadinejad's visit, however, Qatar's foreign minister publicly urged a diplomatic solution, warning of the dangers of war, and said that Qatar would not participate in any military action against Iran launched from Qatar, where the U.S. Central Command is based, although he declined to say whether Qatar could stop the United States from launching an attack from Qatar.[72] Later in the month, UAE President Shaikh Khalifa bin Zayed also publicly said that the UAE will not permit any attack against Iran to be launched from UAE territory.[73] For the most part, if there has been any GCC acquiescence to this option, it must have followed U.S. pressure and must be accompanied by reluctance, worry, and resentment. Some of these states that opposed U.S. military action against Saddam's Iraq in 2003 reluctantly let the U.S. military use their territories then. They can see the outcome is not in their interest, think the U.S. military presence itself is one reason for insurgency and civil war, and fear that the United States will withdraw in a way that results in fragmentation, partition, and widespread ethnic cleansing. They want the United States to withdraw gradually and to be replaced by other forces, including Muslim forces, after stability and Sunni Arab rights have been established. They also fear that in the event of U.S. strikes against Iran, they would be the targets of Iranian retaliation, and they fear that Iran could descend into disorder that the United States could not reverse.[74] Even so, on March 24, the Eisenhower and the Stennis aircraft carrier groups carried out exercises inside the Gulf, in a display of strength obviously meant for Iran's attention.

When the international talks on Iraq occurred, on March 10, the assembled mid-level officials of the various countries discussed how to secure Iraq's borders, i.e., how to stem the flow of fighters, weapons, and money over Iraq's borders, particularly from Iran and Syria; how to handle the problem of two million Iraqi refugees pouring into neighboring countries, particularly into Syria and Jordan; and how to provide for fuel imports into Iraq, some of which Iran transports from Tajikistan to Iraq. Iran denied that it provided weapons to Iraqi Shia militias and pledged to help secure Iraq, but Khalilzad said he would watch events on the ground. The United States and Iran did not engage in direct negotiations, although they had informal conversations on the sidelines of the meeting.[75]

When Iranian Revolutionary Guards seized fifteen British naval personnel on March 23, claiming that they had entered Iranian territorial waters in the northern Gulf, this provided an example of how conflict could occur. The Revolutionary Guards may have done this to use these British hostages as bargaining chips to secure the release of the five Iranians held in Iraq by the U.S. forces. They may have done this to pressure the United States and Britain to cease their possible covert operations inside Iran. They may have done this to subvert any future U.S.-Iran talks. They may have done this to show the United States what they can do if they are attacked. This could, however, have provoked a military retaliation by the United States. When there was no U.S. retaliation, even with two U.S. aircraft carrier groups beginning exercises in the Gulf on March 24, some observers concluded that the administration was *not* waiting for a pretext to attack Iran. The United States did not release the five Iranians held in Iraq, although they did allow the International Red Cross to visit them, and an Iranian diplomat seized in Iraq in February was released. When Iran released the British naval personnel on April 3, the possible explanations were that the hard-liners concluded that they had made their point or that the pragmatists wanted to defuse the crisis and prepare for more talks. At this time, Rice reportedly wanted to release the five Iranians in a reciprocal gesture, but Cheney's office insisted on continuing to hold them to show that even more Iranian officials might be taken and to have a bargaining chip in future talks on Iraq.[76]

On the nuclear front, Russia announced in March that it would not begin the exports of nuclear fuel to Iran that were supposed to begin that month. Russia

initially said publicly that this was because Iran was behind in its monthly payments, but Russian Foreign Minister Ivanov told European officials that it was
a political decision. Indeed, Ivanov subsequently told Iran that Russia would
not begin the fuel deliveries until Iran suspended its enrichment of uranium as
called for by the UN Security Council. Then, on March 24, 2007, in another
unanimous vote, again including Qatar, the UN Security Council passed Resolution 1747, a new resolution that imposed additional sanctions against Iran. The
strongest language of the resolution bans the sale or transfer of Iranian conventional weapons and bans financial transactions with Bank Sepah, which is
thought to finance Iran's nuclear programs and ballistic missile programs, and
which was already under U.S. Treasury Department sanctions. It also expands
the list subject to financial sanctions, including the freezing of their overseas
assets, to fifteen individuals and thirteen organizations, including some affiliated
with the Revolutionary Guards. Milder language of the resolution only calls for
"vigilance and restraint" in sales of conventional weapons to Iran, sales that are
very important to Russia and China, and calls for but does not require a halt to
export credits, grants, and loans to Iran except for humanitarian or development
needs, thus giving European states the option of continuing these programs.
Again, this resolution asked the IAEA to report back in sixty days on whether
Iran had suspended uranium enrichment, and called for stronger sanctions if
the answer was no or for the suspension of sanctions if the answer was yes.[77]

Iranian leaders denounced the resolution as illegal, insisted it would have no
impact on Iran's nuclear programs, and announced that Iran would further limit
its cooperation with the IAEA. Iran would no longer give the IAEA advance
information about the design of facilities for the production of nuclear fuel, they
said. Instead of notifying the IAEA before construction of such facilities begins,
Iran would only notify the IAEA six months before nuclear materials are to be
introduced into the new facility. This is in conformity with previous standards
that have been abandoned by all other nonnuclear weapon members of the
NPT, all of whom now notify the IAEA before construction. Iran did allow the
IAEA to continue inspections to monitor its existing facility at Natanz, but Iran
did not allow an inspection at its heavy water research reactor at Arak in April.
In the wake of this resolution, Ahmadinejad claimed, "We are not after an atomic
bomb because it is not useful and our religion does not allow us to have it."[78]

In April, after the new UN Security Council sanctions had been imposed on
Iran for its nuclear programs, follow-up talks about Iraq were held at a
conference in Sharm al-Shaykh, Egypt. Secretary Rice held private bilateral talks
with Syria's Ambassador Walid Moallem, and by September General Petraeus
was indicating that Syria had reduced the flow of fighters from Syria into Iraq.
There were also some informal U.S.-Iranian conversations on the sidelines of
the conference. Rice intended to speak about Iraq informally to Iran's Foreign
Minister Mottaki at a dinner, but he avoided this by leaving before she could

do so. Nevertheless, it was announced in early May that the United States and Iran would hold bilateral discussions about Iraq in a matter of weeks.

As these May talks approached, Cheney toured a number of GCC states in an effort to develop their support for confronting Iran. The Stennis aircraft carrier group remained in the Gulf and the Eisenhower carrier group had been replaced by the Nimitz carrier group. Cheney stood on the deck of the Stennis inside the Persian Gulf and said: "With two carrier strike groups in the Gulf, we're sending clear messages to friends and adversaries alike. We'll keep the sea lanes open. We'll stand with our friends in opposing extremism and strategic threats. We'll disrupt attacks on our own forces. We'll continue bringing relief to those who suffer, and delivering justice to the enemies of freedom. And we'll stand with others to prevent Iran from gaining nuclear weapons and dominating this region."[79]

Ahmadinejad then visited the UAE to talk about security cooperation, trade, and energy. It was the first visit of an Iranian president to the UAE since its founding in 1971, and followed on the heels of Cheney's visit. When Cheney warned Iran from the deck of the Stennis, Ahmadinejad countered that the United States realizes that Iran would reply with "severe" retaliation to a U.S. military strike on Iran. On the issue of Iran's nuclear programs, he said, "Superpowers cannot prevent us from owning this energy." After noting that Iran would talk with the United States about Iraq, he said, "They know that their plans have failed in Iraq, their vision is wrong. As long as you are plotting against the Iraqi people, failure will be there day after day." He also called for the GCC states to "get rid of" foreign forces, saying, "We in the Persian Gulf are faced by difficulties and enemies. They claim lack of security is the reason for their presence [but] the problem is the intervention of foreign powers."[80]

A week later, the Stennis and Nimitz aircraft carrier groups carried out more exercises in the Gulf. Then the news about Bush's approval in 2006 of covert CIA operations against Iran was leaked to *ABC*, which published the story on May 22, and some speculated that this was intended, perhaps by allies of Cheney, to subvert the upcoming talks between the United States and Iran. Perhaps this was the intent of the leak, but the Iranians already knew about U.S. covert operations and had complained about them previously. Indeed, Iran also announced before the talks that it had discovered U.S. "spy rings" operating in Iran, and this was also seen as a possible effort by Iranian hard-liners to subvert these talks, in this case perhaps by publicizing this and generating domestic Iranian opposition to the talks. Another potential explanation for this leak to *ABC* is that the leakers wanted to put an end to these covert operations. Then, on May 26, the *Boston Globe* reported that the ISOG set up in March 2006 to coordinate covert operations against Iran and headed by Elliott Abrams had been disbanded in March 2007. Some viewed this as a sign that the administration's proponents of "regime change" had been eclipsed, at least temporarily, by the administration's proponents of diplomacy.[81] It may have been due, however, to the fact that the range of activities of this group had only been made public by the same paper on January 2, 2007, the story of CIA covert operations had just been made public on May 22, 2007, and the administration sought to avoid embarrassment only two days before U.S.-Iranian negotiations were to begin, and particularly after Iran's arrests of academics charged with spying. And it did not necessarily mean that the covert operations themselves would come to an end.

On May 8, Haleh Esfandiari, a dual citizen of the United States and Iran, the head of the Middle East Program at the Woodrow Wilson Center for International Scholars in Washington DC, and an advocate of dialogue between American and Iranian academics, was confined in Iran's Evin Prison. The Ministry of Intelligence had held Esfandiari under house arrest since her visit to Iran in December 2006, and this was seen in part as a reaction to various U.S. efforts to promote civil society, democracy, and human rights in Iran, such as the $66 million allocated for these purposes by the Iran Freedom Support Act of October 2006, some of which was allocated to the ISOG. Esfandiari had reportedly not received any of this money. She was specifically charged with receiving funds from George Soros' Open Society Initiative, which also supports civil society, democracy, and human rights in Iran, and this appeared to be true. The Iranian regime saw these efforts as being designed to promote a "soft revolution" or "velvet revolution" to effect "regime change," such as Vaclav Havel's "velvet revolution" in Czechoslovakia, as well as more recent revolutions in the Ukraine and Georgia, and it now charged Esfandiari in May with "seeking to topple the ruling Islamic establishment," specifically through "propaganda" and "espionage."[82] The regime had earlier responded by repressing labor groups, student groups, teachers' groups, human rights groups, and women's rights groups. In addition, after her detention in December 2006, Iranian hard-liners may have seen her as a bargaining chip to use in an effort to obtain the release of the Iranians detained in Iraq since January 2007 and/or as a bargaining chip in the upcoming talks about Iraq with the Bush administration or even as a means of aborting those talks. All of these may also be the reasons for the arrest in January of Iranian-American Parnaz-Azimi, a reporter with the U.S.-funded Radio Farda, and the arrest on May 22 of Iranian-American Kian Tajbakhsh, a consultant to the Open Society Institute and to the World Bank, and the arrest of Iranian-American Ali Shakeri, while they were visiting Iran.

On May 23, a week before the talks on Iraq were scheduled, the IAEA conducted a two-hour advance-notice inspection of the underground facility at Natanz. The IAEA also released another report, again saying that Iran had not complied with suspension of uranium enrichment demanded by the UN Security Council resolutions, and that Iran had continued to expand its enrichment program. The IAEA said Iran was now feeding uranium hexafluoride gas into 1312 centrifuges, or eight 164-centrifuge cascades, that it was testing two more cascades, and building three more. The IAEA noted, however, as it had in April, that Iran was producing relatively small amounts of enriched uranium to about 3–5 percent uranium-235, much lower than the 90 percent necessary for a nuclear weapon. The IAEA also noted that Iran had still not answered outstanding questions previously posed by the IAEA, and that the IAEA had "deteriorating knowledge" about Iran's programs. El-Baradei was now arguing that Iran had acquired sufficient knowledge about the nuclear fuel cycle to overcome the objective of any continued calls for suspension, and that it would be better to fashion an agreement that allowed Iran to engage in limited enrichment activities in return for Iranian commitments not to put more centrifuges into operation and not to expand its enrichment activities and to permit the IAEA to increase its monitoring and inspections. The Bush administration disagreed and once again indicated it would seek tougher sanctions.[83]

On May 28, formal, official, acknowledged, bilateral U.S.-Iran talks were held. New U.S. Ambassador to Iraq Ryan Crocker claimed afterwards that there had been agreement on support for a secure, stable, democratic, federal Iraq that would control its own security and be at peace with its neighbors. Iran's Ambassador Kazemi-Qomi also claimed afterwards that both sides agreed on the question of Iraq's security. But Crocker also said he had insisted that Iran stop financing, training, and arming militias that were attacking U.S. and coalition forces. He reportedly did not provide Iran with a dossier of evidence, although it was later reported that U.S. military forces had already captured two Iraqi Shia brothers and a Lebanese Hezbollah operative who were saying Iran was involved in the killing of U.S. troops in Karbala in January. Kazemi-Qomi reportedly did not directly reply during the meeting, but said afterwards that Iran had already denied these charges many times. He also said he had suggested a trilateral security committee including Iraq, Iran, and the United States and that it could investigate these allegations. He also said he had called the U.S. effort to train and equip Iraqi security forces inadequate and blamed the United States for destroying Iraq's infrastructure. He said Iran was offering to provide training and weapons to the Iraqi forces and to help rebuild Iraq's infrastructure. Kazemi-Qomi reportedly did not raise the issue of the five Iranians still held in Iraq, and Crocker reportedly did not speak about the Iranian-Americans detained on charges of espionage in Iran.[84]

Only days before these talks on Iraq, and only days after talks between Larijani and Solana failed to produce Iranian agreement to suspend uranium enrichment, and only weeks after Cheney's speech on the Stennis in the Persian Gulf, and at a time when the administration, the Congress, and groups such as the American Enterprise Institute were advocating more sanctions against Iran, and at a time when news of Bush's authorization of covert operations against Iran and the disbanding of the ISOG was leaked, it was reported that a member of Cheney's staff had said at the American Enterprise Institute and other conservative and neoconservative think tanks in Washington that Cheney had no confidence in diplomatic contacts with Iran, favored stronger measures, was concerned that Bush would not make "the right decision," and was prepared to make an "end run" around Bush by signaling Israel to launch cruise missiles against Natanz with the expectation that Iran would retaliate and that Bush would be forced to strike Iran.[85] This official was later identified as Deputy National Security Adviser David Wurmser. El-Baradei then warned against "new crazies" who advocated war with Iran after the devastation of the war with Iraq. Wurmser was not, however, a new figure. In fact, Wurmser had been a leading proponent of military action against Syria and "regime change" in Iraq, and a leading critic of the Oslo peace process, since the mid-1990s while working for groups like the Washington Institute for Near East Policy and the American Enterprise Institute and then while serving on the staff of Director of Arms Control and Disarmament John Bolton at the State Department and then Undersecretary for Policy Douglas Feith at the Defense Department, where he had argued that there was a working relationship between al-Qaeda and Iraq's government under Saddam Hussein, an argument that later had been found to be inaccurate by the 9/11 Commission. Senior State Department officials were reportedly furious about Wurmser's remarks, and Rice stated that Bush and his cabinet and Cheney were all supportive of the diplomatic track.[86]

In June, Senator Lieberman, pointing to recent reports that alleged that there were training camps inside Iran where Iraqi Shiites were armed and trained to carry out attacks on U.S. forces in Iraq, and expressing skepticism that talks could prevent Iran from developing nuclear weapons, said on CBS television that the United States should consider air strikes inside Iran.[87] In July, pointing to reports that alleged that Iran was using Lebanese Hezbollah as a surrogate to support Iraqi Shia attacks against U.S. forces in Iraq, expressing dissatisfaction with Iran's diplomatic pledge to Ambassador Crocker in May to stabilize Iraq, and pointing to reports alleging Iranian support even to their historic enemy the Taliban, as well as Hezbollah and Palestinian resistance, Lieberman argued against a U.S. withdrawal from Iraq and argued that there must be a credible threat of U.S. force against Iran to deter Iran in the Middle East.[88] Later that month, Lieberman was a coauthor of Amendment 2073 to the Fiscal Year 2008 National Defense Authorization Act, which condemned the alleged Iranian support for Iraqi attacks against U.S. and Iraqi forces in Iraq and called on the administration to take the issue up with Iran and report back to the Senate. The amendment passed 97-0. But the amendment did say "Nothing in this section shall be construed to authorize or otherwise speak to the use of Armed Forces against Iran."[89] Nevertheless, Senator Brownback said that he would support eventual preventive strikes on Iran.[90]

It did seem that there were elements in the administration who perhaps favored military action over sanctions and diplomacy. The *Guardian* reported in July that at a meeting of White House, Pentagon, and State Department officials in June, Burns had said that the United States could still be on the diplomatic track with Iran in January 2009, that Bush and Cheney had been displeased by this possibility, that neither had faith in any successor to deal firmly with Iran, that they were reluctant to allow Israel to attack Iran, and that Cheney still had the clout to persuade Bush to use force against Iran.[91] Coupled with Lieberman's calls for strikes inside Iran, Brownback's support for eventual strikes, and previous appeals in *Commentary* and the *Wall Street Journal* by Norman Podhoretz, the father-in-law of Elliot Abrams, there appeared to be some in the media and in the Congress who agreed.[92] The intensity of the debate on this was reflected by former Reagan administration official Paul Craig Roberts, who warned that U.S. neoconservatives aligned with Israeli Zionists viewed the use of nuclear weapons against Iran as the only way to force Muslims to accept U.S. hegemony. This was a striking comment because Roberts had also been the associate editor of the *Wall Street Journal's* editorial page, a page that had long championed conservative and neoconservative thought, and a contributing editor to the *National Review,* another noted conservative organ, and his conservative Republican credentials were impeccable.[93] If Iran feared that Roberts was correct, it would give Iranian hard-liners a powerful argument to use against Iranian pragmatists that U.S. calls for Iranian diplomatic cooperation were only another way for the United States to deny Iran its rightful role in the region and the world.

It was reported in June that Israel had launched an Ofek-7 satellite that would pass over Iran, Iraq, and Syria every ninety minutes, providing intelligence that could be used to establish targets for Israel's Shavit missile, which has Iran in its range. Israel's Defense Minister Peretz had told Gates in April that military strikes against Iran must remain an option and Israel's Trade Minister Shaul Mofaz, who formerly served as Defense Minister, told Rice in early June that if sanctions and diplomacy did not halt Iran's uranium enrichment by the end of 2007, Israel would strike Iran's nuclear facilities.[94]

Iran seemed to be preparing for the possibility of U.S. or Israeli strikes. In early June, commercial satellite imagery indicated that Iran was building a tunnel complex inside a mountain two kilometers from their uranium enrichment facility in Natanz, similar to another tunnel complex near their uranium conversion facility in Isfahan. These could be intended to protect nuclear equipment and material from an air attack.[95] Iran also seemed to be seeking a way out. In late June, Mohsen Rezai spoke to the *Washington Post* of the possibility of Iranian cooperation on nuclear issues, Iraq, Afghanistan, Lebanon, and Gaza. This was noteworthy because Rezai had been the top commander of the Revolutionary Guards from 1981 to 1997, had run against Ahmadinejad for the presidency in 2005, and was serving as the secretary of the Expediency Council, where he was an ally of Rafsanjani.[96]

It was later reported that the administration had reached a decision early in the summer that it would concentrate any military strikes on Iranian Revolutionary Guard facilities, because of widespread opposition within the military to attacks on Iran's nuclear installations, and that it would be able to justify such strikes as retaliation for Revolutionary Guard support for Iraqi Shia attacks on U.S. forces in Iraq.[97] In the following months, the administration made significant efforts to document this support.

ANALYZING THE INTELLIGENCE

The state of knowledge about Iran's involvement in Iraq at a time of growing calls for military strikes should be considered here. In June, when U.S. and Iraqi forces undertook a major offensive against AQI (al-Qaeda in Iraq) and other Sunni insurgent forces in Baghdad and in the belt around Baghdad, they again found machine shops where car bombs and IEDs, including EFPs, were being manufactured, clarifying that Sunnis were involved in this activity. There were also U.S. and Iraqi operations in Anbar and in Diyala province, particularly in its capital Baquba, where AQI and other Sunni insurgents had regrouped after escaping U.S. and Iraqi operations in Anbar and Baghdad. The fighting was heavy, with many American casualties from huge roadside IEDs, again clarifying that Sunni insurgents as well as Shia militias were using these weapons.

In early July, Brigadier General Kevin J. Bergner, the newly-arrived spokesman for the U.S. Command in Iraq, said that U.S. forces had captured Ali Musa Daqduq in March, and that he was a senior Lebanese Hezbollah operative who had been sent to Iran in 2005 and had been acting as a surrogate for the Qods Force to finance and train and arm Iraqi Shiites to attack U.S. and Iraqi forces. Bergner said that Daqduq had led an Iraqi Shia cell headed by the al-Khazaali brothers, also captured in March, in carrying out the January attack in Karbala that killed five U.S. forces, and that he had told his interrogators that the cell "could not have conducted this complex operation without the support and direction of the Quds Force."[98] This cell was described as a cell that had broken away from al-Sadr's Mahdi Army. In particular, Bergner said that documents captured with Daqduq showed that the Qods Force had obtained and shared with this cell information about U.S. troop activities at the site in Karbala where they had been attacked. Other documents captured with Daqduq reportedly showed how to attack a convoy and provided a list of his meetings with Iraqi militants. Moreover, Bergner said that Daqduq had been taking groups of Iraqi extremists for training at three separate camps near Tehran for operations inside Iraq, that "our intelligence reveals that the senior leadership in Iran is aware of this activity," that it was "hard to imagine" that Khamenei did not know about it, and that "Both Ali Musa Daqduq and Qais Khazali state that senior leadership within the Quds Force knew of and supported planning for the eventual Karbala attack that killed five coalition soldiers."[99]

Skeptics noted that Bergner had just arrived in Baghdad and had been previously serving on the staff of the National Security Council, where he was an assistant to Elliott Abrams, and suggested that this was administration propaganda, noting in particular that Bergner did not provide complete transcripts of the interrogations or quotations from these captives.[100] It is certainly possible that this information was true, even if the information had been obtained through the use of some of the harsher interrogation techniques then being employed, but still no convincing evidence was actually provided for public scrutiny.

On July 24, a second round of talks were held between Crocker and Kazemi-Qomi. They reportedly began with a somewhat angry exchange, as Crocker argued that the incidence of attacks on U.S. forces attributed to Iraqi Shia militias financed, armed, and trained by Iran had been increasing since their first meeting in late May and Kazemi-Qomi denied Iranian involvement and insisted that Crocker had no proof. Kazemi-Qomi now demanded the release of the five Iranians detained in Iraq, but they were not released. The two sides did agree to establish a subcommittee of experts to continue discussing stabilizing Iraq. Days later, U.S. General Raymond Odierno, the second-in-command in Iraq, said that rocket and mortar attacks against the "Green Zone" in Baghdad had become more accurate during the previous months and he attributed this to the training Iraqi Shia militias were allegedly receiving in Iran. In late July, after a raid in Karbala, U.S. forces claimed to have captured a rogue Mahdi Army militiaman who had allegedly been involved in IED, EFP, and mortar attacks against coalition forces. Farther north, in Diyala province, "allied forces" captured a cell suspected of bringing personnel and weapons, including EFPs, from Iran with Iranian support.[101]

At the same time, *Newsweek* reported in a late July issue that Mohammad Javad Jafari, the former Revolutionary Guard officer and current deputy to the secretary of the Supreme National Security Council who had been the target of the January raid in Irbil but who had escaped, denied that Iran ran camps for training Iraqi Shia extremists or that Iran provided EFPs to Iraqi Shia extremists. He denied that Iran had any connection to the Lebanese Hezbollah operative Daqduq, who had reportedly led the January attack on U.S. forces in Karbala, although he said he did not know if Hezbollah was providing EFPs to Iraqi Shia extremists. He also said that Iran would help establish security in Iraq if the United States withdrew in 2008.[102] He was described in the article as a hard-line associate of Ahmadinejad, but on foreign policy matters, he was a deputy to Larijani and he has reportedly spoken in favor of broad-based negotiations with the United States.

The security subcommittee, a trilateral subcommittee presided over by Talabani with lower level Americans and Iranians, met in early August, and

Crocker and Kazemi-Qomi also had a separate trilateral meeting with Iraqi National Security Adviser Mouaffak al-Rubaie at the same time. Crocker again said Iranian support for Shia militias was increasing and Kazemi-Qomi again said Iran had nothing to do with the attacks on U.S. forces.[103] In early August, as Crocker and Kazemi-Qomi were meeting in Baghdad for the third time, General Odierno said that EFP attacks on U.S.-led forces were climbing, with ninety-nine such attacks in July accounting for one-third of the fatalities of U.S.-led forces. *New York Times* journalist Michael Gordon claimed that most of these attacks were carried out by Shia militias and noted that U.S. officials believed these weapons or their components were supplied by Iran's Qods Force. Odierno said that Iranian financing, training, and arming of Shia militias was "surging" in an effort to increase the U.S. decision-making about withdrawal from Iraq, but it is not clear if he explicitly linked this to the EFPs, as Gordon did.[104] The implication was that Iran was deliberately stoking the conflict, but another explanation was that U.S. forces had vigorously stepped up their operations against the Mahdi Army or rogue units or "special cells" of it, especially in the east of Baghdad, and that rising U.S. casualties from Shia militias was attributable to the resistance they faced during these operations.[105] Moreover, IED/EFP bombs had certainly killed many U.S. troops in June during operations against AQI, and this seemed to be forgotten.

Then in mid-August, the spokesperson for Major General Rick Lynch, in charge of U.S. forces operating in districts south of Baghdad, said that Lynch estimated that there were fifty Iranian Revolutionary Guard Qods Force members actually in the area training Iraqi Shia militants in the use of rockets and mortars, although none of the Revolutionary Guard members had been apprehended.[106] Only four days later, Lynch corrected this, saying thirty of the fifty were "surrogates" for the Revolutionary Guards, presumably Hezbollah.[107] In early September, U.S. forces captured a "highly sought individual" in Karbala who was suspected of being a member of the Revolutionary Guards and of transporting Iraqis to Iran for training and for aiding militias in Iraq. They also seized computers, communication devices, documents, and photographs. Yet when Petraeus testified to Congress on September 11, he said, "The Qods force itself, we believe, by and large those individuals have been pulled out of the country as have the Lebanese Hezbollah trainers that were being used to augment that activity."[108] One week later, U.S. forces detained a member of an Iranian commercial delegation that had been invited to Iraqi Kurdistan, claiming that he was a Qods Force officer involved in bringing IEDs into Iraq and bringing foreign fighters into Iraq.[109]

Some attention should also be given here to allegations that Iran was supporting AQI as well as al-Qaeda and the Taliban in both Pakistan and Afghanistan. These seem to be much less substantial than allegations of Iranian support for Iraqi Shia militias. On January 3, 2007, Eli Lake of the *New York Sun* wrote that the evidence uncovered in the December 2006 raids in Iraq proved that Iran's agents were coordinating with AQI and other Sunni jihadist insurgents as well as Shia militias.[110] The declassified NIE written in January and released on February 2 did *not* make this assertion. It does not seem logical that Iran or SCIRI's Badr Brigade would provide significant support to the Sunni jihadist elements that had incited and perpetuated the civil war with the Shiites. Before his death, AQI's Zarqawi had declared "total war" on Iran and the Iraqi Shia Badr Brigade in September 2005 and had carried out the bombing of a Shia mosque in Samarra in February 2006 that precipitated a new and vicious cycle of bloody reprisals by Shia militias or "death squads" Iran was accused of supporting.[111] But it is not absolutely impossible that some elements of the Qods Force would have limited tactical cooperation with some elements of AQI to tie down and bleed U.S. forces in Iraq and dissuade them from attacking Iran. It may be more likely that Iranian agents seek to penetrate AQI as well as secular Sunni insurgent groups and gather intelligence that could be useful to Iran later.

One month after the *New York Sun* alleged Iranian support for AQI, the CIA notified the NSC that Iran had arrested two operatives from Osama bin Laden's al-Qaeda traveling from Pakistan through Iran on the way to Iraq and that this indicated that Iran was interested in stopping such traffic. But the administration's ISOG was preparing to make public that senior al-Qaeda operatives were under "house arrest" in Iran, that Iran hoped to use them as bargaining chips, and that this was a violation of UNSC resolutions 1267 and 1373 against harboring al-Qaeda members. Among them were Saad Bin Laden, Saif al-Adel, a security chief, and Sulaiman Abu Ghaith, a spokesman. U.S. intelligence said there were suspicions but no proof that one of them, Saif al-Adel, was involved in planning the Riyadh bombing in May 12, 2003.[112] This was in no way a new story, and the suspicion was based on electronic intercepts that did not add proof to the suspicion, and resurfacing this story at this time may have been part of the kind of campaign to build "international outrage" or disseminate propaganda authorized by Bush in 2006 and possibly coordinated by ISOG in an effort to link Iran and al-Qaeda in the minds of the American public. Indeed, the *Washington Post* had reported in January that Elliott Abrams and his colleagues had agreed that the summer war between Israel and Hezbollah "provided an opening to *portray* [author's emphasis] Iran as a nuclear-ambitious link between al-Qaeda, Hezbollah, and the death squads in Iraq."[113]

In fact, al-Qaeda has condemned Iran for helping the United States topple the Taliban in 2001, has denounced Iran for keeping al-Qaeda operatives under house arrest in Iran, has denounced Iranian influence in Iraq, and has even denounced Iran for engaging in talks with the United States about security in Iraq in 2007, eliciting Iranian denunciations of al-Qaeda killings of innocent civilians in Asia, Europe, and the United States. Moreover, former CIA and NSC official Bruce Riedel has written that al-Qaeda may seek to provoke a

U.S. attack against Iran through a "false-flag" operation.[114] Perhaps a "false-flag" operation could include counterfeiting Iranian markings on weapons and then seeing to it that these weapons were captured in Iraq. Or perhaps a "false-flag" operation could include sending al-Qaeda couriers through Iran in the hope that the United States will conclude that Iran permits this.

In early July, the *Financial Times* ran a story titled "Al-Qaeda Linked to Operations from Iran." The story argued that "The group operatives, who link the al-Qaeda leadership in Pakistan with their disciples in Iraq, the Levant, and North Africa, move with relative freedom in the country."[115] It claimed that they had established a hub of operations to provide communications and funds to AQI. The story said that these operatives were not the high-value al-Qaeda operatives Iran had been detaining since 2002. It did mention that Pakistani officials said al-Qaeda operatives from Pakistan had been transiting Iran en route to Iraq since 2004, but it did not mention that one message from al-Qaeda in Pakistan to AQI in 2005 was an appeal for AQI to stop slaughtering Iraqi Shiites, and it did not mention that Iran had apprehended two al-Qaeda operatives from Pakistan trying to transit Iran in February. It did admit that it was not known if Iran supported this or tolerated this. It did not consider the possibility that al-Qaeda may have been disseminating disinformation in order to discredit its enemy Iran, provoke a conflict between Iran and the United States, or carry out a "false-flag" operation that could be pinned on Iran.[116]

AQI did not seem very grateful to Iran. In fact, an audiotape was released in July 2007 in the name of the putative leader of the Islamic State of Iraq, Abu Omar al-Qurayshi al-Baghdadi, who had been reported to be only a fiction created by AQI's new leader Abu Ayyub al-Masri, saying that if the Iranian government did not cease its support for the Shia government of Iraq in two months, AQI would attack Iran, and the speaker, probably al-Masri, evidently included Iranian interests in Iraq, in the Gulf, and in Iran itself in his threat. The speaker also threatened "Persians," which he meant as a derogatory term for Iraqi Shiites supporting the Shia government of Iraq, and he threatened all Sunni Arab businessmen with ties to Iranian business.[117]

Nevertheless, the following week, Eli Lake of the *New York Sun* claimed that the *classified* sections of a new NIE said that an al-Qaeda Council was regularly meeting in eastern Iran, that numerous "instructions" from its leaders to AQI had been intercepted, and that there were differences of opinion within the intelligence community as to whether this was officially sanctioned by Iran or only permitted by elements of the Qods Force.[118] Like the *Financial Times* article, Lake also did not mention that Iran had recently arrested al-Qaeda operatives transiting Iran from Pakistan. He also did not mention that Iran had asked NATO in the fall of 2006 to help seal Iran's border with Afghanistan and that NATO, on U.S. instructions, had refused. The declassified material from the estimate said that al-Qaeda was growing stronger, was determined to attack the U.S. homeland again, and would try to use its contacts with AQI to do so, but it did *not* contain the material in Lake's report. It said AQI was an affiliate of al-Qaeda, i.e., it had some autonomy. It also said Hezbollah might consider attacking the United States if it felt its existence or that of its sponsor Iran was in jeopardy.[119]

At the same time, Bergner claimed that "There is a flow of strategic decision, of prioritizing, of messaging from Al Qaeda senior leaders [believed to be in Pakistan] to Al Qaeda in Iraq leadership," claimed that "al-Qaeda [in Pakistan] had dispatched Khalil, Khalid, and Khattab al-Turki to AQI to help al-Masri strengthen his organization in northern Iraq," and said that U.S. forces had captured a liaison between them, the same individual who claimed that al-Baghdadi was a fiction.[120]

Soon afterwards, Iran's *Fars News Agency,* which is associated with the Revolutionary Guards, reported that eleven Revolutionary Guards were ambushed and killed by drug smugglers in Sistan-Baluchistan, bringing to over 3,300 security personnel killed in this region by drug smugglers since 1979. This area of southeast Iran is a gateway for drug smugglers from Afghanistan and Pakistan who cross into Iran despite the fact that Iran has dug a trench along the border.[121] The story indicates that Iran does not actually control all of the area in which al-Qaeda is claimed to be operating, and therefore suggests that Iran could not necessarily stop al-Qaeda from meeting there.

In fact, the story of Iran's alleged involvement in Afghanistan was also unfolding. In mid-April, Pace reported that allied forces near the southern city of Kandahar in Afghanistan had captured Iranian-made plastic explosives and mortars being transported to the Taliban, although he said it was not clear which Iranian entity was responsible for this shipment.[122] In late May and early June, U.S. officials, who always insisted on anonymity, claimed that the Iranian government was supporting the Taliban against U.S., NATO, and Afghan forces in Afghanistan, as well as supporting AQI in Iraq. It has already been noted that Shia Iran and Sunni al-Qaeda have generally regarded each other as enemies. It has also already been noted that Shia Iran and the Sunni Taliban have regarded each other as enemies. In Iran's case, this is compounded by knowledge that Pakistan has been a patron of the Taliban and has seemed to tolerate al-Qaeda, and that Pakistan, the Taliban, al-Qaeda, and the CIA all reportedly have some relationship with the Sunni Baluchi Jundallah, which sometimes engages in drug smuggling and which has killed Iranian Revolutionary Guards inside Iran. Again, it is conceivable that some in the Qods Force or in some other Iranian entity might want to aid the Taliban in order to bleed or tie down U.S. and other allied forces in Afghanistan and to make a U.S. attack against Iran more difficult and less likely. Reportedly, there is some U.S. intelligence that some Iranian intelligence officers have had some contact with some in the Taliban's leadership. But

Iranian intelligence could be gathering information or complaining and warning when meeting the Taliban. Indeed, the implication of the Iranian government in arms shipments to the Taliban could be a "disinformation" or "false-flag" operation by the Taliban or al-Qaeda or Jundallah in an effort to provoke U.S. action against Iran. Notably, Pakistan's former ambassador to Afghanistan has said the Iranian government is not involved. Implicating Iran could even be another attempt to build "international outrage" or disseminate disinformation to make the same kind of false connection made between al-Qaeda and Iraq that helped rationalize the U.S. invasion of Iraq in 2003.

In June, Gates confirmed that Iranian-made weapons destined for the Taliban were apprehended in Afghanistan, but said there was no evidence the Iranian government was involved and even suggested that some of these weapons might be smuggled out of Iran by Afghan drug smugglers or other criminal gangs. These smugglers do enter Iran with their raw opium and processed heroin by crossing Iran's long and porous border at will, bribing or killing Iranian border guards when necessary, and could bring Iranian weapons back to Afghanistan from these trips. These smugglers provide financial support to the Taliban, and the Taliban protects the Afghan farmers who grow the poppy for these drugs and the smuggling routes of these drug lords. Gates made these remarks at a press conference with Afghan President Karzai, who took the occasion to say that Iranian friendship with his government, which is obviously fighting the Taliban, had never been better. He had in previous months complained that Pakistan was aiding the Taliban. NATO Commander Dan McNeil also said there was no evidence of Iranian government involvement. At the same time, however, unnamed U.S. military officials indicated that EFPs were among the weapons coming from Iran, and unnamed intelligence and Pentagon officials indicated they believed Iran's Revolutionary Guard Qods Force was responsible.[123]

A week later, Gates said that the quantity of the weapons entering Afghanistan from Iran was significant enough that the Iranian government must be aware of it, but still did not say the Iranian government was responsible for it. Undersecretary of State Burns, however, claimed there was "irrefutable evidence" that the weapons were being supplied by the Iranian Revolutionary Guards, and stressed that the Guard is a part of the Iranian government.[124] Burns, however, is not a military or intelligence officer. DNI McConnell said the evidence of this was "a little less clear," although "very plain and, to me, compelling."[125] In August, when Karzai met at Camp David with Bush, Karzai told CNN that Iran was a "helper" in Iran. Bush then said at a joint press conference, "I would be very cautious about whether the Iranian influence in Afghanistan is a positive force."[126] In mid-August, Ahmadinejad visited Kabul and met with Karzai. Ahmadinejad denied the U.S. accusations, and Karzai said Iran and Afghanistan were "brothers" and that Iran as well as the United States was helping in the reconstruction of Afghanistan.[127]

In late June, after El-Baradei and Solana each met with Larijani, it was agreed that the IAEA would travel to Iran in an effort to resolve some of these issues.[128] Also in late June, it was reported that the P5+1 had suggested to Iran that a freeze of the expansion of their uranium enrichment activities would be a sufficient basis for negotiations and for delaying any new UNSC resolution imposing new sanctions. If true, this would mean that the U.S. precondition of suspension was being dropped and that Larijani's earlier proposal and El-Baradei's recommendations were being accepted.[129] This kind of agreement was endorsed by Mohsen Rezai, the secretary of Iran's Expediency Council and the former commander of the Revolutionary Guards from 1981 to 1997.[130] It was also reported, however, that Burns had asked Russia to support stronger UN sanctions in a new resolution, namely inspections of cargo entering or leaving Iran, and that Bush would ask for Putin's support.[131] Subsequently, it became clear that the P5+1 had not adopted the more flexible position on suspension and that this had been only a suggestion by the German government.

When the IAEA traveled to Iran in mid-July, Iran agreed to discuss new measures for IAEA inspections of its uranium enrichment activities at Natanz, agreed to allow an IAEA inspection of the heavy water research reactor at Arak that it had denied earlier in the year, agreed to answer IAEA questions about its previous plutonium experiments, and agreed to replace the IAEA inspectors it had banned from Iran earlier in the year. There were indications that Iran might allow the IAEA to take new samples at a site where highly enriched uranium traces had been found previously and that Iran might answer questions about this and about other projects, including the Green Salt Project, but these indications were not definite. El-Baradei had said earlier in the week that Iran had scaled back its uranium enrichment programs, namely by slowing the construction and operation of the centrifuge cascades at Natanz. These developments seemed to indicate that Iran wanted to ease the crisis, although the latter could also have been due to technical difficulties. It seemed that the centrifuge cascades might be spinning at relatively slow speeds, perhaps because of Iranian concerns that the cascades might break down and crash. It was not clear if Iran could run them continuously at higher speeds with larger amounts of gas fed into them and with larger amounts of enriched uranium produced.[132] If true, this would indicate that Iran is not close to the capability necessary for a nuclear weapon.

The Bush administration was not satisfied, and Rice told European diplomats that if the UN Security Council did not impose new sanctions on Iran, the United States would declare the Iranian Revolutionary Guard Corps to be a "foreign terrorist organization." The United States has long named Iran as a state supporter of terrorism, but this would be the first time the United States had designated a military establishment of another state as terrorists and it would automatically enable the United States to freeze and take control over any financial assets the Revolutionary Guards might have in the United States, probably negligible, or in any U.S. financial institution operating abroad. It would also be intended to discourage any foreign entity from doing business with Iran. It might also be intended by Rice to defuse pressures from those who seek military action against Iran. On the other hand, it could be an effort by those who seek military action to justify a strike in the expectation that by targeting and toppling the Revolutionary Guards, they could disable the main prop for the clerics and thus bring about "regime change." Iranian officials interpreted this as an effort to destabilize the government and an indication that the United States would take action against Iran even if it cooperated with the United States in Iraq and said that it would increase hostility and serve the interests of the real terrorists in the region, evidently a reference to al-Qaeda. Nevertheless, they argued that it would unify Iran.[133] For those in the administration who favored military strikes to bring about "regime change," there was some ammunition in a new NIE that was being finished at the time which argued that popular unrest with economic hardship was unlikely to bring down Iran's clerical regime or change Iran's foreign policies.[134]

It was later revealed, however, that the U.S. intelligence community had received intelligence suggesting that Iran had ceased work on a suspected nuclear weapons program in the fall of 2003, when IAEA inspections had intensified, and that the U.S. intelligence community was briefing senior Bush administration officials about this in July 2007. The new intelligence was based in part on the acquisition of written notes of Iranian military officials and of subsequent electronic intercepts of conversations of Iranian officials in the summer of 2007 and perhaps also on information from other sources, perhaps including Ali Asgari, a former Iranian Revolutionary Guard officer and deputy defense minister who had reportedly defected earlier in the year. U.S. intelligence agencies believed that this new intelligence confirmed the authenticity of the information found on the hard drive of the laptop computer turned over to the IAEA in 2005, namely that Iran had previously been involved in designing a nuclear warhead and related activities, but also believed this new intelligence indicated that Iran had ceased this and other nuclear weapons related work in the fall of 2003. Bush administration officials were skeptical, thinking this new intelligence might be Iranian disinformation, and the U.S. intelligence community delayed a new NIE on Iran's nuclear programs while it tried to verify or debunk this new intelligence. In subsequent months, the Bush administration continued to speak as if Iran were continuing a suspected weapons program.

In August, France's new President Nicolas Sarkozy called the crisis over Iran's nuclear programs "the most serious weighing on the international order today." He praised the dual approach of threatening sanctions if Iran did not suspend enrichment and offering incentives if Iran did suspend enrichment. He called this approach "the only one that can enable us to avoid being faced with an alternative that I call catastrophic: an Iranian bomb or the bombing of Iran." He did not endorse bombing Iran or suggest that France would participate, but he obviously admitted that bombing Iran was a possibility. At the least, it seemed to be a warning to Iran that this was possible. But in an indication of his preferred approach, he reiterated France's opposition to the U.S. invasion and occupation of Iraq, called for a U.S. withdrawal, and pledged that France would seek to avoid confrontation between Islam and the West by helping to mediate resolutions to conflicts inside Iraq, as well as in Lebanon, the Israeli-Palestinian arena, and with Iran, and would send more troops to help train the Afghan army.[135]

In August, the IAEA and Iran announced that they had reached an agreement establishing a work plan and laying out a timetable for Iran to answer all of the IAEA's outstanding questions by December. The United States and France expressed concern that Iran was deliberately dragging out the process. They thought that Iran was doing this in order to continue its uranium enrichment and to make it easier for Russia and China to oppose a third UN Security Council resolution imposing a new round of sanctions. The IAEA indicated, however, that Iran was being unusually cooperative and El-Baradei said he hoped the United States would delay any new sanctions while this process unfolded. The IAEA indicated that Iran had satisfactorily answered questions about its past experiments with plutonium by providing the IAEA with access to an expert and to documentation and other data. The IAEA indicated that Iran was running about 2,000 centrifuges at Natanz, several hundred more than three months earlier, and had 650 more centrifuges under construction. But the IAEA also noted that the uranium being processed was "well below the expected quantity for a facility of this design" and that the uranium was being enriched to a lower level than that claimed by Iran. El-Baradei said, "They could have expanded much faster. Some say it's for technical reasons. My gut feeling is that it's primarily for political reasons."[136]

In July, Iranian media showed brief videoclips of the "confessions" of Esfandiari and Tajbakhsh, after their months in solitary confinement in Evin Prison. In August, Esfandiari was released and she and Arnaz were allowed to leave the country. In September, Tajbakhsh was released from Evin but not allowed to leave Iran. This may also have been an effort to reduce political tensions, particularly when Iran may have believed that it had already intimidated other Iranian-Americans and Iranians. But Bush had requested $108 million for the fiscal year 2008 for IFSA (Iran Freedom and Support Act), the same program that Iran had been reacting against when it detained these Iranian-Americans, and this was roughly double the previous year's appropriation. Moreover, in early September, Iran was shelling a border region in Iraqi Kurdistan from which Iranian Kurdish dissidents were launching attacks against Iran. This group, the Kurdish Free Life Party, or PJAK, had claimed responsibility for attacks inside Iran, was believed to have downed an Iranian helicopter, and was thought to collaborate with the Kurdish Worker's Party, or PKK, a Turkish

Kurdish group that was launching attacks against Turkey from bases in Iraq and eliciting Turkish shelling into Iraq. PJAK's leader, Rahman Haj Ahmadi, had visited Washington in August in what was reported as an effort to develop U.S. support, although Hersh had reported in November 2006 that PJAK already had U.S. and Israeli support. Iran demanded that the United States and Iraq stop PJAK, which Iran believed already had U.S. and Iraqi backing, and Iran seemed willing to push the issue even at this time. By October, the PKK claimed that PJAK had killed 150 Iranian soldiers since August in hit and run attacks from Iraq into Iran.[137]

There were some changes in Iran that might make diplomacy a fruitful endeavor. In early September, Rafsanjani was elected head of the Assembly of Experts, the eighty-six-member body of clerics that appoints, monitors, and can dismiss the Supreme Leader. Rafsanjani was already the head of the Expediency Council, which mediates disputes between the Majlis and the Guardian Council, and where his ally Rezai was the secretary. Furthermore, Khamenei appointed Mohammad Ali Jafari commander-in-chief of the Revolutionary Guards. The *New York Times* referred to Jafari as a hard-liner and noted that he had threatened a crack-down on domestic dissent in the late 1990s. On foreign policy matters, however, some thought he was an ally of Rezai and Rafsanjani, who were rivals of Ahmadinejad and had a record of favoring negotiations with the United States, although Jafari was prepared for war if necessary.[138]

Nevertheless, in mid-September, when Bush announced that the 30,000 U.S. forces "surged" to Iraq earlier in 2007 would be withdrawn from Iraq by the summer of 2008, but that a large U.S. military presence would remain in Iraq even beyond the end of his presidency in 2009, he argued that this was necessary in order to contain Iran. Moreover, the administration pressed for a third round of UN Security Council economic sanctions against Iran, and seemed to have the support of France as well as Italy.[139] Then, when the Israeli Air Force bombed targets in eastern Syria, Israel explained it to the Bush administration as an effort to destroy a Syrian nuclear weapons program supported by North Korea, but the intelligence was questioned.[140] It was possible that Israel might have been trying to test Syria's air defenses for a potential attack against Iran and even if that was not the case Iran could clearly see what Israel's capabilities were. Iran was perhaps relieved, however, when Russian President Putin visited Iran, publicly warned against any military action against Iran, and said he had no evidence that Iran was pursuing nuclear weapons.[141] On the following day, however, Bush warned that an Iranian nuclear weapon could lead to World War III.

In October, there were developments in Iran that might undermine Rafsanjani and his allies. Ali Larijani resigned his posts as Iran's chief nuclear negotiator and as secretary of the Supreme National Security Council, although he would remain on the Council as one of Khamenei's two representatives. Larijani was replaced as nuclear negotiator by Saeed Jalili, a deputy foreign minister said to be an ally of Ahmadinejad, and this suggested that Iran would not be exhibiting much flexibility in future talks on nuclear issues.[142] Meanwhile, the Bush administration, unable to obtain a new Security Council resolution against Iran, in large part because of Russian opposition, announced that it was naming the Qods Force and four Iranian banks as supporters of terror and proliferators of WMD, and called upon foreign banks and companies to stop doing business with these Iranian entities.[143]

It was still not clear that sanctions would have much bite while Iran was earning $100 per barrel for its oil exports, it did not appear that diplomacy was making any progress, and it did not appear that the Bush administration had really made the hard decision to use military force against Iran. In November, El-Baradei reported that Iran was cooperating with the IAEA. In late November, Jalili told Solana that all proposals made in previous negotiations about Iran's nuclear programs were irrelevant and that Iran would now recognize only the IAEA as an interlocutor on the subject. In early December, the declassified key findings of a new NIE on Iran revealed that the new intelligence gathered in 2007 had led the sixteen U.S. intelligence agencies to reverse their May 2005 findings and now "judge with high confidence that in fall 2003, Tehran halted its nuclear weapons program," noting that this referred to "Iran's nuclear weapon design and weaponization work and covert uranium conversion-related and uranium enrichment-related work." The NIE also said, "Tehran's decision to halt its nuclear weapons program suggests it is less determined to develop nuclear weapons than we have been judging since 2005. Our assessment that the program probably was halted primarily in response to international pressure suggests Iran may be more vulnerable to influence on the issue than we judged previously. Indeed, the NIE argued that "some combination of threats of intensified international scrutiny and pressures, along with opportunities for Iran to achieve its security, prestige, and goals for regional influence in other ways, might—if perceived by Iran's leaders as credible—prompt Iran to extend the current halt to its nuclear weapons program. It is difficult to specify what such a combination might be." It seemed that Iran may have halted these programs as IAEA inspections were intensifying and European diplomacy was beginning, and prior to the UN Security Council sanctions of 2006 and 2007.

Bush and others in the administration nevertheless argued that it remained important to continue pressuring Iran to prevent it from even learning more about how to enrich uranium, stressing that Iran might restart a nuclear weapons program, and continued to press for new UNSC sanctions unless Iran met U.S. preconditions for negotiations. Bush also emphasized an Iranian threat during a trip to the GCC states early in 2008 and the bilateral U.S.-Iranian talks on Iraq were not continuing. Meanwhile, Israel rejected the new conclusions of the NIE, arguing that its intelligence indicated that Iran was continuing a nuclear weapons program, and arguing that the military option should not be taken off the table.

In February 2008, the IAEA issued another report, noting that considerable progress had been made in resolving many of its questions about Iran's activities, but also noting that Iran had not suspended uranium enrichment, and had not answered all questions about its alleged weaponization programs, and had not begun to abide by the Additional Protocol to the NPT. Subsequently, in early March, the UNSC did pass Resolution 1803 imposing new sanctions on Iran, particularly to prohibit travel by a list of individuals thought to be involved in nuclear weapons work, and to inspect cargo bound to and from Iran thought to be related to nuclear weapons work. It seemed to be time to think through all of these options again and ask whether war, sanctions, or diplomacy was appropriate, and that is what the next chapter attempts to do.

NOTES

1. One study that makes a strong case for Iran having a nuclear weapons program is Mark Fitzpatrick, "Assessing Iran's Nuclear Programme," *Survival* 48 (Autumn 2006). He points to military funding and administration of some important nuclear programs. See also Paul Kerr, *Bulletin of the Atomic Scientist* 62 (November/December 2006).

2. For a critical analysis of the administration's assertions, see a series of articles by Gareth Porter, beginning with "Bush's New Iran Policy."

3. William Kristol, Reuel Marc Gerecht, Charles Krauthammer, Joshua Muravchik, and Norman Podhoritz were early proponents of the view that military strikes might be necessary. Richard Perle and Max Boot were proponents of striking Syria.

4. See www.whitehouse.gov for text of the National Security Strategy of the United States of America, March 2006, and the National Security Strategy of the United States of America, September 2002.

5. This was reported by Hersh, "The Iran Plans." See also Thomas Ricks, "U.S. Is Studying Military Strike Options on Iran," *Washington Post,* April 9, 2006. The rationale for the possible use of nuclear weapons is set out in Presidential National Security Directive 35, entitled *Nuclear Weapons Deployment and Authorization,* May 2004.

6. Ashton B. Carter and William J. Perry explore this in *Plan B for Iran: What If Nuclear Diplomacy Fails?* A Report Based on a Workshop Hosted by the Preventive Defense Project of Harvard and Stanford Universities, May 22, 2006. See also Lisbeth Gronlund, David Wright, and Robert Nelson, "Earth Penetrating Weapons," Union of Concerned Scientists, May 2005, for some of the drawbacks and shortcomings of these weapons. UK nuclear scientist Frank Barnaby has also explored this in "Would Air Strikes Work?" at www.oxfordresearchgroup.org.uk.

7. Hersh, "The Next Act."

8. Numerous officials from GCC states have said this to the author from the early 1990s through 2007 both in Washington and in the Gulf.

9. Lawrence Kaplan, "Iran Syria Operations Group," *New Republic,* April 10, 2006; Farah Stockman, "US Unit Works Quietly to Counter Iran's Sway: Backs Dissidents, Nearby Nations," *Boston Globe,* January 2, 2007. Elliott Abrams was convicted in 1991 of two misdemeanor charges of withholding information from Congress about the Reagan administration's effort in the mid-1980s to illegally fund the Nicaraguan contras in an effort to destabilize the

Sandinista regime in Nicaragua and was later disbarred from the practice of law. He was pardoned by President George H.W. Bush in 1992.

10. The incentives included possible accession into the World Trade Organization; trade and investment and technical assistance arrangements; and possible access to U.S. commercial aircraft. See www.armscontrol.org for the texts of all relevant proposals regarding Iran's nuclear programs made by Iran; the British, French, and German team known as the E3/EU; and the five permanent members of the Security Council plus Germany known as the P5+1. This Web site also provides the texts of relevant reports by the IAEA and the texts of relevant UN Security Council Resolutions.

11. One administration figure said the prospect of eventual Iranian resumption of uranium enrichment is the "when hell freezes over" clause. *New York Times,* September 12, 2006. The end of Iran's uranium enrichment program is also the stated objective advocated in a study by a progressive research group affiliated with the Democratic Party. See Joseph Cirincione and Andrew J. Grotto, "Contain and Engage: A New Strategy for Resolving the Nuclear Crisis with Iran," the Center for American Progress, February 2007.

12. See www.armscontrol.org.

13. U.S. Central Command Commander John Abizaid said this during the summer 2006 war.

14. Hersh, "The Redirection," *New Yorker,* March 2007, quotes Nasrallah.

15. Seymour M. Hersh, "Watching Israel: Washington's Interest in Israel's War," *New Yorker,* August 21, 2006. Israeli communications were reportedly intercepted, deciphered, and translated by Hezbollah listening posts in southern Lebanon or by Russian-Syrian and Iranian-Syrian listening posts in Syria. Hezbollah reportedly used the advanced RPG-29 antitank weapon, a Russian-made weapon supplied to Syria. Hezbollah may have disabled an Israeli naval vessel with a Chinese-made C-801 antiship missile.

16. It is a 205-mile long stretch of open land and mountains along which the towns are inhabited by Shiites loyal to Hezbollah. Even the Lebanese army border guards are largely Shiites.

17. Brian Ross and Richard Esposito, "Bush Authorizes New Covert Action Against Iran," *ABC News,* May 22, 2007. The story was revealed by former and current U.S. intelligence officials.

18. *New York Times,* June 3, 2007.

19. Dafna Linzer, "Troops Authorized to Kill Iranian Operatives in Iraq," *Washington Post,* January 26, 2007.

20. Hersh, "The Redirection"; David Samuels, "Grand Illusions," *Atlantic,* June 2007.

21. Robert Hunter, "Easing Iran-US Tensions," *United Press International,* April 19, 2007.

22. Retired USAF Colonel Sam Gardiner, "End of the Summer of Diplomacy—Assessing U.S. Military Options on Iran," a report for the Century Foundation, September 27, 2006, www.tcf.org.

23. The Chief of Naval Operations asked in 2006 for a review of plans to blockade two Iranian oil ports in the Persian Gulf. This could conceivably enable the U.S. Navy to block Iranian oil exports, although that would drive the price of oil up for the world's consumers, or to block Iranian imports of refined gas.

24. Hersh, "The Next Act." The BBC ran an Israeli-made documentary that aired Israeli views on October 10, 2006. *Haaretz,* November 20, 2006, reported on the Bush remark to Chirac. Israeli aircraft might need U.S. cooperation to fly through Arab air space without being detected and to refuel on their return to Israel.

25. See H.R. 2168, passed by the House and Senate in September 2006 and signed by President Bush in October 2006, at http://www.iranfocus.com/modules/news/article.php.?storyid=8793.

26. *The Iraq Study Group Report,* James A. Baker, III, and Lee H. Hamilton, Co-Chairs (New York: Vintage Books, 2006). See the Council on Foreign Relations study in 2004 was called "Iran: Time for a New Approach."

27. *New York Times,* November 29, 2006, A24.

28. *New York Times,* December 6, 2006.

29. Joe Klein, "Cheney's Iran Fantasy," May 25, 2007, at Swampland blog at www.time.com.

30. David Ignatius, "The Price of Iran's Help," *Washington Post,* December 6, 2006; Jim Krane, "Iran Urges Arabs to Eject U.S. Military," *Associated Press,* December 5, 2006.

31. *New York Times,* December 15, 2006.

32. *New York Times,* December 21, 2007.

33. For example, the resolution prohibited financial transactions with these individuals and the organizations controlled by them: Major General Yahya Rahim Safavi, the overall commander of the Revolutionary Guards; General Hossein Salimi, the head of the Revolutionary Guards air force; and Ahmad Vahid Dastjerdi, the head of the Aerospace Industries Organization. Ironically, the original UNSC sanctions proposed by Britain, France, and Germany in October would have entailed measures such as a ban on training of Iranian students abroad in fields that could contribute to Iran's nuclear and ballistic missile programs, travel restrictions on Iranians working on these programs, freezing the financial assets of these individuals, restrictions on any international financing of such programs, and restrictions on the export of nuclear equipment or dual use equipment to Iran. Russia and China objected to this draft proposal.

34. Russia and China consider Iran a lucrative market for conventional military exports and for nuclear technology. China sees Iran as an important source of the oil and natural gas China must import for its growing economy, and is investing in these sectors of Iran's economy. Russia may also seek to invest in Iran's oil and gas sectors, perhaps to acquire additional gas supplies to meet its own export contracts through its own pipelines. Germany, France, and Britain, along with Italy and many other EU countries, as well as Japan have billions of dollars of trade with Iran annually, importing Iranian oil and exporting a variety of products. Their firms have also invested billions in Iran's oil and gas sectors. Chirac expressed concern that increasing sanctions could lead to a mutual escalation that ends in conflict, although France did vote for increasing sanctions at the Security Council in December 2006 and again in March 2007. See the *New York Times,* February 1, 2007.

35. It should also be said that Russia and China seek to counter global U.S. hegemony and unilateralism. While they both appear to oppose Iranian acquisition of nuclear weapons, some in both countries may possibly think that Iranian nuclear weapons would contribute to the diminution of American power in the Middle East. See Mark Katz, "Putin, Ahmadinejad and the Iranian Nuclear Crisis," *Middle East Policy* 13 (Winter 2006). China is concerned about U.S. power, but the U.S. security arrangements in the Gulf do permit China to invest and trade there, and especially to import oil and gas reliably. See Steve A. Yetiv and Chunlong Lu, "China, Global Energy and the Middle East," *Middle East Journal* 61 (Spring 2007).

36. Putin and other Russian leaders have expressed concern about the U.S. antiballistic missile defense program involving the deployment of interceptor missiles in Poland and radar guidance systems in the Czech Republic, a program the Bush administration has defended as

necessary in order to counter ballistic missile threats from "rogue nations," particularly Iran. Russian leaders have expressed concern that Iranian missiles would be intercepted and destroyed over Russia, with the debris raining down on Russian people and property. Russia also fears that this program would deter its own missile force and even threatened to aim Russia's missiles at Europe. At the G-8 summit in Germany in June 2007, however, Putin recommended alternatives to the U.S. plan, including a joint assessment of the missile threat, early warning systems in Azerbaijan, and interceptor missiles in Iraq, Turkey, or at sea.

37. *New York Times,* January 11, 2007.

38. *New York Times,* January 29, 2007. Michael Hirsh, "Iran Diplomat: We're Ready to Help in Iraq," *Newsweek,* July 23, 2007.

39. Hersh, "The Redirection."

40. *Star Online,* January 16, 2007.

41. *Al-Siyasa (Politics),* January 27, 2007.

42. *Washington Post,* February 17, 2007, reported on Bandar's remark to Bush administration officials. For a discussion of GCC perceptions of Iran at this time, see Thomas R. Mattair, "Mutual Threat Perceptions in the Arab/Persian Gulf: GCC Perceptions," *Middle East Policy* 14 (Summer 2007): 133–40.

43. *New York Times,* January 17, 2007.

44. *New York Times,* July 28, 2007.

45. *Washington Post,* February 19, 2007; Hersh, "The Redirection"; Samuels, "Grand Illusions."

46. *Los Angeles Times,* February 25, 2007; *New York Times,* July 24, 2007.

47. *New York Times,* January 9, 2007.

48. Trita Parsi, "Bush's Iraq Strategy: Goad Iran into War," *Inter Press Service,* January 12, 2007.

49. *New York Times,* February 19, 2007. Brian Ross and Christopher Isham, "The Secret War Against Iran," *ABC News,* April 3, 2007. This group dates from the late 1990s. It kidnapped nine Iranian soldiers in December 2005. Its leader is Abdulmalik Rigi. The *ABC News* story was based in part on reporting by an individual who subsequently lost his positions at ABC and at the Nixon Center in Washington because of allegations that he had falsified his academic and professional credentials and some earlier interviews. ABC began an investigation into the information he had provided about Jundallah and other topics. Nevertheless, the story about Jundallah was generally consistent with other reporting on U.S. covert action by Hersh and major American newspapers. A subsequent reference to this story by *ABC News* on May 22, 2007 said that Jundallah was also receiving support from the Afghan military and launching attacks into Iran from Afghan territory. The Afghan involvement is questionable inasmuch as Jundallah reportedly has ties with al-Qaeda, the Taliban, and Pakistan's Inter Services Intelligence, all of which have been enemies of the Hamid Karzai government in Afghanistan. But the areas of Afghanistan from which operations against Iran could be launched are far from the Hamid Karzai government's seat of power in Kabul and not really under the control of his government, and could be conducted without the approval of his government.

50. Hersh, "The Redirection." *BBC,* February 19, 2007.

51. Michael Smith and Sarah Baxter, "US Generals 'Will Quit' If Bush Orders Iran Attack," *Sunday Times Online,* February 25, 2007.

52. Gareth Porter, "Commander's Veto Sank Threatening Gulf Buildup," *Inter Press Service,* May 2007.

53. *(London) Sunday Times,* January 2007.

54. Sneh is a former IDF officer and commander in the West Bank, current Knesset member and Deputy Defense Minister, and possible future head of the Labor Party.

55. www.ynetnews.com, Oded Tira, "What to Do with Iran?" December 30, 2006. See also www.today.az.

56. *New York Times,* February 19 and 22, 2007; *Washington Post,* February 23, 2007.

57. *New York Times,* February 22, 2007.

58. *New York Times,* February 28, 2007, and March 1, 2007.

59. Author's personal conversation with former official of Foreign Ministry of Islamic Iran, March 2006.

60. Christiane Amanpour, "Iranian Official Offers Glimpse from Within: A Desire for U.S. Ally," *CNN,* February 21, 2007, at http://www.cnn.com/WORLD/meast/02/21/btsc.iran.amanpour/index.html.

61. "Prospects for Iraq's Stability: A Challenging Road Ahead," Office of the Director of National Intelligence, January 2007. See www.dni.gov.

62. *New York Times,* February 12, 2007. See Gareth Porter, "The Blame Game: Bush's Campaign to Pin the Iraq Quagmire on Iranian Meddling Won't Wash," *American Prospect,* February 2, 2007; and "U.S. Briefing on Iran Discredits the Official Line," *Inter Press Service,* February 13, 2007.

63. *New York Times,* February 14, 2007.

64. *New York Times,* February 26, 2007.

65. *New York Times,* February 28, 2007.

66. *New York Times,* March 4 and 5, 2007.

67. *New York Times,* March 26, 2007.

68. Baker's remark in David E. Sanger, "Dueling Worldviews: Baker's Emphasis on Negotiations Clashes with the Mind-Set of Rice," *New York Times,* December 8, 2006, A16. The assault on the U.S. Embassy in Damascus in 2006 indicates that Islamist radicalism is a problem for the Syrian regime.

69. Michael Slackman, "Iran's Strong Ties with Syria Complicate U.S. Overtures," *New York Times,* December 28, 2006; Hugh Naylor, "Syria, Seeking Investors, Turns Cautiously to Iran," *New York Times,* October 4, 2007.

70. Author's conversation with an official from the Saudi Embassy in Washington, November 2006.

71. *International Herald Tribune,* December 21, 2006. See also Steve Clemons blog at www.thewashingtonnote.com.

72. *Financial Times,* March 15, 2007. See also *Reuters,* March 15, 2007. See www.gulfinthemedia.com.

73. *Gulf News,* March 28, 2007.

74. Mattair, "GCC Perceptions." GCC officials have expressed these views in private to many visiting American academics.

75. *New York Times,* March 11, 2007.

76. For the debate within the administration on releasing the captured Iranians, see Robin Wright, *Washington Post,* April 2007.

77. *New York Times,* March 20 and 25, 2007.

78. *New York Times,* March 26, 2007.

79. *New York Times,* May 12, 2007.

80. *New York Times,* May 14, 2007.

81. Farah Stockman, "US Unit Created to Pressure Iran, Syria Disbanded," *Boston Globe,* May 26, 2007.

82. See Robin Wright, "Tehran Jails U.S. Scholar After Long Arrest," *Washington Post,* May 9, and "Iran Charges U.S. Scholar with Trying to Topple Regime," *Washington Post,* May 21, 2007. Scott MacLeod, "Did U.S. Incite Iranian Arrests?" *Time Magazine,* June 2, 2007.

83. *New York Times,* May 15 and 24, 2007.

84. *New York Times,* May 29, 2007. *Washington Post,* May 29, 2007.

85. Steve Clemons, "Cheney Attempting to Constrain Bush's Choices on Iran Conflict: Staff Engaged in Insubordination Against President Bush," in the May 26 issue of the *Washington Note.* See www.thewashingtonnote.com.

86. *New York Times,* June 2, 2007.

87. "Face the Nation," *CBS,* June 10, 2007.

88. Joseph Lieberman, "Iran's Proxy War," *Wall Street Journal,* July 6, 2007.

89. *New York Times,* July 2007.

90. *Fox News* with Sean Hannity, July 11, 2007.

91. Ewan MacAskill and Julian Borger, "Cheney Pushes Bush to Act on Iran," *Guardian,* July 16, 2007.

92. Norman Podhoretz, "The Case for Bombing Iran," *Wall Street Journal,* May 2007, and *Commentary,* June 2007.

93. Paul Craig Roberts, "The War on Truth and Liberty: The Neocon Threat to American Freedom," *Counterpunch,* June 12, 2007.

94. *New York Times,* April 20, 2007, for Peretz remark; Trita Parsi, "New War Rhetoric Undercuts Iraq Talks," *Inter Press Service,* June 12, 2007, cites *Israel Television 2* for Mofaz remark.

95. See study by David Albright and Paul Brannan, Institute for Science and International Security, July 9, 2007.

96. Michael Hirsh, "Iran Has a Message. Are We Listening?" *Washington Post,* July 1, 2007.

97. Seymour M. Hersh, "Shifting Targets: The Administration's Plan for Iran," *New Yorker,* October 8, 2007.

98. See John F. Burns and Michael R. Gordon, "U.S. Says Iran Helped Iraqis Kill Five G.I.'s," *New York Times,* July 3, 2007. See also Gareth Porter, "The Iran Attack That Wasn't," *American Prospect,* August 2, 2007. Daqduq was also reportedly known as Hamid Muhammad Jabour Alami.

99. *New York Times,* July 3, 2007. Porter, "The Iran Attack That Wasn't."

100. Porter, "The Iran Attack That Wasn't." Porter also noted that prior to the U.S. invasion of Iraq, Gordon and his colleague Judith Miller had reported that Iraq had an active nuclear weapons program, in part based on their reports about aluminum tubes Iraq was supposedly importing for such a program, reports that were later found to be inaccurate. In fact this was one of the reasons the *New York Times* later published an apology for not having vigorously questioned the Bush administration's allegations.

101. *New York Times,* July 24, 27, 28, 2007.

102. Hirsh, "Iran Diplomat: We're Ready to Help."

103. *New York Times,* August 7 and 8, 2007.

104. Michael R. Gordon, "U.S. Says Iran-Supplied Bomb Is Killing More Troops in Iraq," *New York Times,* August 8, 2007.

105. Gareth Porter, "US 'Surges,' Soldiers Die. Blame Iran." *Asia Times,* August 16, 2007.

106. *New York Times,* August 20, 2007.

107. Gareth Porter, "Petraeus Helps Destroy Bush's 'Proxy War' Claim," *Inter Press Service,* September 17, 2007.

108. Ibid.

109. http://news.bbc.co.uk/2/hi/middle_east/7004801.stm.

110. Eli Lake, "Iran's Secret Plan for Mayhem," *New York Sun,* January 3, 2007.

111. Ruhollah Ramazani, "Might U.S., Iran Cooperate on al-Qaeda?" *Daily Progress* (Charlottesville, Virginia), May 27, 2007. Zarqawi's successor was Abu Ayyub al-Masri, an Egyptian. The Islamic State in Iraq, a supposed umbrella group, may have been conceived by him to mask AQI's continuing role, and the titular leader of this state, Abu Omar al-Baghdadi, allegedly an Iraqi, may have been a fictional invention designed to mask the role that foreigners played in the Islamic jihadist resistance. A captured member of al-Qaeda made these claims when interrogated. *New York Times,* July 19, 2007. He was also reputedly a liaison between al-Masri and Zawahri.

112. *Washington Post,* February 10, 2007.

113. Linzer, "Troops Authorized to Kill."

114. Bruce Riedel, "Al-Qaeda Strikes Back," *Foreign Affairs,* May/June 2007.

115. Stephen Fidler, "Al-Qaeda Linked to Operations from Iran," *Financial Times,* July 6, 2007.

116. Ibid.

117. *Associated Press,* July 8, 2007.

118. Eli Lake, "Al-Qaeda Councils in Iran," *New York Sun,* July 17, 2007.

119. *New York Times,* July 18, 2007.

120. *New York Times,* July 19, 2007.

121. *New York Times,* July 23, 2007.

122. *New York Times,* April 18, 2007.

123. *New York Times,* June 4, 2007. For a report that suggests this was an effort by Cheney's office to make an "end run" around Bush, see Gareth Porter, "Cheney's Iran-Arms-to-Taliban Gambit Rebuffed," *Inter Press Service,* June 11, 2007.

124. *New York Times,* June 13, 2007.

125. Robert McMahon interview with DNI McConnell at Council on Foreign Relations, June 28, 2007. See www.cfr.org.

126. *New York Times,* August 7, 2007. Only a day earlier, Nicaragua's President Ortega had announced that Iran had pledged to help with an ocean port, a hydroelectric project, and housing, and that Venezuela, with which Iran was also cooperating, would also participate in the ocean port project. U.S. officials had previously said Iran would be a "problematic" partner for Nicaragua.

127. *New York Times,* August 15, 2007.

128. *New York Times,* June 26, 2007.

129. *Los Angeles Times,* June 30, 2007.

130. *Washington Post,* July 1, 2007.

131. *New York Times,* July 1, 2007.

132. *Associated Press,* July 13, 2007. David Albright of the Institute for Science and International Security has expressed doubts that Iran can run its centrifuges at the high speeds necessary for industrial grade or weapon grade production.

133. *New York Times,* August 15 and 16, 2007.

134. *Associated Press,* August 23, 2007. This NIE remains classified.

135. *New York Times,* August 28, 2007.

136. *New York Times,* August 29 and 31, 2007.

137. *New York Times,* September 4, 2007; Hersh, "The Next Act"; *New York Times,* October 23, 2007.

138. *New York Times,* September 3, 2007.

139. *New York Times,* September 16 and 22, 2007.

140. *Washington Post,* September 21, 2007; *New York Times,* September 22, 2007.

141. *New York Times,* October 17, 2007.

142. *New York Times,* October 21, 2007.

143. *New York Times,* October 26, 2007.

CHAPTER 6

Conclusion

Inasmuch as war is a serious possibility, let us immediately consider one. If U.S. air and sea power, and possibly Israeli, were employed to strike Iran's two dozen known nuclear facilities as well as associated ground-based air defense systems, this will do considerable damage to Iran's nuclear program but may not do more than set it back several years.[1] U.S. naval forces would launch cruise missiles against Iran's air defenses, but these missiles are too small to destroy Iran's hardened underground facilities, such as the uranium enrichment facility at Natanz, although they could open up "tunnels" into which "bunker-busting" weapons could be dropped. U.S. Air Force bombers and perhaps fighter aircraft would have to be deployed to deliver heavy "bunker-busting" bombs, perhaps including nuclear ones. Many scientists say even nuclear bunker-busting weapons cannot penetrate deep enough into the earth to destroy hardened underground facilities and that their use would create radioactive fallout that could spread for hundreds of miles, killing and/or causing disease not only in Iran but throughout the Arab states of the Gulf. Whether nuclear or conventional weapons were used, even if a new generation of conventional bunker busters are more effective, there would likely be repetitive bombing of each target for days. Even without the use of nuclear weapons, there would be heavy Iranian civilian casualties.[2]

It has been suggested that the United States might explicitly tell Iran that only its nuclear facilities and air defenses were targets and that if Iran did not retaliate, the United States would not widen its list of targets. Given the number of days and number of casualties involved, it is hard to say if Iran would comply. Moreover, there have been enough public reports of contingency plans involving all of Iran's military infrastructure and enough reports of administration officials who intend for bombing to bring about "regime change" that Iranian officials might not believe U.S. assurances of limited targets.

More likely, air and sea strikes would involve a wider range of targets, including the regular conventional armed forces and the Revolutionary Guard forces, including their command and control and communication, as well as vital industry and infrastructure, and also intelligence personnel and regime leaders. This is because the U.S. military may want to hit targets suspected to be involved in supporting militants in Iraq and may want to eliminate assets that Iran could use in retaliation in Iraq or elsewhere and because the administration may seek regime change. Again, it will be possible to do enormous damage, but it will not be possible to control developments in Iran after the war, even if U.S. ground forces are there in large numbers, and they very probably will not be there. Some members of Iran's regular and Revolutionary Guard forces, Iran's intelligence agencies, and Iran's regime will survive to play some role in deciding who does or does not rule Iran, just as members of Saddam's regime and military play that role in Iraq. There are likely to be even more civilian casualties in this scenario.

Some of Iran's retaliatory capabilities have been much discussed. Iran can unleash regular military forces and Revolutionary Guards and Basij militia forces to attack U.S. and British forces in Iraq and U.S. and NATO forces in Afghanistan. Iranian forces would be joined by Shia allies in both states. In Iraq, Iranian forces and Iraqi Shia allies could conceivably cut off the supply lines from the south that support all U.S. forces in Iraq. Sunnis in both states may also take the opportunity to strike. Iranian agents could unleash terror and assassinations in the United States and Europe. Iran could encourage Hezbollah, Islamic Jihad, and perhaps Hamas to unleash terror in Israel. Iran could ask Syria, with which it has a recent security cooperation pact, to launch missiles against Israel, although Syria might stay out to avoid Israeli retaliation. Iran itself could launch missiles against Israel and might do so if it thinks it is going down in defeat.

However, the debate about war has unwisely dismissed Iran's ability to engage with and retaliate against the U.S. military and its GCC partners, particularly in the Arab/Persian Gulf, the narrow Strait of Hormuz, and the Gulf of Oman, the route through which tankers carry more than one-fifth of the world's daily oil supplies and much of its liquid natural gas supplies.

Many U.S. analysts argue that the U.S. military can easily deal with "obsolete" Iranian conventional military forces and that Iran cannot close the Strait of Hormuz to shipping.[3] But Iran has modernized its conventional forces since the end of the Iran-Iraq War in 1988 and in response to the increasing U.S. military presence in the Gulf during and after war with Iraq in 1990–91. It has acquired and/or developed Russian-made Sukhoi-24 MK ground attack strike fighter jets; Shahab medium-range ballistic missiles; Chinese-made C-801 and C-802 antiship cruise missiles that can be launched from air, land, or sea; Chinese-made *Houdong*-class fast attack naval craft equipped with these modern antiship missiles; torpedo-firing and mine-laying diesel-electric powered submarines; other mine-laying vessels; midget submarines and submersible swimmer delivery vehicles that can carry divers and explosives to targets throughout the Gulf; amphibious landing craft; and surface-to-air defensive missiles. It also has more than two hundred 155-mm howitzers along its coast. These capabilities bring all of the important economic and military target in the Gulf, in the Strait of Hormuz, and in the GCC states within Iran's range. This includes military facilities used by U.S. forces and the U.S. military personnel themselves.[4] Iran has many types of small craft such as Boghammers and Boston Whalers that along with fast attack craft could harass shipping, even aircraft carriers, by "swarming." Iran's naval exercises in the Strait of Hormuz in 2006 and 2007 have been meant to show that it can retaliate in the Gulf and involved the testing of new torpedoes and missiles. The Revolutionary Guards also announced in February 2007 that it had during recent war games successfully test launched a land based antiship missile that it said has a range of 220 miles and is capable of sinking large warships in the Persian Gulf, the Gulf of Oman, and the northern Indian Ocean.[5] Iran has reportedly recently taken delivery of six new Sukhoi 25T fighter aircraft. The Ukraine has reportedly provided Iran with the Kolchuga air defense system, a system that reportedly can identify enemy aircraft formations, including Stealth aircraft, beyond radar range by tracking their heat emissions, thus potentially enhancing the ability of Iran's fighter aircraft to intercept U.S. and Israeli aircraft.[6]

Other analysts have taken Iran's conventional capabilities seriously enough to ask if Iran would use them irrationally and initiate an overt, attributable attack in the Gulf, knowing that it would suffer worse retaliation. Most U.S. and GCC officials think Iran will not. But history shows how Iran will use its assets. When Iran's oil infrastructure and shipping were attacked by Iraq in the 1980s, Iran retaliated against the shipping and the offshore oil and gas fields of the GCC states supporting Iraq. Iran also retaliated against U.S. naval vessels and U.S. helicopters protecting shipping. These were relatively rational and proportionate retaliations, and after losing their encounters with the U.S. military, they ended the war. Since then, Iran has not acted irrationally, and has initiated no overt, attributable action, even while it has been developing its new capabilities, and even despite its grievances over U.S. and GCC support for Iraq during the Iran-Iraq War, U.S. strikes against Iranian forces in the Gulf during that war, the growing U.S. military presence in the Gulf, U.S. economic sanctions against Iran, and U.S. military sales to and defense agreements with the GCC states. Covert, unattributable acts are another matter, however, and the 1996 Khobar Towers bombing may be an example of this.[7]

But if the United States attacks Iranian nuclear installations and air defenses, and particularly if the U.S. military relies upon logistical support from reluctant GCC states, it would not be irrational for Iran to retaliate with its conventional military assets. Iran could rationally deduce that this attack was about regime change and that U.S. targets could include many other government and conventional military sites. Iran could therefore be expected to engage U.S. bombers and fighters and naval vessels and strike GCC airfields and ports and offshore oil and gas fields and oil tankers and maybe even land marines and special forces on the GCC shore. People would die, including U.S. military personnel. Oil and gas tankers would be crippled in and out of the two shipping lanes while others would refuse to enter the Gulf. Oil and gas prices and insurance rates would skyrocket; oil and gas importers such as the United States could conceivably be sent into deep recession, while exporters such as Russia would profit. U.S. and GCC military forces could not likely put an end to all this before considerable damage had been done, even if Iran's conventional military assets were on the U.S. list of initial targets. Iran would anticipate this and be prepared to wreak havoc in the Gulf at the first sign of strikes. Iran would continue costly covert acts of sabotage around the world even after most of its military assets were destroyed, and in the GCC states, it would employ Iranian Shia elements living there for these purposes. Even limited covert operations by U.S. Special Forces inside Iran could elicit retaliation by Iranian covert forces in the Gulf.

Those who disagree should remember the serious misjudgments in the U.S. military operations in Iraq since 2003. Those who prefer that Israel carry out strikes against Iran should consider that Iran would likely retaliate not only against Israel, but against its principal defender's interests as well. Iran would likely think the United States had colluded, even if the United States publicly deplored the Israeli strikes, and in fact the Israeli air force would probably need U.S. permission to fly over Iraq. It would be harder for Iran to justify overt, attributable attacks against U.S. interests, but covert, unattributable retaliation in Iraq, the GCC states, the Gulf, and around the world would be deniable.

In conclusion, military strikes would "blow back" on the United States, the GCC, Israel, and the world economy in ways that would be more difficult to manage than many Bush administration officials think. Moreover, the civilian casualties and economic damage caused by war with Iran would increase anti-Americanism to a level that will severely undermine U.S. power and influence in Iran, throughout the region, and possibly throughout the Islamic world, thus undermining the very objectives that the Bush administration is pursuing. Indeed, even Iran's most noteworthy activists in the fields of human rights and democracy believe that U.S. military strikes against Iran will subvert their efforts and bolster the clerical regime.

Having considered the potential consequences of war, it should be noted that it is widely agreed that Iran does not have nuclear weapons. In fact, the NIE released in December 2007 concluded that Iran has halted a secret nuclear weapons program.[8] The Israeli assessment that Iran may have these weapons by 2009 may be a worst case scenario. Iran had difficulty continuously running the two 164-centrifuge cascades in its aboveground experimental research pilot plant at Natanz using centrifuges in the P-1 class. It has been behind schedule in its effort to construct additional centrifuge cascades in the P-1 class for its underground industrial fuel enrichment unit at Natanz, although it had numerous cascades by early 2008. It has fed only small amounts of uranium hexafluoride gas into the centrifuges and has produced only a small amount of enriched uranium 235 to a very low level of 3–5 percent purity, called LEU, and there are considerable technological hurdles to overcome before it can produce LEU at an industrial scale sufficient to power a reactor or to enrich (the gas from) the tons of uranium to the high level of about 90 percent, called HEU, necessary for weapons. Iran has developed a new generation of P-2 centrifuges, which it calls IR-2 centrifuges, but as of February 2008 it had installed only one small cascade at its pilot enrichment facility at Natanz and had tested only one with nuclear fuel. Iran is constructing a heavy water plant and heavy water research reactor at Arak, and these would eventually give Iran the ability to produce small amounts of plutonium, but these are also not close to completion. Finally, IAEA officials have said that most Western intelligence on suspected Iranian nuclear weapons programs has proven to be inaccurate or suspicious and that they have found no evidence of any nuclear material having been diverted to a weapons program.[9]

One argument made for making sure that Iran does not get nuclear weapons in the future is that Iran may be an irrational actor undeterred by normal cost/benefit calculations and might use such weapons in a first strike against the United States, Israel, or other U.S. friends. This is suggested by some who note that Iranian President Ahmadinejad has said the mission of Islamic Iran is to prepare the way, or even hasten the way, for the return of the religious figure known as the Hidden Imam or Mahdi, arguing that Ahmadinejad and some of his associates think this will be preceded by Armageddon. This leads these analysts to fear that Iran would use nuclear weapons in a first strike even knowing that Iran would subject itself to the assured destruction of a retaliatory second strike.[10] But Ahmadinejad has no constitutional power to make foreign policy or command the armed forces and he may be losing favor with the Iranian who does have this power, Ayatollah Khamenei. Moreover, Shia eschatology expects the Hidden Imam to restore the Shiites to their rightful place and redeem their suffering when he returns and until the Day of Judgment and the end of time, and it is hard to understand how Shiites could be restored and redeemed after Armageddon. Indeed, Ayatollah Khomeini thought that the Hidden Imam's return would be brought about by social justice, not war. And the Hojjatieh Society, an underground society to which some think Ahmadinejad belongs, and which others think is now defunct, evidently does not believe that Iran can *hasten* the return of the Hidden Imam, even though they want to prepare the way for it. Shia eschatology would therefore not likely lead Ahmadinejad or others to a first strike with nuclear weapons.[11] Others argue that the normal laws of deterrence would prevail and that Iran would make the rational calculation that it should not launch a first strike that would provoke a devastating second strike.[12] This logic could also deter Iran from providing weapons to any other actor if the United States issued an explicit warning. Moreover, Iran would likely fear that it would have no control over what another actor would do with any weapon provided by Iran. Still others have argued that the significance of Iranian nuclear weapons is that they would change the distribution of power in the region, deterring attacks against Iran, and therefore allowing Iran to be more assertive, forcing Israel and other U.S. friends and the United States itself to be more cautious.[13] This outcome could conceivably serve the interest of Russia and China in limiting or balancing U.S. global power, but it would also enhance Iran's posture vis-à-vis these two major powers. This kind of change in the distribution of power in the region may be a sufficient reason for all major and regional powers to seek to deny Iran nuclear weapons.

Inasmuch as there is some record of sanctions and diplomacy, let us consider the outcomes to this point and the prospects for the future of these strategies.

Unilateral U.S. sanctions imposed since the 1980s and especially since the Executive Orders in 1995 and the Iran-Libya Sanctions Act in 1996 and more recently the IFSA of 2006 and the new sanctions announced in 2007 against Iran's Revolutionary Guards apply to a wide range of military and nonmilitary commercial transactions and have slowed somewhat the development of Iran's oil and gas industry and Iran's nuclear industry. One aim of these sanctions has been to deny Iran the kind of capital and sophisticated technology that would enable Iran to develop, repair, maintain, and modernize its oil and natural gas infrastructure, and this has been partially successful. Non-American firms have made relatively modest investments in Iran, even though the punitive measures against these firms that are incorporated within the U.S. sanctions laws have generally not been carried out and in the case of Total an exemption was actually granted. But there have been some investments and they are important and will be only reluctantly given up.

U.S. efforts to persuade others to impose sanctions have only slowly produced results. In October 2006, Japan's INPEX Holding Company reduced its participation from 75 percent to 10 percent in a $2 billion project for the development of Iran's largest onshore oil field at Azedegan, and Iran has reportedly not found alternate financing. Credit Suisse First Boston and UBS, both Swiss banks, indicated in 2006 that they would do no more new business with Iran, and other European banks have been agreeing to cease business with Bank Sepah and Bank Saderat, the first accused by the United States of involvement in Iran's nuclear and ballistic missile programs and the second accused by the United States of financing terror by Hezbollah and others. Indeed, UNSC Resolution 1747 now prohibits dealings with Bank Sepah, and UNSC Resolution 1803 urges caution in dealing with Bank Melli. The Japan Bank for International Cooperation also announced it would issue no new loans for projects in Iran. In this case, as in

Japan's decision regarding the oil field, Japan, a major importer of Persian Gulf oil, cited concerns over Iran's nuclear programs. But China and Russia are stepping into this vacuum. China's major state-owned oil and gas companies, for example, are making and planning investments in Iran's Yadavaran onshore oil field and in Iran's North Pars and South Pars offshore gas fields.

UN Security Council resolutions in 2006, 2007, and 2008 have focused on blocking Iran's acquisition of materials or equipment or financing necessary for uranium enrichment and reprocessing, and for ballistic missiles. In other respects, however, UNSC Resolution 1747 calls only for "vigilance and restraint" in sales of conventional weapons to Iran, sales that are very important to Russia and China, and Resolutions 1747 and 1803 call for but do not require a halt to export credits, grants, and loans to Iran, thus giving European and other states the option of continuing these programs.

In May 2007, the American Enterprise Institute released a study identifying major business relations between Iran and foreign governments, corporations, and banks in an effort to generate citizen and shareholder pressure against these relations.[14] Moreover, new legislation to identify foreign companies and overseas subsidiaries of U.S. companies investing more than $20 million in Iran's oil and gas industry, to require the application of U.S. sanctions against them, and to encourage divestment was being sponsored by Tom Lantos, a California Democrat and the Chairman of the House International Relations Committee, and by Democratic presidential candidate Senator Barak Obama. It was being supported by AIPAC and was being called the Iran Sanctions Enabling Act.[15] In addition, the U.S. Congress is developing legislation that would impose sanctions on any company that sells refined gas to Iran. At the same time, Venezuela has agreed to sell refined gas to Iran and this could be important if other suppliers, such as India, the Netherlands, France, and the UAE, were deterred by sanctions.[16]

In evaluating the impact of sanctions, however, it is also important to note that Iran places restrictions on foreign investment, offers unattractive terms to foreign companies, tries to rely on its own indigenous technology and expertise, which fall below Western standards, and makes its own political decisions about its oil and gas industry, and that these policies add to Iran's problems.

For all these reasons, Iran's oil production and exports are stalled at 3.7 million barrels per day and 2.6 million barrels per day, respectively, and may slowly contract without substantial new foreign investment and technology. Iran's refineries are insufficient for domestic demand, in part because Iran has chosen not to expand its refinery capacity, and Iran must therefore also import refined products and subsidize them to meet growing domestic demand, particularly demand for gasoline for automobiles. Iran must also inject much of its natural gas into its aging oil fields in order to keep them pumping and must utilize much of its natural gas in its home heating infrastructure, so its ability to export natural gas is limited. The high price of oil and gas means that Iran's export revenues are substantial, but the price per barrel of oil has fluctuated from $77 to the low $50s in 2006 and then climbed back to the low $90s in October 2007 and topped $100 in early 2008. Despite these revenues, Iran's economy has been under stress, with 15 percent of its GDP spent on imported and subsidized refined products, and with high inflation and unemployment and underemployment, with capital flight as well as declining foreign investment. In mid-2007, Iran raised the price of the imported and subsidized refined products for its domestic consumers by 25 percent and then rationed these products, which led to mobs burning gas stations, banks, and government buildings in Tehran and other cities. Iran's government did note that its reliance on these imports made it vulnerable to sanctions and it did have a plan to spend $12 billion to expand its existing refineries and build new ones in order to boost its refined product from 1.6 billion barrels per day to 3.1.[17] Even with the current impact of sanctions and the domestic Iranian anger about Iran's economy, a recent NIE concluded that these factors did not endanger the Iranian regime's hold on power.[18]

It can be argued that economic sanctions are slowly producing pressures that may lead Iran to agree to some compromises. If so, intelligent diplomacy may be in order. It can also be argued that as the United States dissuades American, European, and Japanese firms from investing in Iran's oil and gas sector, Chinese and Russian state-owned companies will move into the vacuum. This might ease some of the pressures that would lead Iran to compromise. Iran's own domestic investments may also ease the pressures to compromise. Diplomacy at an early date might therefore be more successful than diplomacy at a later date, when Iran may have less need for Western oil and gas partners and when Iran's nuclear programs are more advanced. Moreover, it can also be argued that Iran's need to export its production for revenue and to import for its domestic consumption has actually created a need for the development of an alternative source of energy, namely nuclear power, for Iran's domestic electricity needs and that sanctioning Iran's oil and gas industry has increased Iran's quest for nuclear energy. Thus, any diplomatic compromise would have to accommodate Iran's need for civilian nuclear energy, but could also reduce Iran's need for it if sanctions on Iran's oil and gas industry could be dropped.

The diplomatic prospects are not as poor as they may appear. The United States and Iran would simply have to consider the trade-offs and calculate if they can gain more than they can lose. If Iran were to abide by the Additional Protocol to the NPT and extend its provisions to allow intrusive inspections of military facilities, this would improve the chances of discovering any possible future covert nuclear weapons program. This would be more advantageous to the United States than the current situation, in which Iran limits IAEA inspections, or to the possible future, in which Iran may eject the IAEA and withdraw from the NPT in response to UNSC sanctions. Ejecting the IAEA completely might allow Iran to attempt to enrich uranium to the 90 percent purity necessary for a nuclear weapon, whereas this would be extremely difficult for Iran if the IAEA inspectors remained in Iran doing their work. The United States has argued that international inspections could not definitely discover a possible secret Iranian nuclear weapons facility, but if that is the case, then even Iranian acceptance of a long-term suspension of enrichment at known facilities would not stop Iran from enriching uranium at facilities that may not be known. This subverts the logic of the demand that Iran suspend enrichment as a precondition for negotiations or as an outcome of negotiations. Moreover, it is too late to stop Iran from acquiring human understanding of the nuclear fuel cycle. They have it.

In order to get satisfactory agreements from Iran, it may be worthwhile to offer Iran the kinds of security guarantees it has been seeking and the Bush administration has been unwilling to offer since 2003. But this would probably require the kind of "grand bargain" Iran suggested in 2003 and that the United States has been unwilling to consider. Iran must consider it highly unlikely that its cooperation on nuclear issues alone, or on Iraq alone, or even on both issues, would be sufficient to satisfy the United States, but if the United States is unwilling to discuss and reach agreements on all outstanding disputes, including the Persian Gulf and Arab-Israeli issues, then Iran cannot likely satisfy the United States on these issues. Talks on any issue may be more productive from everyone's point of view if there is movement on other issues.

Both developments, if accepted by Iran, may ease U.S. concerns about Iran and some of the U.S.-Iranian tensions that are played out in the Gulf. And there is little chance of persuading Iran to moderate its behavior in the Gulf if the United States and Iran do not reach compromises on the above issues and Iran continues to feel threatened.

On the question of Iraq, Iran knows that the fragmentation of this country could destabilize the larger region. Iran knows the civil war in Iraq could spill over into Iran, including its oil-rich and Arab-populated Khuzistan province, particularly if Iraqi Sunni Arabs were supported by Sunni Arab states. Iran also knows that U.S. military forces in Iraq and the larger array of U.S. military forces in the Gulf region, which are growing, could be used against Iran over a U.S. perception or misperception that Iran is fomenting unrest in Iraq.

If Iran could influence the competing Iraqi Shia factions to unite or compromise, to share more power with Iraqi Sunnis in a federal structure, and to find a way to distribute national oil revenues equitably to all groups, including the Kurds and the Sunnis, this could help stabilize Iraq. It could bolster the Iraqi Shiites who have ties both with Iran and with the United States. It could potentially reduce the anxieties of neighboring Sunni Arab states that deplore the marginalization of Iraqi Sunnis and who may have been tacitly acquiescing in the flow of private funds and individual fighters to the Sunni insurgency and who are now funding Sunni groups fighting AQI but who may later turn on the Iraqi Shia-led government. It could alleviate Turkey's anxiety that Iraqi Kurds may press for independence and inspire Turkey's Kurds to do the same. But how could Iran do any of this?

The Bush administration or the administration that follows in 2009 should not ask Iran to do more to promote compromise and subdue militias in Iraq than Iran can actually do. Iraq's civil war is primarily the result of a poorly planned U.S. invasion and occupation and the sectarian and ethnic interests it has unleashed, not Iranian behavior. Iran's influence with Iraqi Shiites may be exaggerated by the United States. Iraqi Shiites, who are Arabs, have their own grievances and ambitions; they are friendly to Iran but not pawns of Iran. As long as Iraqi Sunni Arabs are attacking Iraqi Shia Arabs, Shia militias will likely retaliate against Sunni communities, even if Iran urges restraint on its core-ligionists. Iran seeks an Iraq with relatively strong provinces and a relatively weak central government, because this ensures the power of friendly Shia elements, may satisfy Kurdish aspirations, and contains Sunnis, but Iran does not favor real disenfranchisement of Sunnis and a possible fragmentation of Iraq into three states. If al-Hakim's Shia SIIC continues to press for a highly autonomous Shia super-province in the south that controls Iraq's richest oil resources, despite Sunni efforts to oppose this through constitutional amendments, and despite objections by other Shia forces such as Moqtada al-Sadr and the Fadhila party, Iran may not be able to mediate successfully, despite its close ties to SIIC, even if this threatens to lead to the breakup of the country. If al-Maliki and his Shia Islamic al-Dawa Party and his SIIC partners resist U.S. calls for his government to include more Sunnis and Kurds, Iran may not be able to change Maliki's mind.

To the extent Iran supports Shia militias, this is in part because Shiites have been attacked by Sunnis, in part to prevent the reestablishment of a Sunni government that could threaten Iran as previous Sunni governments have done, in part an effort to demonstrate a deterrent to the U.S. military and intelligence forces, which may be involved in special operations inside Iran and which could be used to attack Iran, and generally to discourage military actions against Iran and to motivate the United States to withdraw from Iraq, but not in a precipitous way that would be followed by even worse civil war that could spill over into Iran. It may also be in part because of the U.S. and Iraqi effort to confront and disarm rogue Shia militias, an effort that even the al-Maliki government itself has been inconsistent in carrying out.

Even if al-Sadr were involved in IED/EFP and RPG attacks against U.S. forces, he is an Arab nationalist who is suspicious of Iran. He would accept support from Iran on a primarily tactical basis and Iran would offer it on a tactical basis, worrying that al-Sadr might use these weapons against SIIC and its Badr Brigade as well as al-Dawa, both of which Iran favors over al-Sadr's Mahdi Army and both of which are prominent in Iraq's government and security forces.

Renegade Shia militias that are not answerable to al-Sadr might be more likely to be involved in these attacks against U.S. and Shia-dominated Iraqi security forces. Members of Iraq's Shia-dominated security forces, who are more likely from SIIC's Badr Brigade than from al-Sadr's Mahdi Army, have also been implicated in IED/EFP attacks on U.S. forces. But Shia militias need not rely exclusively on Iranian support any more than Sunni insurgents rely exclusively on neighboring Sunni states. They can provide much of their own funding and arms by oil smuggling, organized crime, bank robberies, the black market, and their own machine shops. Iran cannot stop this and could not actually disarm Shia militias without fighting them.

While the Bush administration should certainly insist that Iran do all it can to stem the flow of weapons and components involved in Shia militia attacks against U.S. forces, the administration should also try to understand the extent to which Iran can realistically influence developments in Iraq. The administration should also try to understand the potential consequences of U.S. conflict with Shia militias and Iranian agents. U.S. operations against Shia militias and Iranian agents could lead even moderate Shia government officials to think that the United States is leaving the Shia community more vulnerable to Sunni attacks. And even if the United States does not confront Shia militias, there are other ways for such conflict to occur. For example, Iraqi Shiites, even those like Maliki who were brought to power by the United States, were incensed by U.S. support for Israel's military campaign in Lebanon in 2006. U.S. intelligence argues that some Shia militia fighters have been trained in Iraq and in Lebanon and in Iran by Hezbollah fighters, and that this has been facilitated by Iran and Syria. U.S. acquiescence in an escalation of Israel's use of force in the Gaza Strip and the West Bank and/or a resumption of Israeli force against Hezbollah in Lebanon or U.S.-Israeli-Saudi covert operations against Hezbollah could motivate elements of Iraqi Shia militias trained by and/or sympathetic to Hezbollah to attack U.S. and British troops in Iraq. U.S. support for Fatah against Hamas may have the same result. Perhaps more importantly, Moqtada al-Sadr has intimated that his forces would fight U.S. forces if there is U.S. military action against Iran. U.S. actions against Sadrists could be seen as an effort to weaken them prior to U.S. action against Iran. This could encourage even more Iranian involvement in Iraq. The U.S. military in Iraq relies upon fuel shipments from the Shiite-inhabited south of Iraq, and if these were cut, U.S. forces would be even more vulnerable than they are now.

In the Persian Gulf, Iran is concerned about U.S. military forces in the Gulf and U.S. security partnerships with GCC states armed by the United States and offering bases and facilities to the United States. Iran sees them as part of an effort to deny Iran its rightful role in the Gulf and because Iran knows they could be used to attack Iran. This increased U.S. military presence in the Gulf region was in part a response to Iraq's invasion of Kuwait in 1990 but was also a response to Iran's program to modernize its military after the Iran-Iraq War ended in 1988 and its military exercises in the area. In turn, this U.S. presence fuels Iran's continuing military modernization and exercises and perhaps even a covert nuclear weapons program that Iran could see as a necessary deterrent. But if agreements over nuclear issues, and Iraq, and Israel were attainable and enabled the United States to offer the possibility of security guarantees to Iran, it could lead to Iranian restraint in the Gulf. Iran has sought the withdrawal of U.S. forces from the Gulf and the abrogation of U.S. security pacts with the GCC states, and they should not and will not obtain this, but at least U.S. security guarantees and Iranian restraint would permit some reduction of U.S. forces in the Gulf and some redeployment "over the horizon."

This would be good for the GCC states. They have been concerned about Iran's military acquisitions and exercises in the Gulf, its insistence on occupying the strategic islands of Abu Musa and the Tunbs, its past efforts to subvert GCC regimes, and rumors that Iran has increased its contacts with Shia opposition forces inside the GCC states, and they are concerned that Iran's acquisition of nuclear weapons would make it more assertive in the Gulf. But their relations with Iran are complex, involving considerable trade and the possibility of cooperation in many areas, and there has been a thaw in recent years. As they said at their summit in Riyadh in May 2006, and as they say in private, they want their problems with Iran resolved through diplomacy rather than force because they fear they would be targets of Iranian retaliation.

U.S. talks with Iran could possibly help resolve the nexus of terror and Arab-Israeli conflicts. In the "grand bargain" Iran proposed in 2003, Iran intimated it might accept the Saudi-proposed Arab League offer in 2002 to establish normal relations with Israel within its 1967 borders in exchange for a Palestinian state with East Jerusalem as its capital and a "fair and agreed" resolution of the Palestinian refugee problem, and that it would not support rejectionism by Hezbollah, Islamic Jihad, and Hamas. Khamenei said in 2006 that Iran supports the Arab position. If the Bush administration were to agree to talk about this with Iran in the context of a "grand bargain," perhaps in a wide-ranging regional security forum, and if the administration were to learn that Iran's intimations were genuine, this would be a very advantageous breakthrough for Israel. Yet there is not much evidence that the administration is really prepared to mediate this kind of two-state resolution of the Palestinian-Israeli conflict after seven years of not doing so, and not much evidence that Israel will consider this. It is not likely that this kind of agreement will emerge from the meetings held in Annapolis, Maryland in November 2007. This is the Achilles heel in U.S. foreign policy.

Nevertheless, a "grand bargain" may be attainable and would support most U.S. objectives. More generally, the anti-Americanism rampant in the Sunni and the Shiite street throughout the Arab world is the result of specific U.S. policies such as invasion and occupation of Muslim lands and lack of evenhandedness in Arab-Israeli affairs. A "grand bargain" is the best way for the United States to reverse the growing trend of anti-Americanism.

Does Iran really want a "grand bargain"? Would an Iran that gives up the future option of nuclear weapons be at a disadvantage vis-à-vis neighbors that have nuclear weapons to the north, east, south, and west? Would an Iran that enjoys popularity in a Shia crescent but also in the Sunni populations of the region lose some of this popularity if it abandoned its opposition to Israel? Would a stable federal Iraq limit Iran's influence? Would any remaining U.S. forces in the Gulf cramp Iran's ambitions? Would the lifting of sanctions and an increase in foreign trade and investment also increase foreign influence and challenge regime control? The answer to these questions is yes, but the survival of the regime is more important.

Indeed, it may be that the disadvantages of a "grand bargain" would be felt most by some leaders of the Revolutionary Guards, who have considerable financial interests in Iran's foreign trade, industry, nuclear and missile programs, influence in the Levant, influence in the Persian Gulf, and influence throughout Iran's government, and who might lose much of this if Iran became a status quo power and was admitted to and bound by the rules of the WTO.

But none of these costs are absolute for the larger Iranian regime. Iran's need for a nuclear deterrent may be obviated by agreements that end U.S. and Israeli threats. No Iranian regime can use nuclear weapons in a first strike without dooming itself and the country to a devastating second strike. Iranian nuclear weapons could lead several GCC neighbors to acquire their own, thus neutralizing Iranian power. Iran does not have to possess these weapons or to create or exploit turmoil or support a Hezbollah coup in Lebanon or subvert Israel to be a regional power. Iran will have a measure of influence with Shiites in Lebanon and Iraq after the settlements of those conflicts. It cannot dominate these confessionally mixed Arab countries. Iran could retain some popularity by claiming some credit for the emergence of an independent Palestine from a two-state solution to that conflict. Iran will be a power in the Gulf even with some remaining U.S. forces present. The GCC states recognize Iran's need for a military presence sufficient for Iran's self-defense. And Iran's economy will grow if economic sanctions are lifted and normal economic relations are established, easing the burden that high unemployment, inflation, interest rates, and subsidies place on the regime. There will be a struggle within the Iranian regime over these considerations and trade-offs, and some in the Revolutionary Guards could be expected to resist, but Khamenei is likely to accept the benefits, and to be supported by allies like the pragmatic former president Rafsanjani, and to win the struggle as long as negotiations take place soon. The absence of a deal could strengthen radical conservatives like Ahmadinejad, whose obnoxious pronouncements about Israel and the Holocaust are given more weight than they deserve when he is only one of the many actors who have a say in these matters. But to the extent that he is challenging the authority of the traditional conservative clerics in what some close observers think is a domestic power struggle, and to the extent that he is seeking to build support from the Revolutionary Guards, which is essentially loyal to Khamenei rather than to him, then further marginalizing him and his supporters like Ayatollah Mezbah-Yazdi would be good.

Iranian concerns about military action and economic sanctions have led Iran's Supreme Religious Leader Khamenei to want talks with the United States. The more vocal and less important President Ahmadinejad may or may not be a challenge to Khamenei, but even he claims to want talks and cannot decide what Iran's positions in talks will be.

The United States should talk to Iran about the entire range of differences before Iran concludes that talks would be useless. The United States should find out if these talks can produce agreements. If agreements are possible, Iran will expect assurances that it will not be attacked and the United States and its friends can avoid the consequences of war, but the Bush administration would have to give these assurances and give up the neoconservative dreams of quick regime change and work instead for gradual political evolution in Iran. If the Bush administration does not take this path, and it does not seem likely that it will, then the next administration should negotiate in this spirit. This may be the best way to boost the eventual prospects of pragmatists and reformists in Iran, a country whose young population wants normal ties with the United States and more freedom at home. Indeed, these forces already asserted their importance in the municipal council elections and elections for the Assembly of Experts in December 2006, handing the hard-line followers of Ahmadinejad a stinging defeat. Moreover, 150 of the 290 members of the parliament, including most of Ahmadinejad's hard-line supporters, important business groups, and important newspapers have criticized his nuclear and economic policies. It appears that Khamenei and Larijani have, through newspapers they own, conveyed dissatisfaction with Ahmadinejad's defiant rhetoric about and involvement in the nuclear issue, signaling that he may be losing their support as they confront the consequences of the UNSC resolutions and other U.S. threats. Rafsanjani's recent election as chairman of the Assembly of Experts also weakens Ahmadinejad. Jalili's appointment to replace Larijani does seem to signal that Iran will not make significant concessions on uranium enrichment, but this does not signal a commitment to nuclear weapons or subvert the possibility of a reasonable "grand bargain." And even though conservatives dominate the new Majlis after the elections in March 2008, in large part because so many reformist candidates were disqualified, many of these conservatives are dissatisfied with Ahmadinejad and his positions on foreign policy. Indeed, a "grand bargain" may be possible and would be the best way for the United States to reverse the growing trend of anti-Americanism in both the Shiite and the Sunni street in the Middle East and the Islamic world.

NOTES

1. Carter and Perry explore this in *Plan B for Iran: What If Nuclear Diplomacy Fails?*

2. The U.S. Air Force has concluded that it could take out 85 percent of Iran's nuclear facilities. Gardiner says 400 "aim points" or targets would have to be hit repeatedly over five nights in order to disable the two dozen nuclear facilities. If the bombing took place during the day, in an effort to kill Iranian nuclear scientists at work, civilian casualties would likely be even higher.

3. Congressional Research Agency analyst Kenneth Katzman, MIT Professor Barry Posen, and Washington Institute for Near East Policy analyst Dennis Ross have made this argument.

4. Mattair, *Three Occupied UAE Islands.*

5. *New York Times,* February 9, 2007.

6. Iran seeks and will probably acquire more modern weapons, including Russian fighter aircraft and SAMs and Chinese antiship missiles, in the coming years.

7. Mattair, *Three Occupied UAE Islands.*

8. *New York Times,* December 4, 2007.

9. *New York Times,* February 22, 2007; Borger, "US Iran Intelligence 'Is Incorrect'"; Drogin and Murphy, "UN Calls US Data Unreliable."

10. Dennis Ross, "A New Strategy on Iran," *Washington Post,* May 1, 2006.

11. See Noah Feldman, "Islam, Terror and the Second Nuclear Age," *New York Times Magazine,* October 29, 2006. Feldman argues that the Hojjatieh Society does *not* believe that humans can hasten the return of the Hidden Imam, whereas Ahmadinejad's possible membership is usually and mistakenly taken to mean that he would try to hasten the Hidden Imam's return by provoking Armageddon. Many dispute that Ahmadinejad belongs to this society. Nasr suggests that he does, but then writes that he wants to hasten the Mahdi's return, although Nasr seems to be relying on a *Newsweek International* article and one can question the accuracy of the translation in an English-language publication. See Nasr, *Shia Revival,* 133–34.

12. Barry R. Posen, "We Can Live with a Nuclear Iran," *New York Times,* February 27, 2006. Chirac also suggested that Iran would understand this logic or that major powers would have the capability to destroy any Iranian weapon launched against a target soon after it was launched. See *New York Times,* February 1, 2007.

13. Parsi, *Treacherous Alliance.*

14. See www.aei.org/IranInteractive1.

15. See Jim Lobe blog at www.ips.org/blog/jimlobe/.

16. *New York Times,* July 4, 2007.

17. *New York Times,* June 29, 2007. The former Petroleum Minister, Bijan Zangeneh, did not want to expand Iran's refinery capacity, in part because he feared it would encourage the continued high domestic demand that forced the government to continue low prices and price subsidies. The Ahmadinejad government has decided to increase refinery capacity as a way of meeting the high demand, but has coupled this by raising prices and imposing rationing.

18. Pauline Jelilnek and Katherine Shrader, "Draft Report Logs Bleak Outlook for Iran," *Associated Press,* August 23, 2007. This NIE remained classified.

Biographies

MOHAMMAD REZA PAHLAVI

Shah Mohammad Reza Pahlavi (born October 26, 1919; died July 27, 1980) was the ruler of Iran from 1941 until 1979, when he was overthrown in a popular revolution.

He was born in Tehran. His father, an officer in the Persian Cossack brigade, deposed the Qajar dynasty in 1923 and established the Pahlavi dynasty in 1925, ruling as Shah Reza Pahlavi.

Mohammad Reza, who had an identical twin sister named Ashraf, became crown prince as a child. He was educated at a private boarding school in Switzerland and returned to Iran in 1936 to enter the Tehran Military Academy. He was married three times and was the father of five children.

Mohammad Reza succeeded his father in September 1941, after British and Soviet forces occupied Iran and forced his pro-German father to abdicate the throne. Shah Mohammad Reza Pahlavi would be the second and last shah in the Pahlavi dynasty. Throughout this period of foreign occupation and intrigue over the future of the country, the Shah reigned as monarch but did not rule.

The Shah's concerns about Soviet designs in Iran were based on their efforts to support the pro-Soviet Tudeh Party during the war, by the Soviet refusal to withdraw from Iran after World War II, and by Soviet support for autonomous Tudeh rule in Iranian Azerbaijan as well as support for an independent Kurdish republic that broke away from Iran. His friendly attitude toward the United States was based in part on the U.S. pressure that led the Soviets to withdraw in May 1946, which in turn enabled Iran to reassert control over Azerbaijan and Kurdistan, and on the economic and political assistance the United States provided over the next two decades. In 1949, he survived an assassination attempt by an alleged member of the Tudeh Party, which he then outlawed.

The Shah's political power was still limited in the early 1950s, when Iran's parliament nationalized the AIOC and Britain orchestrated an international boycott of Iranian oil. When the Shah attempted to remove Prime Minister Muhammad Mossadeq from office and he refused, the Shah briefly fled the country but was quickly restored to the throne after loyal military officers, the CIA, and British military intelligence, or MI6, removed Mossadeq from office.

Mohammad Reza Shah now set out to be a ruling monarch and became an autocrat. He outlawed Mossadeq's National Front party. He established a loyal military and security apparatus, including a domestic intelligence and security force known as SAVAK, which ruthlessly repressed political opposition. In 1961, he dissolved the parliament and reestablished it in 1963 as a powerless institution. He also exiled Ayatollah Khomeini, a vociferous critic of his rule, and his military suppressed antigovernment demonstrations with force in 1963. He introduced a series of domestic reforms known as the "White Revolution," which included measures such as redistributing land to peasants and promoting women's rights and literacy and widening access to public services, and these were also intended in part to weaken opponents in the landed aristocracy and in the clergy. He also embarked on a drive to industrialize Iran, modernize its armed forces, and make it a leading regional and world power. He took special care to make sure that his forces would be dominant in the Persian Gulf after the British withdrew their forces at the end of 1971. He also negotiated new contracts with Western oil firms, giving Iran ownership of its oil industry and increasing its revenues.

The Shah attempted to establish the strength and continuity of the institution of the monarchy. In a coronation ceremony in 1967, he took the title of His Imperial Majesty Mohammad Reza Pahlavi Aryamehr (Light of the Aryans), Shahanshah (King of Kings) of Iran, while his third wife Farah was crowned as empress, and their young son Reza became crown prince. In 1971, celebrations were held in Persepolis to commemorate the 2500th anniversary of the Achaemenid Empire. This was meant to stress and celebrate the pre-Islamic roots of Iran. In 1975, the 50th anniversary of the Pahlavi dynasty was celebrated.

In 1973, the Shah led a successful drive to quadruple the price of a barrel of oil and thus dramatically increased Iran's oil revenues. He used those revenues to finance arms purchases, industrialization, and imports of consumer goods. Political opposition was growing during the 1970s, however, based in part on the unequal distribution of wealth and indeed the corruption associated with the country's rapid economic development, the repressive character of the regime, and the Shah's close relations with the United States and his relations with Israel. In 1978, this opposition, which was fanned by the exiled Ayatollah Khomeini, burst into mass demonstrations and strikes and became a revolution.

The Shah tried liberalization and he also tried brute force, and neither could subdue the revolution. In January 1979, the Shah and his family went into exile again. When he was admitted to the United States for treatment for lymphatic cancer later in 1979, Iranian students seized the U.S. Embassy in Tehran and its personnel and demanded the return of the Shah and his assets. The United States refused and the U.S. personnel were held hostage in Iran for 444 days. Even before they were released, Mohammad Reza Pahlavi died of lymphatic cancer on July 27, 1980, in Cairo, where he is buried at the Al Rifai Mosque.

The Shah authored three books. *Mission for My Country* was published in 1961. *The White Revolution of Iran* was published in 1967. *Answer to History* was published in 1980.

RUHOLLAH KHOMEINI

Grand Ayatollah Seyyed Ruhollah Musavi Khomeini (born *circa* 1900–1902; died June 3, 1989) was a Shia Muslim cleric and leader of the Islamic revolution which overthrew Shah Mohammad Reza Pahlavi in January 1979. After consolidating his power, Khomeini became the Supreme Leader of the Islamic Republic of Iran on December 3, 1979 and held this position until his death.

Khomeini's father was also a cleric and was from a family that claimed to be descendents of the Prophet Mohammad, which is why Khomeini was called a seyyed and wore a black turban. His mother's father was also a cleric and had supported the 1891–92 boycott of tobacco after Shah Nasser ed-Din of the Qajar dynasty had granted a tobacco concession to a British company in 1889, a concession the Shah was then forced to cancel.

In 1921, Khomeini began his religious studies under Ayatollah Sheikh Abdol-Karim Haeri-Yazdi, spending most of these years in Qom, an Iranian city that was beginning to rival Najaf in Iraq as a center of Shia learning. After becoming a mojtahed, or doctor of Islam, he taught Islamic jurisprudence (fiqh), philosophy, and mysticism and wrote books on these subjects. He married the daughter of an ayatollah in 1929 and was the father of five children, including two sons who became clerics themselves.

Iran's clerical class, or ulama, had been challenged by Shah Reza Pahlavi and his secular and anticlerical policies after his rise to power in the 1920s. Khomeini criticized these secular policies in his book, *Kashf-e Assrar* (*Discovery of Secrets*), in 1942, although this book did express acceptance of limited rule by a monarch under the 1906–7 constitution if the monarch ruled according to sharia, or Islamic law. For Khomeini, sharia applied not only to religious affairs but also to all social, economic, and political affairs.

In the 1950s, Khomeini became recognized as an ayatollah, which means "sign of God," a cleric who attracts a wide following and raises large donations because of the popularity of his publications and lectures. He became a grand ayatollah, or leading marja' al-taqlid, or source of imitation or emulation, i.e., one who is most highly qualified to guide the community in understanding the sharia, in 1963, following the death in 1962 of Grand Ayatollah Seyyed Husayn Borujerdi, who had been the sole marja in the Shia world and had been a proponent of quietism, i.e., the belief that the clergy should not play a major role in politics.

Khomeini and many of Iran's clerics now saw the secular and authoritarian rule of Shah Mohammad Reza Pahlavi and his relations with the United States and Israel as a threat. In 1963, after the Shah had announced the "White Revolution," Khomeini's criticisms of the Shah intensified. Khomeini made speeches and issued statements that accused the Shah of numerous violations of the sharia and the constitution, accused the Shah of being an agent of U.S. imperialism and Israeli Zionism, and blamed him for opening Iran to corrupting Western cultural influences. He was a vehement opponent of capitulations, namely, granting legal immunity to U.S. military personnel. He skillfully called upon Shia history to mobilize opposition to the Shah. In June 1963, on the festival of Ashoura commemorating the killing of the revered Imam Husain at Karbala at the hands of the Ummayad Caliph Yazid, Khomeini delivered a speech comparing the Shah to Yazid. Khomeini was then arrested, provoking a week of antigovernment riots and clashes with the police and army throughout Iran in which hundreds died. Khomeini was subsequently deported.

Khomeini spent most of his exile in Najaf, the center of Shia learning in southern Iraq, until then-Vice President Saddam Hussein exiled him in 1978. He then went to Neauphle-le-Château, a suburb of Paris, France.

During these years in exile, he continued to denounce the Shah's policies, for example, in a lengthy letter to Prime Minister Hoveyda in 1967, in letters to religious scholars and students in Qom, and in messages to Muslims making the annual pilgrimage, or hajj, to Mecca. While in exile, he rejected the institution of monarchy and rejected Iran's 1906 constitution. In his book, *Islamic Government (Hokumat-e Islami)*, which is a collection of lectures he gave in 1971 in Najaf, he argued that the Shah's government was an un-Islamic, illegitimate government and that legitimate authority should rest with a supreme religious leader (Faqih), who should rely on his superior knowledge of the sharia in governing the religious and political affairs of the Muslim community (Umma) in order to root out injustice, oppression, corruption, un-Islamic practices, and threats to Islam. This is the theory of velayat-e faqih, the "guardianship of the jurist."

By 1978, Khomeini was the most important spiritual leader of the growing opposition to the Shah. He forged tactical alliances with Islamist reformers and secular opponents of the Shah, including some influenced by Marxism, in order to bolster his impact. Cassette recordings of his lectures denouncing the Shah were widely circulated in the bazaars, or traditional markets, of Iran as opposition turned into revolution. His growing stature was marked by the stream of visitors to his residence near Paris during the latter months of 1978, with not only Iranian opponents of the Shah but international scholars and journalists making the journey to talk with him. He was even referred to as "Imam," and he did not discourage this.

When Khomeini returned to Iran on February 1, 1979, after the Shah had fled, millions of Iranians celebrated in the streets. Khomeini challenged the provisional government established by the Shah and headed by Shahpour Bakhtiar, huge crowds demanded Bakhtiar's resignation, the Shah's Imperial Army was attacked and overcome, government buildings were seized, the armed forces declared neutrality, followed by defections and the losses of armories, and the Bakhtiar government fell.

Khomeini appointed a government led by his secular, democratic, liberal, and liberal Islamist allies such as the new prime minister, Mehdi Bazargan, and members of the National Front. They began to draft a constitution for the Islamic Republic that stressed popular representation and individual rights and did not include the position of supreme religious leader. Moreover, although they were committed to a nonaligned foreign policy, they did favor normal diplomatic relations with the United States. But Khomeini and some of his clerical allies, including Ali Akbar Hashemi Rafsanjani, Ali Khamenei, and Muhammad Beheshti, formed the Council of the Revolution, and along with local revolutionary committees they challenged this official government. In the following months, hundreds of former officials of the Shah's government and military faced summary trials, many were executed by firing squads, and many fled the country. In the midst of this, on March 31, 1979, a referendum to replace the monarchy with an Islamic Republic passed with 98 percent voting yes.

Khomeini took full advantage of the Iran hostage crisis to consolidate his domestic power. On November 4, soon after the Shah had been admitted into the United States for cancer treatment, students loyal to Khomeini seized the U.S. Embassy in Tehran, taking the American staff hostage. Bazargan and other moderates in the government opposed this, but Khomeini endorsed it, understanding that framing this as a struggle between Islam and the "Great Satan" would help him mobilize the popular support necessary to consolidate his power, sweep away his secular allies, and establish a theocracy. Bazargan resigned, Khomeini's candidates won control of the new Assembly of Experts, which revised the proposed constitution to include a Supreme Leader, to enshrine the sharia, and to establish a Council of Guardians that would screen candidates for elective office and veto un-Islamic legislation. The new constitution was passed by a popular referendum in December 1979 and Khomeini became the Supreme Leader. On February 4, 1980, Abolhassan Bani-Sadr was elected as Iran's first president. The Majlis, or parliament, which was now dominated by Khomeini loyalists, began its work. During the hostage crisis, Khomeini demanded that the United States extradite the Shah to Iran for trial and return the Shah's wealth to Iran. Although the Shah died in July, Khomeini did not consent to the release of the hostages until immediately after the inauguration of Ronald Reagan as U.S. President, on January 20, 1981, after 444 days of captivity.

Khomeini also sought to export Iran's Islamic revolution throughout the Muslim world, Sunni as well as Shia, and to topple regimes he saw as tyrannical agents of Western imperialism, Israeli Zionism, and Soviet communism. This applied to Iraq, and he called upon Iraq's Shia Arabs to rise up against Saddam Hussein, Iraq's Sunni Arab nationalist Baathist leader. Alarmed about this, and calculating that Iran was too weak and chaotic to resist, and perhaps hoping to assert Iraq's border claims and also occupy Iran's adjacent oil-rich province of Khuzestan, in September 1980 Saddam ordered his forces to invade Iran, starting the Iran-Iraq War, which only ended eight years later, in August 1988.

Khomeini again understood that a crisis provided him with an opportunity to consolidate his leadership. Early in the war, he portrayed Banisadr as an agent of the West and intimidated him into fleeing the country. He cracked down on clerics who opposed rule by a Supreme Leader, even defrocking Ayatollah Ali Shariatmadari and many others and imprisoned many. He also cracked down on secular domestic opponents in a reign of terror that resulted in many executions. In 1982, when Iran recovered most of the territory Iraq had captured, Khomeini rejected Saddam Hussein's offer of a truce and reparations, insisting that he would not agree to peace until Saddam's regime was replaced by an Islamic Republic. The war thus continued for another six years, with major tank battles, missile attacks against Iranian and Iraqi cities, attacks against Iranian and Arab shipping in the Gulf, and perhaps a million casualties, including young Iranian boys sent as "human waves" to detonate land mines and swarm Iraqi tanks. Throughout this, Khomeini successfully mobilized popular support by invoking Shia history, comparing this war to Karbala. Khomeini secretly accepted arms from Israel and the United States, but did not moderate his opposition to these countries, as seen in Iran's simultaneous support for the Lebanese Hezbollah. He deeply resented GCC, U.S., and other Western support for Iraq. In 1988, with most of his military and political advisors arguing that the war could not be won, and some warning that the United States might attack Iran, Khomeini finally accepted a truce mediated by the United Nations, saying that it was like "drinking a chalice of poison."

In 1988, Khomeini ordered a review of the cases of political prisoners in Iran and the execution of any who did not repent their opposition to the regime. This reportedly resulted in the execution of thousands of political prisoners. In 1989, after Grand Ayatollah Hossein Ali Montazeri, who had been favored by Khomeini and elected by the Assembly of Experts to succeed him as Supreme Leader, protested these executions and called for liberalization in domestic and foreign policy, Khomeini repudiated him as his successor.

In December 1988, before the fall of the Berlin Wall and three years before the fall of the Soviet Union, Khomeini sent a letter to USSR Premier Mikhail Gorbachev predicting the fall of communism and inviting him to study and research Islam.

In February 1989, Khomeini issued a call for the killing of Salman Rushdie, the Indian-born British author of *The Satanic Verses,* arguing that this novel blasphemed the Prophet Mohammad. This led to a rupture of diplomatic relations with Britain for almost a decade.

Khomeini died of cancer on June 3, 1989. Grieving Iranians thronged the streets of Iran mourning his death. The crowd at Khomeini's funeral procession was so intent on touching his wooden coffin or tearing off a piece of the shroud that the coffin almost fell to the ground, forcing officials to rush the coffin to safety. A second funeral was conducted under much greater security measures. He is buried in a mausoleum in Tehran.

ALI KHAMENEI

Ayatollah Seyyed Ali Khamenei (born July 17, 1939) is a Shia cleric who actively opposed the Shah's rule, was a close associate of Ayatollah Khomeini in establishing the Islamic Republic of Iran after the revolution in 1978–79, and succeeded Khomeini as the Supreme Leader after Khomeini's death in 1989. He is generally considered a hard-line follower of Khomeini, but has provided some opportunities for more pragmatic and reformist members of the clerical elite to introduce change, particularly in the field of foreign policy.

Khamenei was born in Meshad, a city in northeast Iran, into a family reputedly descended from the Prophet. His father was an ethnic Azeri and an ayatollah. Two of his brothers are clerics and one of these two, Hadi, is a prominent newspaper editor. He is married and has six children.

Khamenei began advanced religious training in Najaf, Iraq in 1957. (Some sources claim that Khamenei also undertook limited paramilitary training in Palestinian camps in Lebanon and Libya.) He continued his religious studies in Qom, in 1958, where he was a student of Ayatollah Khomeini. Khamenei was involved in the protests against the Shah's rule in 1963 and was briefly jailed. He then resumed his studies in Meshad and went on to lecture and write there about Islamic jurisprudence, history, and science. He was imprisoned on numerous occasions in the 1960s and 1970s for his teaching and opposition to the Shah and was banned from teaching after imprisonment in 1975–76.

Khamenei was a relatively young man during the revolution of 1978–79, and it is well known that he had not gained the reputation and following of a great Islamic thinker at that time. His language skills in Arabic and Turkish had enabled him to translate and critique a variety of works on Islamic science, history, and Western civilization. He also wrote a book about the role of Muslims in the liberation of India. There is some debate as to whether he was accorded the title of hojjatoleslam ("authority on Islam"), a rank one step below ayatollah. But he was active from his base in Meshad in organizing the demonstrations and protests that brought the shah down in 1979.

Khamenei went to Tehran in 1979 and played a key role in helping Khomeini gradually consolidate his power after the shah fell. He was a member of the Revolutionary Council, a cofounder of the Islamic Republican Party, the Friday Prayer Leader for Tehran, a member of the first Majlis, and was involved in the establishment and ideological training of the Revolutionary Guards. Like Khomeini, he supported the students who seized U.S. diplomats in November 1979 and held fifty-two of them hostage for 444 days. And like Khomeini, he supported the war with Iraq and the refusal to accept Saddam Hussein's offers to end it. He was Khomeini's first representative on the powerful Supreme Defense Council, visiting the war front, and helped orchestrate the removal of then-president Bani-Sadr in 1981.

Khamenei survived an assassination attempt by the Mojahedin-e Khalq in June 1981, and has had limited use of his right arm since then. On October 2, 1981, after a major bombing by the Mojahedin-e Khalq killed Bani-Sadr's successor, Mohammad Ali Rejai, Khamenei was elected as Iran's third president. He was reelected for a second term in 1985. The presidency has limited power in Iran, but Khamenei used this position to support strict Islamic social and cultural norms, to protect the business interests of Iran's bazaar merchants, who have traditionally been important allies of the clergy, to mobilize domestic support for the continuation of the war with Iraq, and to reject foreign domination.

Khamenei supported the advice of the leaders of Iran's regular armed forces and Revolutionary Guards that Khomeini agree to a cease-fire with Iraq in August 1988. He served as the first chairman of the new Expediency Council in 1988 and 1989, a body established to resolve disputes between the Majlis and the Guardian Council, and empowered to overturn Guardian Council vetoes of Majlis legislation. He rarely differed with Khomeini, but when he suggested in 1989 that the condemned author Salman Rushdie could redeem himself, Khomeini publicly reversed Khamenei, saying that Rushdie could not repent from his blasphemy.

In 1989, Ayatollah Khomeini rejected Ayatollah Montazeri as his successor as Supreme Leader. Khamenei was now a hojjatoleslam but was not a marja or an ayatollah and was therefore not qualified under the constitution to serve in this position. But when Khomeini died in June 1989, the Assembly of Experts revised the constitution to select Khamenei as the new Supreme Leader. A number of Iran's grand ayatollahs opposed this. Later in 1989, after assuming the position of Supreme Leader, Khamenei was referred to as Ayatollah Khamenei, although he had not attained this rank through the normal means of attracting a large following through his teaching and writing. In 1994, after several years of study and tutoring, Khamenei was named a marja. Again, a number of Iran's marjas and grand ayatollahs opposed this. Khamenei himself declined to serve as marja for Iran's Shia, saying he would serve in that role for Shia abroad.

As Supreme Leader, Khamenei has carried on Khomeini's legacy of keeping power in the hands of the clergy, particularly in institutions such as the Supreme Leader, the Assembly of Experts, the Expediency Council, the Guardian Council, and the judiciary, and keeping the elected institutions such as the presidency and the Majlis in a secondary status. He has also used his control of the bonyads, or economic foundations, and his position as head of the Revolutionary Guards to maintain his power and promote his agenda. But he has been more pragmatic than Khomeini and has played the role of balancing the competing interests of the conservative hard-line followers of Khomeini, and the pragmatics and the reformers within the ruling clergy. He limited the efforts of the pragmatic Ali Rafsanjani, who succeeded him as president from 1989 to 1997, to relax strict Islamic codes for the society and to develop relations with the United States, but he accepted Rafsanjani's efforts to develop trade relations with major international powers and to obtain international loans and investment for the economic reconstruction of Iran after the devastation of the war with Iraq. He endorsed conservative hard-liner Ali Akbar Nateq Nouri for president in 1997 but accepted the election results that brought the reformist cleric Mohammad Khatami into office. Nevertheless, he acquiesced in only a very limited liberalization and then resisted it with renewed repression of reformist intellectuals and reformist media. The Guardian Council, half of whose members are appointed by Khamenei, vetoed much of the reformists' legislation and disqualified many reformers from running for the parliament in 2004 or for the presidency in 2005. He is thought to have supported Mahmoud Ahmadinejad's candidacy for the presidency in 2005. He has created a new bureaucratic structure to limit Ahmadinejad's power, but has not stopped him from public statements that have outraged many foreign audiences, although Khamenei has rejected some of Ahmadinejad's most offensive comments.

Khamenei has also presided over a foreign policy that has been somewhat more pragmatic than Khomeini's. Khamenei favored efforts to eject Iran's adversary Iraq from Kuwait in 1990 and 1991 and did nothing to interfere. But he opposed the long-term presence of U.S. forces in Saudi Arabia and in the larger Gulf region, particularly U.S. security arrangements with the GCC countries, a position shared by both Rafsanjani and Khatami, and he has supported the development of Iran's conventional military capabilities as well as its covert capabilities. He acquiesced in Khatami's "Dialogue of Civilizations," i.e., exchanges of scholars and artists, which had been occurring even under Rafsanjani, but he opposed Iranian government talks with the Clinton administration in the late 1990s, as he also had in 1993. In 2001 and 2002, he did approve Iranian cooperation with the United States in efforts to unseat the Taliban and al-Qaeda in Afghanistan, both of them adversaries of Iran, and to establish the Karzai government there. He also approved of the offer to discuss all disputes with the Bush administration in 2003, including Iran's possible acceptance of Israel alongside an independent Palestinian state, i.e., the "grand bargain," and the limited talks with the Bush administration on stabilizing Iraq in 2007, possibly because he sees negotiation as a way of avoiding U.S. military action against Iran. This has not received much media attention in the United States or other Western countries, even though Khamenei is the Supreme Leader and has significantly more power than Ahmadinejad. Khamenei has strongly supported Iran's development of scientific and technological knowledge, particularly nuclear power, but he has issued a religious ruling, or fatwa, banning the development, stockpiling, or use of nuclear weapons by Iran. Iran's actual policy on developing nuclear weapons is not known.

ALI AKBAR HASHEMI RAFSANJANI

Hojjatoleslam Ali Akbar Hashemi-Rafsanjani (born August 25, 1934) is a Shia cleric who opposed the Shah, was an associate of Khomeini, and has served in numerous important positions in the Islamic Republic of Iran. He is known as a pragmatist.

Rafsanjani was born in a village near Rafsanjan, in the southeastern province of Kerman. His father was a local cleric and pistachio farmer, and Rafsanjani was one of nine children. He began his religious studies at the age of 14 in Qom, where he was a student and disciple of Ayatollah Khomeini, and where he attained the rank of hojjatoleslam by the late 1950s. He married in 1958 and is the father of five children. Faezeh, his daughter, has served in the Majlis and as publisher of the newspaper Zan. Mehdi, his son, ran the state-owned Iran Gas Company. Rafsanjani is, reportedly, one of the wealthiest individuals in Iran, having numerous property holdings and involvement in foreign trade and in the oil and gas industry.

Rafsanjani helped organize demonstrations against the Shah in June 1963. During Khomeini's exile, Khomeini relied on Rafsanjani for fund-raising and contacts with the wide range of domestic opponents of the Shah, a responsibility that called upon and developed his skills as a pragmatist and coalition-builder. He was imprisoned and reportedly tortured on several occasions in the 1960s and 1970s, including from 1975 until 1978. Upon Khomeini's return to Iran in 1979, Rafsanjani served on the Revolutionary Council with Khamenei, and was a cofounder, again with Khamenei, of the Islamic Republican Party. He served as Deputy Minister of the Interior after the Bazargan government resigned in the wake of the November 1979 seizure of American hostages. He was elected to the Majlis in 1980 and served as Speaker of the Majlis from 1980 to 1989. After the MEK killed the president and many members of the parliament, Rafsanjani supported a violent campaign to kill and imprison MEK members.

He served on the Supreme Defense Council and also as a Friday Prayer Leader in Tehran during his years as Speaker, and he used all of these positions to support the continuation of the war with Iraq. His associates were involved in the secret negotiations to acquire Israeli and U.S. arms during the early years of the war with Iraq and eventually to obtain the release of some Western hostages in Lebanon, behavior that illustrates his basic pragmatism. When these negotiations were revealed by his rivals in 1986, Khomeini intervened to prevent a domestic political crisis that might have ended Rafsanjani's career. Rafsanjani then served as Acting Commander in Chief of the Armed Forces from June 1988 until 1989 and was instrumental in persuading Khomeini to accept the UN cease-fire resolution in July 1988, a position that Khamenei also supported.

After Khomeini's death in 1989, Rafsanjani supported the Assembly of Experts' selection of Khamenei as Supreme Leader. Rafsanjani was then elected as Iran's fourth president, and he was reelected in 1993. During his presidency, he led the pragmatist faction of Iran's clerical elite and was able to wield more power than technically authorized by the constitution because of the stature earned in his previous positions and because of his relatively close relations with Khamenei. He sought to promote modest liberalization in the society, for example, in the press and the universities, which Khamenei constrained. He labored more successfully, with Khamenei's blessing, to rebuild an economy devastated by war, opening Iran to foreign investments, loans, and trade, much of it from Europe, and reducing the role of the state in the economy in favor of more private ownership. He established a group known as the Executives of Construction to support these economic efforts. He also sought to engineer Iran's reintegration into the international community, by building ties with the Soviet Union (and then Russia) and China, by not interfering with the U.S.-led coalition efforts to eject Iraq from Kuwait in 1991 and by generally adhering to the UN sanctions imposed on Iraq, by helping to obtain the release of more Western hostages in Lebanon in 1991 and 1992, by seeking trade with and investments from western Europe, by attempting to repair relations with some GCC states, and by secretly exploring the possibility of talks with the Clinton administration, and even by offering an oil and gas concession to an American oil company, which the Clinton administration vetoed. Rafsanjani was and remains, however, a fierce critic of the U.S. military presence in the Gulf region and of GCC security ties with the Western powers and a staunch supporter of Iran's conventional military rearmament. He is suspected of having ordered or supported the killings of regime opponents abroad, and Argentine prosecutors have called for his arrest for alleged involvement in the bombing of a Jewish cultural center in Buenos Aires in 1994.

Unable to seek a third consecutive term as president in 1997, Rafsanjani supported the candidacy of the reformist Khatami, who won. Rafsanjani was appointed later in 1997 as chairman of the Expediency Council. He barely won a seat in the Majlis in 2000, however, in part because he did not have the support of reformists and in part because of rumors of financial corruption, and he gave up his seat. He offered some endorsement of the Arab League's proposal in 2002 for recognition of Israel in exchange for a Palestinian state. He is thought to have supported Iran's "grand bargain" overture to the United States in 2003. He has argued that Iran should negotiate over its nuclear programs and reconsider its support for Hezbollah. He ran for president again in 2005, but lost in a runoff election to Mahmoud Ahmadinejad. In December 2006, however, he and his supporters were elected to the Assembly of Experts, in a vote that reflected dissatisfaction with Ahmadinejad and that enhanced Rafsanjani's power even more, inasmuch as the Assembly of Experts monitors, dismisses, and chooses the Supreme Leader. In September 2007, he was elected chairman of the Assembly of Experts, defeating an ally of Ahmadinejad. Moreover, he still retained his position as chairman of the Expediency Council.

MOHAMMAD KHATAMI

Hojjatoleslam Seyyed Mohammad Khatami (born on September 29, 1943) is a Shia cleric who served as Iran's president from 1997 until 2005. He is a member of the Society of Militant Clerics, a reformist movement within the clergy, and is indeed considered one of the leading reformists in Iran.

Khatami was born in Ardakan, in the province of Yazd, in central Iran. His father was a prominent cleric and from a family claiming to be descendents of the Prophet. One brother, Mohammad, has served in Iran's Majlis and as the head of Iran's major reformist political party, the Islamic Iran Participation Front. Khatami is married and has three children.

Khatami earned a B.A. in Western philosophy at Isfahan University and then completed advanced studies in Islamic theology in Qom, attaining the rank of hojjatoleslam. He was an opponent of the Shah's rule throughout these years.

During the revolution in 1978 and 1979, Khatami was the head of the Islamic Center in Hamburg, Germany, where many Iranians were studying. He returned to Iran in 1979 and was named to head the Kayhan Publishing Group. He was elected to the Majlis in 1980. He served as Minister of Culture and Islamic Guidance from 1982 until 1992. After Khomeini's death in 1989, with hard-liner Khamenei as Supreme Leader and pragmatist Rafsanjani as president, Khatami relaxed restrictions on the press and the arts, angering hard-liners, who forced his resignation in 1992. He then served as the head of the National Library from 1992 until 1997, continued to serve as a cultural adviser to President Rafsanjani, and wrote a number of books on Western philosophy and Islam.

Khatami ran for the presidency in 1997, advocating economic and social reforms, and was the surprise winner, receiving support from Rafsanjani, reform-minded clerics, intellectuals, the middle class, students, and women.

Khamenei supported his opponent but accepted Khatami's victory. As president, he sought to promote the rule of law, civil society, democracy, and to champion the primacy of Iran's elected bodies over its unelected institutions, including the institution of the Supreme Leader, believing that Islam called upon rulers to consult with the ruled, to be accountable, and to respect human freedom and equality, and believing that democracy in Iran would insure the maintenance of the Islamic character of the state. One result of his policies was the emergence of numerous newspapers that called for reform and investigated corruption in state institutions. Another result was a backlash that resulted in the murder and repression of reformists in 1998. Khatami removed those in the Ministry of Information and Security who were thought to be responsible for this. A raid on Tehran University in 1999 by police and hard-line vigilantes killed one student and injured twenty others, and led to the largest demonstration in Iran since the revolution in 1979, showing popular support for the students. Given the limited constitutional authority of Iran's presidency, however, hard-liners in the security apparatus and in the judiciary were able to frustrate many of his reform efforts and send some reform politicians to prison. Reformists won seats in the Majlis in 2000, however, and Khatami won a second term in 2001. In his second term, Khatami was again not able to implement his desired reforms in the face of hard-line opposition, leading many reformers to blame him for not confronting hard-liners. In fact, hard-liners in the Council of Guardians prevented most reformists from running for the Majlis in 2004.

In the sphere of economics, President Khatami continued with the policies of his predecessor, Rafsanjani, to encourage growth of private enterprise, industrialization, and foreign investment and trade, although state-owned enterprises remained strong. In the realm of foreign policy, he used an appearance on CNN to advocate a "dialogue of civilizations" to foster understanding and reconciliation, and promoted exchanges of Iranian and foreign intellectuals, artists, and athletes. Khatami and Khamenei made it clear that this would not entail talks with the U.S. government. Khatami did, however, travel to the United States in 1998, where he met with journalists, and he also did meet with French President Jacques Chirac and with Pope John Paul II. Khatami also called for better relations with the GCC states. Like Khomeini, Khamenei, and Rafsanjani, however, he was opposed to the large U.S. military presence in the Gulf region and the security relations that GCC states maintain with the United States and other Western powers. He condemned the September 11, 2001 attacks on the United States. He also reportedly endorsed Iran's cooperation with the United States in Afghanistan and vigorously denied that his government had authorized a shipment of arms to Palestinian Authority President Yasser Arafat in January 2002, which became known as the *Karine-A* incident. He also reportedly supported the May 2003 "grand bargain" offer to the Bush administration, as did his foreign minister, Kamal Kharrazi, and Khamenei.

After stepping down from the presidency, Khatami has continued his efforts to promote a "dialogue of civilizations." He has established the Institute for the Dialogue of Civilizations with offices in Iran and in Geneva, Switzerland, has lectured at Harvard University and at the National Cathedral in Washington DC, and has been awarded numerous honorary doctorates around the world.

MAHMOUD AHMADINEJAD

Mahmoud Ahmadinejad (born on October 28, 1956) is an Iranian politician who was elected to Iran's presidency in 2005. He is considered a leading figure in a new generation of hard-line followers of Ayatollah Khomeini.

Ahmadinejad was born in Garmsar, near Tehran. His father was an iron-worker, a devout Muslim, and a father of seven. Ahmadinejad is married and has three children and is noted for having lived very modestly, even after being elected to the presidency.

Much of Ahmadinejad's personal history is disputed by international scholars, and this profile will acknowledge this when necessary. Ahmadinejad began study-ing civil engineering at Tehran's University of Science and Technology in the mid-1970s and after several interruptions earned a PhD in transportation planning in 1997. He was a hard-line conservative Islamist student activist and opponent of the Shah's rule, but was not arrested during these years. He may have been a member of the secretive Hojjatieh Society, a society that looks forward to the return of the Twelfth Imam, or Mahdi, a society which was report-edly disbanded after the revolution, but that is also disputed. He was reportedly a member of the student union that decided to take U.S. Embassy personnel hostage in 1979, but he reportedly favored a plan to capture the Soviet Embassy at the same time, and he reportedly did not participate in the actual storming of the U.S. Embassy. Some of the American hostages who were held from Novem-ber 1979 until January 1981 claim that he was one of the students who guarded them, but Ahmadinejad and some of the students involved have denied this and the CIA has also cast doubt on it. He may have served in low-level positions in the Ministry of Education and the Ministry of Interior from 1980 to 1982 and may have been posted in Iran's northwest, in Maku and Khoi, from 1982 to 1986. Some biographies indicate that he served in the Revolutionary Guards during the Iran-Iraq War in combat or in covert operations, and that he partici-pated in assassinations of dissidents abroad and the torture and execution of regime opponents inside Evin Prison, but these may not be reliable accounts. It does seem that he served a stint as an engineer in a Revolutionary Guard logistical corps during the latter years of the war.

After the war, he lectured at the University of Science and Technology. In 1993 he was appointed governor of the province of Ardabil, in northwest Iran, on the recommendation of Ayatollah Beheshti, and served until 1997, when he was

replaced by the newly elected Khatami government. After this, he was again a
lecturer at Tehran's University of Science and Technology. After a very low voter
turnout, he was selected as mayor of Tehran in 2003 by a new city council dominated by hard-line members of Abadgaran, or the Association of Builders of
Islamic Iran, an ultraconservative movement wanting to return Iran to the vision
of Khomeini and shaped by the Iran-Iraq War. He then reversed reforms introduced by previous mayors, stressed Islamic culture, and increased welfare for
the poor. He won the presidency in 2005, running on a populist platform of
social and economic justice, promising to fight corruption and to insure that
the people shared in Iran's oil wealth. Moreover, he insisted that Iran would not
submit to foreign pressures, and especially not give up its right to nuclear power,
and dismissed the need for relations with the United States. He surprisingly
defeated better known hard-line candidates in the first round, and then defeated
the pragmatist Rafsanjani in a second round. The Basij, or Mobilization Resistance Force, a paramilitary force under the Revolutionary Guards, worked
actively to mobilize votes for him, especially in poor and rural areas of Iran,
and conservative clerics in Iran's mosques also did so. Rafsanjani and others considered the election rigged, and it has been suggested that Khamenei supported
Ahmadinejad. It has also been suggested that President Bush's disparaging
remarks about the upcoming election mobilized Ahmadinejad's supporters and
enabled his campaign to portray Rafsanjani as misguided in his ideas that negotiations with the United States could be fruitful for Iran.

Ahmadinejad is a member of the Islamic Society of Engineers and also of
Abadgaran, the Association of Builders of Islamic Iran. His religious mentor is
the conservative Ayatollah Mesbah-Yazdi, who runs the Haqqani seminary in
Qom, and who is very popular with many in the Revolutionary Guards and
the Basij. It is not clear whether Ahmadinejad has an independent base of support in the Revolutionary Guards or whether he depends on Khamenei and
Mesbah-Yazdi for the support of the Revolutionary Guards. Again, Ahmadinejad
is said by some to belong to the Hojjatieh Society, a disbanded or underground
society that is thought to long for the return of the Hidden Imam, or the Mahdi.
He is also said to belong to Osulgarayan, the principalists, who strive to adhere to
the principles of Islam and the Iranian revolution in political matters.

As president, Ahmadinejad's power is limited by the constitution. He does
not command the armed forces and does not make Iran's foreign policy. These
are the prerogatives of Supreme Leader Khamenei, who has also established
a new body to oversee the new president. Ahmadinejad is one of a dozen members of the Supreme National Security Council, which advises the Supreme
Leader on foreign policy and military issues. He has, however, alarmed the world
with his public challenges to Israel. On October 25, 2005, he said, "The Imam
[i.e. Khomeini] said this regime occupying Jerusalem must vanish from the page
of time." It was widely mistranslated as "Israel must be wiped off the map." This

mistranslation led to the interpretation that Ahmadinejad was threatening the military destruction of Israel. Some in the West fear that his alleged membership in the Hojjatieh Society, and its longing for the return of the Mahdi, means that Ahmadinejad might use nuclear weapons against Israel or the United States in order to bring about Armageddon and hasten the return of the Twelfth Imam. Others argue that this society does not believe that humans can hasten the return of the Mahdi. Moreover, there are different interpretations of Shia thought about the end of time, and in some of them, the Mahdi is to introduce a long reign of justice on earth before the Day of Judgment and end of the world, which would suggest that launching a nuclear war resulting in nuclear retaliation that devastates Iran would not make sense. Ahmadinejad has also claimed that he does not want Iran to acquire nuclear weapons, and perhaps more importantly Ahmadinejad does not have the power to pursue or use these weapons. It seems more likely that Ahmadinejad has been expressing opposition to Israel as a Jewish state and expressing hope that a non-Zionist regime representing both Palestinians and Jews will replace it, rather than calling for Iran to militarily defeat Israel, although even this position is no comfort to Israelis. He has also questioned whether the Holocaust actually took the lives of six million Jews, and has indicated that since the Holocaust took place in Europe, then Israel should be situated in Europe instead of displacing and occupying Palestinians to situate Israel there. He has insisted that Iran will not give up the right to nuclear energy for peaceful purposes, which again is the decision of those more powerful than he is. He has also claimed that Iran is willing to help stabilize Iraq if the United States begins withdrawal.

On the domestic front, Ahmadinejad has not successfully tamed Iran's high inflation and unemployment, despite Iran's rising oil revenues. His modest and unexpected efforts on behalf of women, such as allowing them to attend soccer events, have been overturned by Khamenei. His repression of reformist thinkers in academia has led to demonstrations by students. His followers fared poorly in municipal council elections and elections for the Assembly of Experts in late 2006, and his domestic and foreign policies were rebuked by newspapers considered close to Rafsanjani and Khamenei, suggesting that he is losing support and may be a one-term president. One particular criticism of Ahmadinejad is that his confrontational rhetoric has galvanized more opposition to Iran in the United States and in other Western governments, increasing sanctions on Iran, and diminishing the prospects for negotiations. In 2007, Ahmadinejad and his Intelligence Minister Mohseni-Ejehi and his Interior Minister Pour-Mohammedi, both involved in the violent repression of intellectuals after the election of Khatami in 1997, led a campaign to arrest reformers and to detain dual citizens such as Iranian-American scholar Haleh Esfandiari when visiting Iran, charging the latter with efforts to subvert the regime. This was seen by some as an effort to reassert his position in the face of criticism by pragmatists and reformers and to shore up his own conservative base. In August and September, after televised "confessions," they were released and allowed to leave the country. In the summer of 2007, he reluctantly supported modest gasoline price hikes and gasoline rationing in order to alleviate the cost of the subsidies Iran provides on gas and the vulnerability this entails, but this led to riots and mobs burning gas stations in various cities in Iran. Students have also continued to demonstrate against him in 2007. In September 2007, the victory of Rafsanjani over Ahmadinejad's mentor Mesbah-Yazdi to head the Assembly of Experts, the body that chooses, monitors, and can replace the Supreme Leader, was interpreted as another blow to Ahmadinejad's standing. In general, it may be that the Western media may pay more attention to Ahmadinejad than he merits in terms of his real power in Iran.

APPENDIX B

Chronology

559 BC–330 BC	The Achaemenid Empire
AD 224–AD 641	The Sassanid Empire
AD 642	Arab armies defeat the Persians at the Battle of Nehavend and begin converting the Persians to Islam.
AD 680	The Prophet Mohammad's descendant Imam Husayn is killed at the Battle of Karbala by the Ummayyad Caliph Yazid, marking the split in the Islamic world between the Shia followers of Husayn and the Sunnis.
AD 939	The Twelfth Imam, or Mahdi, goes into hiding until his return to usher in a reign of justice before the end of the world.
AD 1217	The Mongol invasion of Persia
AD 1501–AD 1722	The Safavid Dynasty rules and declares Shiism the state religion of Persia.
AD 1794–AD 1925	The Qajar Dynasty rules and Persia is subjected to Russian and British encroachments and competition.
AD 1925	Shah Reza Pahlavi establishes the Pahlavi Dynasty, seeks to emancipate Persia from Soviet Russian and British pressures, and declares the official name of the country Iran.
AD 1941	The Soviet Union and Great Britain occupy Iran, depose Shah Reza Pahlavi, and install Shah Mohammad Reza Pahlavi to the throne.
AD 1951–AD 1953	Iran nationalizes the AIOC, Iran suffers an international boycott of its oil, and British intelligence agency MI6 and the U.S. CIA overthrow Prime Minister Muhammad Mossadeq to restore the Shah's power and negotiate new oil concessions.
AD 1959	Iran and the United States sign a bilateral defense pact.

AD 1963	Ayatollah Ruhollah Khomeini leads domestic opposition to the Shah's autocratic rule and relations with the United States and Israel and is deported.
AD 1971	Britain withdraws it military forces from the Persian Gulf and the Shah asserts Iranian military preeminence in the region, with sophisticated weapons systems supplied by the United States and Britain.
AD 1973–AD 1974	The Shah takes advantage of reduced oil supplies after the 1973 Arab-Israeli war to orchestrate a fourfold increase in the price of a barrel of oil.
AD 1978–AD 1979	The Iranian revolution, inspired by Ayatollah Khomeini, challenges and overthrows the Shah and ushers in the Islamic Republic of Iran.
AD 1979–AD 1981	Iranian students seize U.S. Embassy personnel in Tehran and hold them captive for 444 days.
AD 1980–AD 1988	The Iran-Iraq War claims a million lives and hundreds of billions of dollars in damages to the economies of Iran and Iraq.
AD 1995–AD 1996	The United States imposes significant economic sanctions on Iran, arguing that Iran seeks nuclear weapons and supports terrorism.
AD 2001–AD 2002	Iran cooperates with the United States after September 11, 2001 in defeating their common enemies the Taliban and al-Qaeda in Afghanistan, but Iran is accused of supplying weapons to Palestinian Authority President Yasser Arafat. An Iranian opposition group reveals that Iran has been secretly constructing two nuclear facilities.
AD 2003	Iran sends the United States a proposal for negotiating all of the disputes between the two countries in what has become known as the "grand bargain" proposal and the Bush administration rejects the offer.
AD 2003–AD 2005	Iran engages in unsuccessful negotiations over its nuclear programs with Britain, France, Germany, and the European Union (the EU-3).
AD 2006	The United States joins the five permanent members of the UN Security Council plus Germany (the P5+1) to offer new negotiations with Iran on its nuclear programs if Iran agrees to suspend sensitive elements of its programs as a precondition of the talks and Iran rejects this offer.
AD 2007	Iran and the United States hold bilateral discussions on the future of Iraq while U.S. threats of military action against Iran and U.S.-orchestrated Security Council sanctions against Iran presage a possible war between the two countries.

APPENDIX C

Documents

DOCUMENT 1

Letter from Swiss Ambassador to Iran to U.S. Department of State with Iranian Proposal for a "Grand Bargain" with the United States

May 4, 2003

1. On April 21, I had a longer discussion with Sadeq Kharrazi who came to see me (S.Kh is the Iranian Ambassador in Paris, former Deputy-FM and nephew of the Foreign Minister, his sister is married to the son of the Religious Leader Khamenei). During this discussion a first draft of the enclosed Roadmap was developed. He said that he would discuss this with the Leader and the Foreign Minister.

2. On May 2, I met him again for three hours. He told me that he had two long discussions with the Leader on the Roadmap. In these meetings, which both lasted almost two hours, only President Khatami and FM Kharrazi were present; "we went through every word of the this paper". (He additionally had a series of separat meetings with both). The question is dealt with in high secrecy, therefore no one else has been informed, (S.Kh. himself has become also very discreet in our last contacts). – S.Kh. presented the paper to the Leader as a proposal which he had discussed , with a friend in Europe who has close contacts with higher echelons in the DoS'. The Leader explicitly hat asked him whether this is a US-proposal and S.Kh. denied this, saying that, if it is accepted, this friend could convey it to Washington as the basis for opening the bilateral discussion.

3. Then S.Kh. told me that the Leader uttered some reservations as for some points; the President and the Foreign Minister were very positive, there was no problem from their side. Then he said „They (meaning above all the Leader) agree with 85%-90% of the paper. But everthing can be negotiated." (By 'agree' he meant to agree with the points themselvers referred to as 'US aims' in the Roadmap, and not only to agree that the US puts these points on the agenda). "There is a clear interest to tackle the problem of our relations with the US. I told them, this is a golden opportunity, one day we must find a solution". – Then S.Kh. asked me whether I could present the enclosed Roadmap very confidentially to someone very high in the DoS in order to get to know the US-reaction on it. - He asked me to make some minor changes in the Roadmap draft of our previous meeting, we re-wrote for instance the Iranian statement on the Middle East, and he said that he thinks, that this statement would be acceptable - "the peace process is a reality".

4. Then he said: „If the Americans agree to have a discreet bilateral meeting on the basis of this Roadmap, then this meeting could be arranged very soon. In this meeting our remaining reservations could be discussed as well as the US would bring in their reservations on this paper. I am sure that these differences can be eliminated. If we can agree on a Roadmap to clarify the procedure, as a next step it could already be decided in this first meeting that the two Foreign Ministers could meet for starting the process" along the lines of the Roadmap „to decide on how to proceed to resolve everything from A till Z". – Asked whether the meeting between the two foreign ministers has been agreed by the Leader, he said: „Look, if we can agree on the procedure, I believe honestly that it is O.K. for the meeting of the foreign ministers in Paris or Geneva, there is soon an occasion." – Asked whom he thinks would participate in the first discreet meeting, he mentioned Armitage, referring to the positive positions of the latter on Iranian democracy. - I told him that I think that this is impossible, but then he mentioned a meeting these days between Khalilzad and Zarif (Ambassador to the UN) in Geneva on terrorism and said it could be a similar level from the DoS and on their side maybe him or Zarif or both.

5. When I tried to obtain from him a precise answer on what exactly the Leader explicitly has agreed, he said that the lack of trust in the US imposes them to proceed very carefully and very confidentially. After discussing this problem with him I understood that they want to be sure that if this initiative failed, and if anything about the new Iranian flexibility outlined in it became known, they would – also for internal reasons – not be bound to it. – However, I got the clear impression that there is a strong will of the regime to tackle the problem with the US now and to try it with this initiative.

Roadmap

<u>US aims:</u> (Iran agrees that the US puts the following aims on the agenda)

- WMD: full transparency for security that there are no Iranian endeavours to develop or possess WMD, full cooperation with IAEA based on Iranian adoption of all relevant instruments (93+2 and all further IAEA protocols)
- Terrorism: decisive action against any terrorists (above all Al Qaida) on Iranian territory, full cooperation and exchange of all relevant information.
- Iraq: coordination of Iranian influence for actively supporting political stabilization and the establishment of democratic institutions and a democratic government representing all ethnic and religious groups in Iraq
- Middle East:
  1. stop of any material support to Palestinian opposition groups (Hamas, Jihad etc.) from Iranian territory, pressure on these organisations to stop violent action against civilians within borders of 1967.
  2. action on Hisbollah to become an exclusively political and social organization within Lebanon
  3. acceptance of the two-states-approach.

<u>Iranian aims:</u> (the US accepts a dialogue „in mutual respect" and agrees that Iran puts the following aims on the agenda)

- US refrains from supporting change of the political system by direct interference from outside
- Abolishment of all sanctions: commercial sanctions, frozen assets, refusal of access to WTO
- Iraq: pursuit of MKO, support of the repatriation of MKO-members, support of the Iranian claims for Iraqi reparation, no Turkish invasion in North Iraq, respect for the Iranian national interests in Iraq and religious links to Najaf/Kerbala.
- Access to peaceful nuclear technology, biotechnolgy and chemical technology
- Recognition of Iran's legitimate security interests in the region with the according defense capacity
- Terrorism: action against MKO and affiliated organizations in the US

<u>Steps:</u>

1. Communication of mutual agreement on the following procedure
2. Mutual simultanous statements „we have always been ready for direct and authoritative talks with the US/with Iran with the aim of discussing – in mutual respect – our common interests and our mutual concerns, but we have always made it clear that, such talks can only be held, if genuine progress for a solution of our own concerns can be achieved".
3. A direct meeting on the aproprate level will be held with the previously agreed aims
   a) of a decision on the first mutual steps:
      - Iraq: establishment of a common working group on Iraq, active Iranian support for Iraqi stabilization, US-commitment to resolve MKO problem in Iraq, US comitment to take Iranian reparation claims into the discussion on Iraq foreign debts.
      - Terrorism: Iranian comitment for decisive action against Al Qaida members in Iran, agreement on cooperation and information exchange
      - Iranian statement „that it supports a peaceful solution in the Middle East, that it accepts a solution which is accepted by the Palestinians and that it follows with interest the discussion on the Roadmap, presented by the Quartett."
      - US-acceptance of iranian access to WTO-membership negotiations
   b) of the establishment of three parallel working groups on disarmament, regional security, and economic cooperation. Their aim is an agreement on three parallel road maps, for the discussions of these working groups each side accepts that the other side's aims (see above) are put on the agenda:
      1) Disarmament: road map, which combines the mutual aims of, on the one side, full transparency by international comittments and guarantees to abstain from WMD with, on the other side, access to western technology (in the three areas),
      2) Terrorism and regional security: road map for above mentioned aims on Middle East and terrorism
      3) Economic cooperation: road map for the lifting of the sanctions and the solution of the frozen assets
   c) and of a public statement after this first meeting on the achieved agreements

Source: A link to this document can be found in the electronic version of Nicholas D. Kristof, "Iran's Proposal for a 'Grand Bargain,'" *New York Times,* April 28, 2007. Or see http://www.washingtonpost.com/wp-srv/world/documents/us_iran_1roadmap.pdf.

DOCUMENT 2

Final Edited Version of Iran's "Grand Bargain" Proposal, May 12, 2003

IRANIAN AIMS

(The US accepts a dialogue **"in mutual respect"** and agrees that Iran puts the following aims on the agenda)

- **Halt US hostile behavior and rectifications of status of Iran in the US:** (interference in internal or external relations, "axis of evil", terrorism list.)
- **Abolishment of all sanctions:** commercial sanctions, frozen assets, judgments (FSIA), impediments in international trade and financial institutions.
- **Iraq:** democratic and fully representative government in Iraq, support of Iranian claims for Iraqi reparations, respect for Iranian national interests in Iraq and religious links to Najaf/Karbal.
- **Full access to peaceful nuclear technology, biotechnology and chemical technology.**
- Recognition of **Iran's legitimate security interests** in the region with according defense capacity.
- **Terrorism:** pursuit of anti-Iranian terrorists, above all the MKO and support for repatriation of their members in Iraq, decisive actions against anti-Iranian terrorists, above all MKO and affiliated organizations in the US.

US AIMS

(Iran accepts a dialogue **"in mutual respect"** and agrees that the US puts the following aims on the agenda)

- **WMD:** full transparency for security that there are no Iranian endeavors to develop or possess WMD, full cooperation with IAEA based on Iranian adoption of all relevant instruments (93+2 and all further IAEA protocols)
- **Terrorism:** decisive action against any terrorists (above all Al Qaida) on Iranian territory, full cooperation and exchange of all relevant information.
- **Iraq:** coordination of Iranian influence for activity supporting political stabilization and the establishment of democratic institutions and a nonreligious government.
- **Middle East:**
    1. stop of any material support to Palestinian opposition groups (Hamas, Jihad etc.) from Iranian territory, pressure on these organizations to stop violent actions against civilians within borders of 1967.
    2. action on Hizbollah to become a mere political organization within Lebanon
    3. acceptance of the Arab League Beirut declaration (Saudi initiative, two-states-approach)

STEPS

I. communication of **mutual agreement on the following procedure**

II. **mutual simultaneous statements** "we have always been ready for direct and authoritative talks with the US/with Iran in good faith and with the aim of discussing—in mutual respect—our common interests and our mutual concerns based on merits and objective realities, but we have always made it clear that, such talks can only be held, if genuine progress for a solution of our own concerns can be achieved."

III. **a first direct meeting** on the appropriate level (for instance in Paris) will be held **with the previously agreed aims**

    a. of a **decision on the first mutual steps**

       ◦ **Iraq:** establishment of a common group, active Iranian support for Iraqi stabilization, US-commitment to actively support Iranian reparation claims within the discussions on Iraq foreign debts.

       ◦ **Terrorism:** US-commitment to disarm and remove MKO from Iraq and take action in accordance with SCR1373 against its leadership, Iranian commitment for enhanced action against Al Qaida members in Iran, agreement on cooperation and information exchange

       ◦ Iranian general statement "to support a peaceful solution in the **Middle East** involving the parties concerned"

       ◦ US general statement that "Iran did not belong to the 'axis of evil'"

       ◦ US-acceptance to halt its impediments against Iran in international financial and trade institutions

    b. **of the establishment of three parallel working groups** on disarmament, regional security and economic cooperation. Their **aim is an agreement on three parallel road maps,** for the discussions of these working groups, each side accepts that the other side's aims (see above) are put on the agenda:

       1. **Disarmament:** road map, which combines the mutual aims of, on the one side, full transparency by international commitments and guarantees to abstain from WMD with, on the other side, full access to western technology (in the three areas)

       2. **Terrorism and regional security:** road map for above mentioned aims on the Middle east and terrorism

       3. **Economic cooperation:** road map for the abolishment of the sanctions, rescinding of judgments, and un-freezing of assets

    c. of agreement on a time-table for implementation

    d. and **of a public statement after this first meeting on the achieved agreements**

Source: A link to this document can also be found in the electronic version of Nicholas D. Kristof, "Iran's Proposal for a 'Grand Bargain,'" *New York Times,* April 28, 2007. See also the Web site of the Arms Control Association at www.aca.org.

DOCUMENT 3

Elements of a Revised Proposal to Iran Made by the E3+3 (June 6, 2006)

Our goal is to develop relations and cooperation with Iran based on mutual respect and the establishment of international confidence in the exclusively peaceful nature of Iran's nuclear programme. We propose a fresh start in negotiations of a comprehensive agreement with Iran. Such an agreement would be deposited with the IAEA and endorsed in a Security Council resolution.

To create the right conditions for negotiations:

We will:

- reaffirm Iran's right to develop nuclear energy for peaceful purposes in conformity with its NPT obligations, and in this context reaffirm their support for the development by Iran of a civil nuclear energy programme;
- commit to actively support the building of new light water reactors in Iran through international joint projects, in accordance with the IAEA Statute and the NPT;
- agree to suspend discussion of Iran's nuclear programme at the Security Council on resumption of negotiations.

Iran will:

- commit to addressing all the outstanding concerns of the IAEA through full cooperation with the IAEA;
- suspend all enrichment-related and reprocessing activities to be verified by the IAEA, as requested by the IAEA Board of Governors and the UN Security Council, and commit to continue this during these negotiations; and
- resume implementation of the Additional Protocol;

AREAS OF FUTURE COOPERATION TO BE COVERED IN NEGOTIATIONS ON A LONG TERM AGREEMENT

Nuclear

We will take the following steps:

Iran's Rights to Nuclear Energy

- reaffirm Iran's inalienable right to nuclear energy for peaceful purposes without discrimination and in conformity with Articles I and II of the NPT, and co-operate with Iran in the development by Iran of a civil nuclear power programme.
- negotiate and implement a Euratom/Iran nuclear cooperation agreement.

Light Water Reactors

- actively support the building of new light water power reactors in Iran through international joint projects, in accordance with the IAEA Statute and the NPT, using state-of-the-art technology, including by authorising the transfer of necessary goods and the provision of advanced technology to make its power reactors safe against earthquakes.

- provide co-operation with the management of spent nuclear fuel and radioactive waste through appropriate arrangements.

Research & Development in Nuclear Energy

- provide a substantive package of research and development co-operation, including possible provision of light water research reactors, notably in the fields of radioisotope production, basic research and nuclear applications in medicine and agriculture.

Fuel Guarantees

- give legally binding, multi-layered fuel assurances to Iran, based on:
  - participation as a partner in an international facility in Russia to provide enrichment services for a reliable supply of fuel to Iran's nuclear reactors. Subject to negotiations, such a facility could enrich all the UF6 produced in Iran.
  - establishment on commercial terms of a buffer stock to hold a reserve of up to 5 years' supply of nuclear fuel dedicated to Iran, with participation and under supervision of the IAEA.
  - development of a standing multilateral mechanism for reliable access to nuclear fuel with the IAEA based on ideas to be considered at the next Board of Governors.

Review of Moratorium

The long-term agreement would, with regard to common efforts to build international confidence, include a clause for review of the agreement in all its aspects, to follow:

- confirmation by the IAEA that all outstanding issues and concerns reported by the IAEA, including those activities which could have a military nuclear dimension, have been resolved; and
- confirmation that there are no undeclared nuclear activities or materials in Iran and that international confidence in the exclusively peaceful nature of Iran's civil nuclear programme has been restored.

Political and Economic

Regional Security Co-operation

Support for a new conference to promote dialogue and cooperation on regional security issues.

International Trade & Investment

Improving Iran's access to the international economy, markets and capital, through practical support for full integration into international structures, including the

WTO, and to create the framework for increased direct investment in Iran and trade with Iran (including a Trade and Economic Cooperation Agreement with EU). Steps would be taken to improve access to key goods and technology.

Civil Aviation

Civil aviation cooperation, including the possible removal of restrictions on US and European manufacturers, from exporting civil aircraft to Iran, thereby widening the prospect of Iran renewing its fleet of civil airliners.

Energy Partnership

Establishment of a long-term energy partnership between Iran and the EU and other willing partners, with concrete and practical applications.

Telecommunications Infrastructure

Support for the modernisation of Iran's telecommunication infrastructure and advanced internet provision, including by possible removal of relevant US and other export restrictions.

High Technology Co-operation

Co-operation in fields of high technology and other areas to be agreed.

Agriculture

Support for agricultural development in Iran, including possible access to US and European agricultural products, technology and farm equipment.

Source: http://www.diplomatie.gouv.fr/en/article-imprim.php3?id_article =5314.

DOCUMENT 4

Resolution 1747 (2007)

ADOPTED BY THE SECURITY COUNCIL AT ITS 5647TH MEETING ON 24 MARCH 2007

The Security Council,

Recalling the Statement of its President, S/PRST/2006/15, of 29 March 2006, and its resolution 1696 (2006) of 31 July 2006, and its resolution 1737 (2006) of 23 December 2006, and *reaffirming* their provisions,

Reaffirming its commitment to the Treaty on the Non-Proliferation of Nuclear Weapons, the need for all States Party to that Treaty to comply fully with all their obligations, and recalling the right of States Party, in conformity with Articles I and II of that Treaty, to develop research, production and use of nuclear energy for peaceful purposes without discrimination,

Recalling its serious concern over the reports of the IAEA Director General as set out in its resolutions 1696 (2006) and 1737 (2006),

Recalling the latest report by the IAEA Director General (GOV/2007/8) of 22 February 2007 and *deploring* that, as indicated therein, Iran has failed to comply with resolution 1696 (2006) and resolution 1737 (2006),

Emphasizing the importance of political and diplomatic efforts to find a negotiated solution guaranteeing that Iran's nuclear programme is exclusively for peaceful purposes, and *noting* that such a solution would benefit nuclear non-proliferation elsewhere, and *welcoming* the continuing commitment of China, France, Germany, the Russian Federation, the United Kingdom and the United States, with the support of the European Union's High Representative to seek a negotiated solution,

Recalling the resolution of the IAEA Board of Governors (GOV/2006/14), which states that a solution to the Iranian nuclear issue would contribute to global non-proliferation efforts and to realizing the objective of a Middle East free of weapons of mass destruction, including their means of delivery,

Determined to give effect to its decisions by adopting appropriate measures to persuade Iran to comply with resolution 1696 (2006) and resolution 1737 (2006) and with the requirements of the IAEA, and also to constrain Iran's development of sensitive technologies in support of its nuclear and missile programmes, until such time as the Security Council determines that the objectives of these resolutions have been met,

Recalling the requirement on States to join in affording mutual assistance in carrying out the measures decided upon by the Security Council,

Concerned by the proliferation risks presented by the Iranian nuclear programme and, in this context, by Iran's continuing failure to meet the requirements of the IAEA Board of Governors and to comply with the provisions of Security Council resolutions 1696 (2006) and 1737 (2006), *mindful* of its primary responsibility under the Charter of the United Nations for the maintenance of international peace and security,

Acting under Article 41 of Chapter VII of the Charter of the United Nations,

1. *Reaffirms* that Iran shall without further delay take the steps required by the IAEA Board of Governors in its resolution GOV/2006/14, which are essential to build confidence in the exclusively peaceful purpose of its nuclear programme and to resolve outstanding questions, and, in this context, *affirms* its decision that Iran shall without further delay take the steps required in paragraph 2 of resolution 1737 (2006);

2. *Calls upon* all States also to exercise vigilance and restraint regarding the entry into or transit through their territories of individuals who are engaged in, directly associated with or providing support for Iran's proliferation sensitive nuclear activities or for the development of nuclear weapon delivery systems, and *decides* in this regard that all States shall notify the Committee established pursuant to paragraph 18 of resolution 1737 (2006) (herein "the Committee") of the entry into or transit through their territories of the persons designated in the Annex to resolution 1737 (2006) or Annex I to this resolution, as well as of additional persons designated by the Security Council or the Committee as being engaged in, directly associated with or providing support for Iran's proliferation sensitive nuclear activities or for the development of nuclear weapon delivery systems, including through the involvement in procurement of the prohibited items, goods, equipment, materials and technology specified by and under the measures in paragraphs 3 and 4 of resolution 1737 (2006), except where such travel is for activities directly related to the items in subparagraphs 3 (b) (i) and (ii) of that resolution;

3. *Underlines* that nothing in the above paragraph requires a State to refuse its own nationals entry into its territory, and that all States shall, in the implementation of the above paragraph, take into account humanitarian considerations, including religious obligations, as well as the necessity to meet the objectives of this resolution and resolution 1737 (2006), including where Article XV of the IAEA Statute is engaged;

4. *Decides* that the measures specified in paragraphs 12, 13, 14 and 15 of resolution 1737 (2006) shall apply also to the persons and entities listed in Annex I to this resolution;

5. *Decides* that Iran shall not supply, sell or transfer directly or indirectly from its territory or by its nationals or using its flag vessels or aircraft any arms or related materiel, and that all States shall prohibit the procurement of such items from Iran by their nationals, or using their flag vessels or aircraft, and whether or not originating in the territory of Iran;

6. *Calls upon* all States to exercise vigilance and restraint in the supply, sale or transfer directly or indirectly from their territories or by their nationals or using their flag vessels or aircraft of any battle tanks, armoured combat vehicles, large calibre artillery systems, combat aircraft, attack helicopters, warships, missiles or missile systems as defined for the purpose of the United Nations Register on Conventional Arms to Iran, and in the provision to Iran of any technical assistance or training, financial assistance, investment, brokering or other services, and the transfer of financial resources or services, related to the supply, sale, transfer, manufacture or use of such items in order to prevent a destabilizing accumulation of arms;

7. *Calls upon* all States and international financial institutions not to enter into new commitments for grants, financial assistance, and concessional loans, to the Government of the Islamic Republic of Iran, except for humanitarian and developmental purposes;

8. *Calls upon* all States to report to the Committee within 60 days of the adoption of this resolution on the steps they have taken with a view to implementing effectively paragraphs 2, 4, 5, 6 and 7 above;

9. *Expresses* the conviction that the suspension set out in paragraph 2 of resolution 1737 (2006) as well as full, verified Iranian compliance with the requirements set out by the IAEA Board of Governors would contribute to a diplomatic, negotiated solution that guarantees Iran's nuclear programme is for exclusively peaceful purposes, *underlines* the willingness of the international community to work positively for such a solution, *encourages* Iran, in conforming to the above provisions, to re-engage with the international community and with the IAEA, and *stresses* that such engagement will be beneficial to Iran;

10. *Welcomes* the continuous affirmation of the commitment of China, France, Germany, the Russian Federation, the United Kingdom and the United States, with the support of the European Union's High Representative, to a negotiated solution to this issue and *encourages* Iran to engage with their June 2006 proposals (S/2006/521), attached in Annex II to this resolution, which were endorsed by the Security Council in resolution 1696 (2006), and *acknowledges* with appreciation that this offer to Iran remains on the table, for a long-term comprehensive agreement which would allow for the development of relations and cooperation with Iran based on mutual respect and the establishment of international confidence in the exclusively peaceful nature of Iran's nuclear programme;

11. *Reiterates* its determination to reinforce the authority of the IAEA, strongly supports the role of the IAEA Board of Governors, *commends and encourages* the Director General of the IAEA and its secretariat for their ongoing professional and impartial efforts to resolve all outstanding issues in Iran within the framework of the IAEA, *underlines* the necessity of the IAEA, which is internationally recognized as having authority for verifying compliance with safeguards agreements, including the non-diversion of nuclear material for non-peaceful purposes, in accordance with its Statute, to continue its work to clarify all outstanding issues relating to Iran's nuclear programme;

12. *Requests* within 60 days a further report from the Director General of the IAEA on whether Iran has established full and sustained suspension of all activities mentioned in resolution 1737 (2006), as well as on the process of Iranian compliance with all the steps required by the IAEA Board and with the other provisions of resolution 1737 (2006) and of this resolution, to the IAEA Board of Governors and in parallel to the Security Council for its consideration;

13. *Affirms* that it shall review Iran's actions in light of the report referred to in paragraph 12 above, to be submitted within 60 days, and:

    a. that it shall suspend the implementation of measures if and for so long as Iran suspends all enrichment-related and reprocessing activities, including research and development, as verified by the IAEA, to allow for negotiations in good faith in order to reach an early and mutually acceptable outcome;

    b. that it shall terminate the measures specified in paragraphs 3, 4, 5, 6, 7 and 12 of resolution 1737 (2006) as well as in paragraphs 2, 4, 5, 6 and 7 above as soon as it determines, following receipt of the report referred to in paragraph 12 above, that Iran has fully complied with its obligations under the relevant resolutions of the Security Council and met the requirements of the IAEA Board of Governors, as confirmed by the IAEA Board;

c. that it shall, in the event that the report in paragraph 12 above shows that Iran has not complied with resolution 1737 (2006) and this resolution, adopt further appropriate measures under Article 41 of Chapter VII of the Charter of the United Nations to persuade Iran to comply with these resolutions and the requirements of the IAEA, and underlines that further decisions will be required should such additional measures be necessary;

14. *Decides* to remain seized of the matter.

Annex I

Entities Involved in Nuclear or Ballistic Missile Activities

1. Ammunition and Metallurgy Industries Group (AMIG) (aka Ammunition Industries Group) (AMIG controls 7th of Tir, which is designated under resolution 1737 (2006) for its role in Iran's centrifuge programme. AMIG is in turn owned and controlled by the Defence Industries Organisation (DIO), which is designated under resolution 1737 (2006))

2. Esfahan Nuclear Fuel Research and Production Centre (NFRPC) and Esfahan Nuclear Technology Centre (ENTC) (Parts of the Atomic Energy Organisation of Iran's (AEOI) Nuclear Fuel Production and Procurement Company, which is involved in enrichment-related activities. AEOI is designated under resolution 1737 (2006))

3. Kavoshyar Company (Subsidiary company of AEOI, which has sought glass fibres, vacuum chamber furnaces and laboratory equipment for Iran's nuclear programme)

4. Parchin Chemical Industries (Branch of DIO, which produces ammunition, explosives, as well as solid propellants for rockets and missiles)

5. Karaj Nuclear Research Centre (Part of AEOI's research division)

6. Novin Energy Company (aka Pars Novin) (Operates within AEOI and has transferred funds on behalf of AEOI to entities associated with Iran's nuclear programme)

7. Cruise Missile Industry Group (aka Naval Defence Missile Industry Group) (Production and development of cruise missiles. Responsible for naval missiles including cruise missiles)

8. Bank Sepah and Bank Sepah International (Bank Sepah provides support for the Aerospace Industries Organisation (AIO) and subordinates, including Shahid Hemmat Industrial Group (SHIG) and Shahid Bagheri Industrial Group (SBIG), both of which were designated under resolution 1737 (2006))

9. Sanam Industrial Group (subordinate to AIO, which has purchased equipment on AIO's behalf for the missile programme)

10. Ya Mahdi Industries Group (subordinate to AIO, which is involved in international purchases of missile equipment)

Iranian Revolutionary Guard Corps Entities

1. Qods Aeronautics Industries (Produces unmanned aerial vehicles (UAVs), parachutes, para-gliders, para-motors, etc. Iranian Revolutionary Guard Corps (IRGC) has boasted of using these products as part of its asymmetric warfare doctrine)

2. Pars Aviation Services Company (Maintains various aircraft including MI-171, used by IRGC Air Force)

3. Sho'a' Aviation (Produces micro-lights which IRGC has claimed it is using as part of its asymmetric warfare doctrine)

Persons Involved in Nuclear or Ballistic Missile Activities

1. Fereidoun Abbasi-Davani (Senior Ministry of Defence and Armed Forces Logistics (MODAFL) scientist with links to the Institute of Applied Physics, working closely with Mohsen Fakhrizadeh-Mahabadi, designated below)

2. Mohsen Fakhrizadeh-Mahabadi (Senior MODAFL scientist and former head of the Physics Research Centre (PHRC). The IAEA have asked to interview him about the activities of the PHRC over the period he was head but Iran has refused)

3. Seyed Jaber Safdari (Manager of the Natanz Enrichment Facilities)

4. Amir Rahimi (Head of Esfahan Nuclear Fuel Research and Production Center, which is part of the AEOI's Nuclear Fuel Production and Procurement Company, which is involved in enrichment-related activities)

5. Mohsen Hojati (Head of Fajr Industrial Group, which is designated under resolution 1737 (2006) for its role in the ballistic missile programme)

6. Mehrdada Akhlaghi Ketabachi (Head of SBIG, which is designated under resolution 1737 (2006) for its role in the ballistic missile programme)

7. Naser Maleki (Head of SHIG, which is designated under resolution 1737 (2006) for its role in Iran's ballistic missile programme. Naser Maleki is also a MODAFL official overseeing work on the Shahab-3 ballistic missile programme. The Shahab-3 is Iran's long range ballistic missile currently in service)

8. Ahmad Derakhshandeh (Chairman and Managing Director of Bank Sepah, which provides support for the AIO and subordinates, including SHIG and SBIG, both of which were designated under resolution 1737 (2006))

Iranian Revolutionary Guard Corps Key Persons

1. Brigadier General Morteza Rezaie (Deputy Commander of IRGC)

2. Vice Admiral Ali Akbar Ahmadian (Chief of IRGC Joint Staff)

3. Brigadier General Mohammad Reza Zahedi (Commander of IRGC Ground Forces)

4. Rear Admiral Morteza Safari (Commander of IRGC Navy)

5. Brigadier General Mohammad Hejazi (Commander of Bassij resistance force)

6. Brigadier General Qasem Soleimani (Commander of Qods force)

7. General Zolqadr (IRGC officer, Deputy Interior Minister for Security Affairs)

Annex II

Author's Note: Annex II was a repetition of the proposal presented as Document 3.

Source: www.un.org.

DOCUMENT 5

Understandings of the Islamic Republic of Iran and the IAEA on the Modalities of Resolution of the Outstanding Issues, Tehran—21 August 2007

Pursuant to the negotiations between H. E. Dr. Larijani, I. R. of Iran's Secretary of Supreme National Security Council and H. E. Dr. El-Baradei, Director General of the IAEA, in Vienna; following the initiative and good will of the Islamic Republic of Iran and the agreement made, a high ranking delegation consisting of the directors of technical, legal and political departments of the IAEA, paid a visit to Tehran from 11 to 12 July 2007 during which "Understandings of The Islamic Republic of Iran and the IAEA on the Modalities of Resolution of the Outstanding Issues, Tehran 12 July 2007" were prepared.

A second meeting took place in Vienna on 24 July 2007 followed by a further meeting in Iran from 20 to 21 August 2007. The Agency's delegation had the opportunity to have meetings with H. E. Dr. Larijani during both visits to Tehran. Following these three consecutive meetings, both Parties reached the following understandings:

I. LATEST DEVELOPMENTS:

Based on the modalities agreed upon on 12 July 2007, the following decisions were made:

1. Present Issues:

A. Enrichment Programme

The Agency and Iran agreed to cooperate in preparing the safeguards approach for the Natanz Fuel Enrichment Plant in accordance with Iran's Comprehensive Safeguards Agreement. The draft text of the safeguards approach paper, and the facility attachment of IRN, were provided to Iran on 23 July 2007. The safeguards approach and the facility attachment were discussed during technical meetings in Iran between the Agency and the AEOI from 6 to 8 August 2007. Further discussions will be held with the aim of finalizing the facility attachment by the end of September 2007.

B. Heavy Water Research Reactor in Arak

Iran agreed with the Agency's request to visit the heavy water research reactor (IR40) site in Arak. A successful visit took place on 30 July 2007.

C. Designation of New Inspectors

On 12 July 2007, Iran accepted the designation of five additional inspectors.

D. Issue of Multiple Entry Visas

On 12 July 2007, Iran agreed to issue one year multiple entry visas for 14 inspectors and staff of the Agency.

2. Past Outstanding Issues:

A. Plutonium Experiments

In order to conclude and close the file of the issue of plutonium (Pu), the Agency provided Iran with the remaining questions on 23 July 2007. During a meeting in Iran between representatives of the Agency and Iran, Iran provided clarifications to the Agency that helped to explain the remaining questions. In addition, on 7 August 2007, Iran sent a letter to the Agency providing additional clarifications to some of the questions. On 20 August 2007 the Agency stated that earlier statements made by Iran are consistent with the Agency's findings, and thus this matter is resolved. This will be communicated officially by the Agency to Iran through a letter.

B. Issue of P1-P2:

Based on agreed modalities of 12 July 2007, Iran and the Agency agreed the following procedural steps to resolve the P1-P2 issue. The proposed timeline assumes that the Agency announces the closure of the Pu-experiments outstanding issue by 31 August 2007, and its subsequent reporting in the Director General's report to the September 2007 Board of Governors.

The Agency will provide all remaining questions on this issue by 31 August 2007. Iran and the Agency will have discussions in Iran on 24–25 September 2007 to clarify the questions provided. This will be followed up by a further meeting in mid-October 2007 to further clarify the written answers provided. The Agency's target date for the closure of this issue is November 2007.

C. Source of Contamination

Based on the agreed modalities on 12 July 2007 and given the Agency's findings which tend, on balance, to support Iran's statement about the foreign origin of the observed HEU contamination, the only remaining outstanding issue on contamination is the contamination found at a Technical University in Tehran.

Iran and the Agency agreed on the following procedural steps to address this issue, starting once the P1-P2 issue is concluded and the file is closed.

The Agency will again provide Iran with the remaining questions regarding the contamination found at a Technical University in Tehran by 15 September 2007. After 2 weeks of the closure of the P1-P2 issue, Iran and the Agency will have discussions in Iran on this issue.

D. U Metal Document

Upon the request of the Agency, Iran agreed to cooperate with the Agency in facilitating the comparison of the relevant sections of the document. Iran is presently reviewing the proposals already made during the first meeting on 12 July 2007. After taking this step by Iran, the Agency undertakes to close this issue.

II. MODALITIES OF RESOLUTION OF OTHER OUTSTANDING ISSUES

A. Po210

Based on agreed modalities of 12 July 2007, Iran agreed to deal with this issue, once all the above mentioned issues are concluded and their files are closed. Iran and the Agency agreed upon the following procedural steps: regarding this issue, the Agency will provide Iran in writing with all its remaining questions by 15 September 2007.

After 2 weeks from conclusion and closure of the issues of the source of contamination and U-metal, reflected in the Director General's report to the Board of Governors, Iran and the Agency will have discussions in Iran where Iran will provide explanations on the Po210.

B. Ghachine Mine

Based on agreed modalities of 12 July 2007, Iran agreed to deal with this issue, once the issue of Po210 is concluded and its file is closed. Iran and the Agency agreed upon the following procedural steps: regarding this issue, the Agency will provide Iran in writing with all its remaining questions by 15 September 2007.

After 2 weeks from conclusion and closure of the issue of Po210, reflected in the Director General's report to the Board of Governors, Iran and the Agency will have discussions in Iran where Iran will provide explanations to the Agency about Ghachine Mine.

III. ALLEGED STUDIES

Iran reiterated that it considers the following alleged studies as politically motivated and baseless allegations. The Agency will however provide Iran with access to the documentation it has in its possession regarding: the Green Salt Project, the high explosive testing and the missile re-entry vehicle.

As a sign of good will and cooperation with the Agency, upon receiving all related documents, Iran will review and inform the Agency of its assessment.

IV. GENERAL UNDERSTANDINGS

1. These modalities cover all remaining issues and the Agency confirmed that there are no other remaining issues and ambiguities regarding Iran's past nuclear program and activities.

2. The Agency agreed to provide Iran with all remaining questions according to the above work plan. This means that after receiving the questions, no other questions are left. Iran will provide the Agency with the required clarifications and information.

3. The Agency's delegation is of the view that the agreement on the above issues shall further promote the efficiency of the implementation of safeguards in Iran and its ability to conclude the exclusive peaceful nature of the Iran's nuclear activities.

4. The Agency has been able to verify the non-diversion of the declared nuclear materials at the enrichment facilities in Iran and has therefore concluded that it remains in peaceful use.

5. The Agency and Iran agreed that after the implementation of the above work plan and the agreed modalities for resolving the outstanding issues, the implementation of safeguards in Iran will be conducted in a routine manner.

Source: www.iaea.org

DOCUMENT 6

Resolution 1803 (2008)

ADOPTED BY THE SECURITY COUNCIL AT ITS 5848TH MEETING, ON 3 MARCH 2008

The Security Council,

Recalling the Statement of its President, S/PRST/2006/15, of 29 March 2006, and its resolution 1696 (2006) of 31 July 2006, its resolution 1737 (2006) of 23 December 2006 and its resolution 1747 (2007) of 24 March 2007, and *reaffirming* their provisions,

Reaffirming its commitment to the Treaty on the Non-Proliferation of Nuclear Weapons, the need for all States Party to that Treaty to comply fully with all their obligations, and recalling the right of States Party, in conformity with Articles I and II of that Treaty, to develop research, production and use of nuclear energy for peaceful purposes without discrimination,

Recalling the resolution of the IAEA Board of Governors (GOV/2006/14), which states that a solution to the Iranian nuclear issue would contribute to global non-proliferation efforts and to realizing the objective of a Middle East free of weapons of mass destruction, including their means of delivery,

Noting with serious concern that, as confirmed by the reports of 23 May 2007 (GOV/2007/22), 30 August 2007 (GOV/2007/48), 15 November 2007 (GOV/2007/58) and 22 February 2008 (GOV/2008/4) of the Director General of the International Atomic Energy Agency (IAEA), Iran has not established full and sustained suspension of all enrichment related and reprocessing activities and heavy water-related projects as set out in resolution 1696 (2006), 1737 (2006), and 1747 (2007), nor resumed its cooperation with the IAEA under the Additional Protocol, nor taken the other steps required by the IAEA Board of Governors, nor complied with the provisions of Security Council resolution 1696 (2006), 1737 (2006) and 1747 (2007) and which are essential to build confidence, and *deploring* Iran's refusal to take these steps,

Noting with concern that Iran has taken issue with the IAEA's right to verify design information which had been provided by Iran pursuant to the modified Code 3.1, *emphasizing* that in accordance with Article 39 of Iran's Safeguards Agreement Code 3.1 cannot be modified nor suspended unilaterally and that the Agency's right to verify design information provided to it is a continuing right, which is not dependent on the stage of construction of, or the presence of nuclear material at, a facility,

Reiterating its determination to reinforce the authority of the IAEA, strongly supporting the role of the IAEA Board of Governors, *commending* the IAEA for its efforts to resolve outstanding issues relating to Iran's nuclear programme in the work plan between the Secretariat of the IAEA and Iran (GOV/2007/48, Attachment), *welcoming* the progress in implementation of this work plan as reflected in the IAEA Director General's reports of 15 November 2007 (GOV/2007/58) and 22 February 2008 (GOV/2008/4), *underlining* the importance of Iran producing tangible results rapidly and effectively by completing implementation of this work plan including by providing answers to all the questions the IAEA asks so that the Agency, through the implementation of the required transparency measures, can assess the completeness and correctness of Iran's declaration,

Expressing the conviction that the suspension set out in paragraph 2 of resolution 1737 (2006) as well as full, verified Iranian compliance with the requirements set out by the IAEA Board of Governors would contribute to a diplomatic, negotiated solution, that guarantees Iran's nuclear programme is for exclusively peaceful purposes,

Stressing that China, France, Germany, the Russian Federation, the United Kingdom and the United States are willing to take further concrete measures on exploring an overall strategy of resolving the Iranian nuclear issue through negotiation on the basis of their June 2006 proposals (S/2006/521), and *noting* the confirmation by these countries that once the confidence of the international community in the exclusively peaceful nature of Iran's nuclear programme is restored, it will be treated in the same manner as that of any Non-Nuclear Weapon State party to the Treaty on the Non-Proliferation of Nuclear Weapons,

Having regard to States' rights and obligations relating to international trade,

Welcoming the guidance issued by the Financial Actions Task Force (FATF) to assist States in implementing their financial obligations under resolution 1737 (2006),

Determined to give effect to its decisions by adopting appropriate measures to persuade Iran to comply with resolution 1696 (2006), resolution 1737 (2006), resolution 1747 (2007) and with the requirements of the IAEA, and also to constrain Iran's development of sensitive technologies in support of its nuclear and missile programmes, until such time as the Security Council determines that the objectives of these resolutions have been met,

Concerned by the proliferation risks presented by the Iranian nuclear programme and, in this context, by Iran's continuing failure to meet the requirements of the IAEA Board of Governors and to comply with the provisions of Security Council resolutions 1696 (2006), 1737 (2006) and 1747 (2007), *mindful* of its primary responsibility under the Charter of the United Nations for the maintenance of international peace and security,

Acting under Article 41 of Chapter VII of the Charter of the United Nations,

1. *Reaffirms* that Iran shall without further delay take the steps required by the IAEA Board of Governors in its resolution GOV/2006/14, which are essential to build confidence in the exclusively peaceful purpose of its nuclear programme and to resolve outstanding questions, and, in this context, *affirms* its decision that Iran shall without delay take the steps required in paragraph 2 of resolution 1737 (2006), and *underlines* that the IAEA has sought confirmation that Iran will apply Code 3.1 modified;

2. *Welcomes* the agreement between Iran and the IAEA to resolve all outstanding issues concerning Iran's nuclear programme and progress made in this regard as set out in the

Director General's report of 22 February 2008 (GOV/2008/4), *encourages* the IAEA to continue its work to clarify all outstanding issues, *stresses* that this would help to re-establish international confidence in the exclusively peaceful nature of Iran's nuclear pro-gramme, and *supports* the IAEA in strengthening its safeguards on Iran's nuclear activities in accordance with the Safeguards Agreement between Iran and the IAEA;

3. *Calls upon* all States to exercise vigilance and restraint regarding the entry into or transit through their territories of individuals who are engaged in, directly associated with or providing support for Iran's proliferation sensitive nuclear activities or for the develop-ment of nuclear weapon delivery systems, and *decides* in this regard that all States shall notify the Committee established pursuant to paragraph 18 of resolution 1737 (2006) (herein "the Committee") of the entry into or transit through their territories of the per-sons designated in the Annex to resolution 1737 (2006), Annex I to resolution 1747 (2007) or Annex I to this resolution, as well as of additional persons designated by the Security Council or the Committee as being engaged in, directly associated with or pro-viding support for Iran's proliferation sensitive nuclear activities or for the development of nuclear weapon delivery systems, including through the involvement in procurement of the prohibited items, goods, equipment, materials and technology specified by and under the measures in paragraphs 3 and 4 of resolution 1737 (2006), except where such entry or transit is for activities directly related to the items in subparagraphs 3 (b) (i) and (ii) of resolution 1737 (2006);

4. *Underlines* that nothing in paragraph 3 above requires a State to refuse its own nationals entry into its territory, and that all States shall, in the implementation of the above paragraph, take into account humanitarian considerations, including religious obliga-tions, as well as the necessity to meet the objectives of this resolution, resolution 1737 (2006) and resolution 1747 (2007), including where Article XV of the IAEA Statute is engaged;

5. *Decides* that all States shall take the necessary measures to prevent the entry into or transit through their territories of individuals designated in Annex II to this resolution as well as of additional persons designated by the Security Council or the Committee as being engaged in, directly associated with or providing support for Iran's proliferation sensitive nuclear activities or for the development of nuclear weapon delivery systems, including through the involvement in procurement of the prohibited items, goods, equipment, materials and technology specified by and under the measures in paragraphs 3 and 4 of resolution 1737 (2006), except where such entry or transit is for activities directly related to the items in subparagraphs 3 (b) (i) and (ii) of resolution 1737 (2006) and provided that nothing in this paragraph shall oblige a State to refuse its own nationals entry into its territory;

6. *Decides* that the measures imposed by paragraph 5 above shall not apply where the Committee determines on a case-by-case basis that such travel is justified on the grounds of humanitarian need, including religious obligations, or where the Committee concludes that an exemption would otherwise further the objectives of the present resolution;

7. *Decides* that the measures specified in paragraphs 12, 13, 14 and 15 of resolution 1737 (2006) shall apply also to the persons and entities listed in Annexes I and III to this res-olution, and any persons or entities acting on their behalf or at their direction, and to entities owned or controlled by them and to persons and entities determined by the Council or the Committee to have assisted designated persons or entities in evading

sanctions of, or in violating the provisions of, this resolution, resolution 1737 (2006) or resolution 1747 (2007);

8. *Decides* that all States shall take the necessary measures to prevent the supply, sale or transfer directly or indirectly from their territories or by their nationals or using their flag vessels or aircraft to, or for use in or benefit of, Iran, and whether or not originating in their territories, of:

   a. all items, materials, equipment, goods and technology set out in INFCIRC/254/Rev.7/ Part 2 of document S/2006/814, except the supply, sale or transfer, in accordance with the requirements of paragraph 5 of resolution 1737 (2006), of items, materials, equipment, goods and technology set out in sections 1 and 2 of the Annex to that document, and sections 3 to 6 as notified in advance to the Committee, only when for exclusive use in light water reactors, and where such supply, sale or transfer is necessary for technical cooperation provided to Iran by the IAEA or under its auspices as provided for in paragraph 16 of resolution 1737 (2006);

   b. all items, materials, equipment, goods and technology set out in 19.A.3 of Category II of document S/2006/815;

9. *Calls upon* all States to exercise vigilance in entering into new commitments for public provided financial support for trade with Iran, including the granting of export credits, guarantees or insurance, to their nationals or entities involved in such trade, in order to avoid such financial support contributing to the proliferation sensitive nuclear activities, or to the development of nuclear weapon delivery systems, as referred to in resolution 1737 (2006);

10. *Calls upon* all States to exercise vigilance over the activities of financial institutions in their territories with all banks domiciled in Iran, in particular with Bank Melli and Bank Saderat, and their branches and subsidiaries abroad, in order to avoid such activities contributing to the proliferation sensitive nuclear activities, or to the development of nuclear weapon delivery systems, as referred to in resolution 1737 (2006);

11. *Calls upon* all States, in accordance with their national legal authorities and legislation and consistent with international law, in particular the law of the sea and relevant international civil aviation agreements, to inspect the cargoes to and from Iran, of aircraft and vessels, at their airports and seaports, owned or operated by Iran Air Cargo and Islamic Republic of Iran Shipping Line, provided there are reasonable grounds to believe that the aircraft or vessel is transporting goods prohibited under this resolution or resolution 1737 (2006) or resolution 1747 (2007);

12. *Requires* all States, in cases when inspection mentioned in the paragraph above is undertaken, to submit to the Security Council within five working days a written report on the inspection containing, in particular, explanation of the grounds for the inspection, as well as information on its time, place, circumstances, results and other relevant details;

13. *Calls upon* all States to report to the Committee within 60 days of the adoption of this resolution on the steps they have taken with a view to implementing effectively paragraphs 3, 5, 7, 8, 9, 10 and 11 above;

14. *Decides* that the mandate of the Committee as set out in paragraph 18 of resolution 1737 (2006) shall also apply to the measures imposed in resolution 1747 (2007) and this resolution;

15. *Stresses* the willingness of China, France, Germany, the Russian Federation, the United Kingdom and the United States to further enhance diplomatic efforts to promote resumption of dialogue, and consultations on the basis of their offer to Iran, with a view to seeking a comprehensive, long-term and proper solution of this issue which would allow for the development of all-round relations and wider cooperation with Iran based on mutual respect and the establishment of international confidence in the exclusively peaceful nature of Iran's nuclear programme, and inter alia, starting direct talks and negotiation with Iran as long as Iran suspends all enrichment-related and reprocessing activities, including research and development, as verified by the IAEA;

16. *Encourages* the European Union High Representative for the Common Foreign and Security Policy to continue communication with Iran in support of political and diplomatic efforts to find a negotiated solution including relevant proposals by China, France, Germany, the Russian Federation, the United Kingdom and the United States with a view to create necessary conditions for resuming talks;

17. *Emphasizes* the importance of all States, including Iran, taking the necessary measures to ensure that no claim shall lie at the instance of the Government of Iran, or of any person or entity in Iran, or of persons or entities designated pursuant to resolution 1737 (2006) and related resolutions, or any person claiming through or for the benefit of any such person or entity, in connection with any contract or other transaction where its performance was prevented by reason of the measures imposed by the present resolution, resolution 1737 (2006) or resolution 1747 (2007);

18. *Requests* within 90 days a further report from the Director General of the IAEA on whether Iran has established full and sustained suspension of all activities mentioned in resolution 1737 (2006), as well as on the process of Iranian compliance with all the steps required by the IAEA Board and with the other provisions of resolution 1737 (2006), resolution 1747 (2007) and of this resolution, to the IAEA Board of Governors and in parallel to the Security Council for its consideration;

19. *Reaffirms* that it shall review Iran's actions in light of the report referred to in the paragraph above, and:

   a. that it shall suspend the implementation of measures if and for so long as Iran suspends all enrichment-related and reprocessing activities, including research and development, as verified by the IAEA, to allow for negotiations in good faith in order to reach an early and mutually acceptable outcome;

   b. that it shall terminate the measures specified in paragraphs 3, 4, 5, 6, 7 and 12 of resolution 1737 (2006), as well as in paragraphs 2, 4, 5, 6 and 7 of resolution 1747 (2007), and in paragraphs 3, 5, 7, 8, 9, 10 and 11 above, as soon as it determines, following receipt of the report referred to in the paragraph above, that Iran has fully complied with its obligations under the relevant resolutions of the Security Council and met the requirements of the IAEA Board of Governors, as confirmed by the IAEA Board;

   c. that it shall, in the event that the report shows that Iran has not complied with resolution 1696 (2006), resolution 1737 (2006), resolution 1747 (2007) and this resolution, adopt further appropriate measures under Article 41 of Chapter VII of the Charter of the United Nations to persuade Iran to comply with these resolutions and the requirements of the IAEA, and underlines that further decisions will be required should such additional measures be necessary;

20. *Decides* to remain seized of the matter.

Annex I

1. Amir Moayyed Alai (involved in managing the assembly and engineering of centrifuges)
2. Mohammad Fedai Ashiani (involved in the production of ammonium uranyl carbonate and management of the Natanz enrichment complex)
3. Abbas Rezaee Ashtiani (a senior official at the AEOI Office of Exploration and Mining Affairs)
4. Haleh Bakhtiar (involved in the production of magnesium at a concentration of 99.9%)
5. Morteza Behzad (involved in making centrifuge components)
6. Dr. Mohammad Eslami (Head of Defence Industries Training and Research Institute)
7. Seyyed Hussein Hosseini (AEOI official involved in the heavy water research reactor project at Arak)
8. M. Javad Karimi Sabet (Head of Novin Energy Company, which is designated under resolution 1747 (2007))
9. Hamid-Reza Mohajerani (involved in production management at the Uranium Conversion Facility (UCF) at Esfahan)
10. Brigadier-General Mohammad Reza Naqdi (former Deputy Chief of Armed Forces General Staff for Logistics and Industrial Research/Head of State Anti-Smuggling Headquarters, engaged in efforts to get round the sanctions imposed by resolutions 1737 (2006) and 1747 (2007))
11. Houshang Nobari (involved in the management of the Natanz enrichment complex)
12. Abbas Rashidi (involved in enrichment work at Natanz)
13. Ghasem Soleymani (Director of Uranium Mining Operations at the Saghand Uranium Mine)

Annex II

A.   Individuals Listed in Resolution 1737 (2006)

1. Mohammad Qannadi, AEOI Vice President for Research & Development
2. Dawood Agha-Jani, Head of the PFEP (Natanz)
3. Behman Asgarpour, Operational Manager (Arak)

B.   Individuals Listed in Resolution 1747 (2007)

1. Seyed Jaber Safdari (Manager of the Natanz Enrichment Facilities)
2. Amir Rahimi (Head of Esfahan Nuclear Fuel Research and Production Center, which is part of the AEOI's Nuclear Fuel Production and Procurement Company, which is involved in enrichment-related activities)

Annex III

1. Abzar Boresh Kaveh Co. (BK Co.) (involved in the production of centrifuge components)

2. Barzagani Tejarat Tavanmad Saccal companies (subsidiary of Saccal System companies) (this company tried to purchase sensitive goods for an entity listed in resolution 1737 (2006))

3. Electro Sanam Company (E. S. Co./E. X. Co.) (AIO front-company, involved in the ballistic missile programme)

4. Ettehad Technical Group (AIO front-company, involved in the ballistic missile programme)

5. Industrial Factories of Precision (IFP) Machinery (aka Instrumentation Factories Plant) (used by AIO for some acquisition attempts)

6. Jabber Ibn Hayan (AEOI laboratory involved in fuel-cycle activities)

7. Joza Industrial Co. (AIO front-company, involved in the ballistic missile programme)

8. Khorasan Metallurgy Industries (subsidiary of the Ammunition Industries Group (AMIG) which depends on DIO. Involved in the production of centrifuges components)

9. Niru Battery Manufacturing Company (subsidiary of the DIO. Its role is to manufacture power units for the Iranian military including missile systems)

10. Pishgam (Pioneer) Energy Industries (has participated in construction of the Uranium Conversion Facility at Esfahan)

11. Safety Equipment Procurement (SEP) (AIO front-company, involved in the ballistic missile programme)

12. TAMAS Company (involved in enrichment-related activities. TAMAS is the overarching body, under which four subsidiaries have been established, including one for uranium extraction to concentration and another in charge of uranium processing, enrichment and waste)

Source: www.un.org.

Glossary

Al-Hizb al-Dawa al-Islamiya — Literally "the Party of the Call to Islam," often referred to as *al-Dawa,* or "the Call." An Iraqi Shia party funded and trained by Iran to resist Saddam Hussein's government and compete for power in a post-Saddam Iraq.

Al-Qaeda — Literally "the Base." A fundamentalist Sunni network dedicated to ejecting Western and Zionist forces from the land of Islam and to establishing an Islamic Empire.

Ayatollah — Literally "the sign of God." One who is popularly recognized as a high-ranking cleric in Shia Islam because of a distinguished record of scholarship and fund-raising.

Baath Party — The Arab Socialist Renaissance Party, which ruled Iraq from 1968 until 2003.

Ballistic missile — A missile that uses rocket power in its first stage but that continues on to its target without it, and whose trajectory is influenced by gravity, air, wind, and other variables.

Basij — The Mobilization Resistance Force. An Iranian volunteer paramilitary force trained by the Islamic Revolutionary Guard Corps.

Hamas — An Arabic acronym for "the Islamic Resistance Movement." A large Palestinian Arab Sunni Islamist organization that emerged in the late 1980s, resorted to terrorism against Israelis, provided welfare to Palestinians in the West Bank and the Gaza Strip, and won control of the Palestinian legislature in early 2006.

Hezbollah — Literally "the Party of God." The Lebanese Shia party that emerged in 1982, mounted resistance to Israel, provided social welfare to the disadvantaged Lebanese Shia population, and entered parliament in 1992.

Hojjatoleslam — Literally "proof of God." A mid-level Shia cleric.

Imam — A ruler and teacher for the Shia Muslims who is unsurpassed by others because he is a descendent of and has the spiritual qualities and understanding of the Prophet Mohammad. The last of these, the Twelfth Imam, or the Mahdi, went into hiding in AD 939 and is expected to return to bring a reign of justice before the end of the world.

Islam — Literally "submission." A monotheistic religion, worshipping the God of the Jewish and Christian faiths, Allah.

Littoral states — States situated on the shore of a sea or other body of water, such as the Persian Gulf.

Majlis — Iran's parliament.

Mojahedin-e Khalq (MEK or MKO) — Literally "Fighters of the People." A movement mixing Islamist and Marxist thought and resisting first the Shah and then the Islamic Republic of Iran. Also known as the National Council of Resistance of Iran.

Mujahideen — A network of Afghan fighters, joined by other Muslims from Saudi Arabia and other countries, resisting Soviet occupation from 1979 to 1989.

Mujtahed — A lower-ranking Shia cleric who is qualified to interpret the faith for the flock.

Northern Alliance — A coalition of Afghan tribes and parties, largely composed of ethnic Afghan Tajiks and of Afghan Shia forces from the north, opposed to the rule of the Taliban after 1995.

Palestinian Islamic Jihad (PIJ) — Literally "Palestinian Islamic Holy War." A small Palestinian Arab Sunni Islamist organization that rejects any peace with Israel and resorts to terror against Israelis.

Pan-Arabism — An ideology that holds that all Arab states should unite or collaborate closely.

Pasdaran — The Islamic Revolutionary Guard Corps. The ideological armed forces of the Islamic Republic of Iran, a parallel organization to the regular armed forces. Its Quds Force, or Jerusalem Force, is focused on foreign operations.

Preemptive war — An attack against an enemy when there is an imminent threat of an attack by that enemy.

Preventive war — An attack against an enemy when there is a growing future threat.

Propaganda — A political message that uses the deliberate commission of falsehoods and/or the deliberate omission of truths in order to mobilize the support of a population for a policy.

SAVAK — An acronym for National Organization for Information and Security, Shah Mohammad Reza Pahlavi's domestic intelligence/secret police organization.

Shah — King.

Shia Islam — The sect of Islam that believes legitimate religious authority is vested only in the descendents of the Prophet Mohammad.

Sunni Islam — The sect of Islam that has accepted the authority of leaders, such as caliphs and sultans and kings, if they are protecting the stability and order of the Islamic community.

Supreme Islamic Iraq Council (SIIC) — Called the Supreme Council for the Islamic Revolution in Iraq, or SCIRI, until 2006, is an Iraqi organization trained and funded by Iran to resist the Saddam Hussein regime and to compete for power in the post-Saddam Iraq. Its Badr Brigade, a militia, has members inside and outside Iraq's official security forces.

Taliban — Literally "the students." A fundamentalist Sunni movement that ruled Afghanistan from 1995 to 2001.

Terrorism — The deliberate killing of innocent civilians in order to instill fear in a population and bring about a change in its government's policy.

Ulama — The Islamic religious clergy.

Uranium conversion — The conversion of raw uranium into uranium hexafluoride gas.

Uranium enrichment — The enrichment of uranium hexafluoride gas to the low level of 3–5 percent uranium-235 which is necessary to fuel a nuclear reactor and produce power, or to the high level of 90 percent uranium-235 which is necessary in a nuclear bomb.

Uranium reprocessing — The chemical treatment (rather than disposal) of the spent fuel, or "waste," after enriched uranium is used in a nuclear reactor to produce power, in order to extract separated uranium/reprocessed uranium for reuse, or "recycling," in the reactor to produce more power.

Velayat-e Faqih — Literally "rule by the jurisprudent." The theory that Iran must be governed by a supreme religious authority, the Supreme Leader, according to the principles of Islam.

Zionism — An ideology that advocates a Jewish right to an independent state, Israel, in the ancient home of the Jewish people, also called Palestine.

Selected Bibliography

Abdullah, Muhammad Morsy. *The United Arab Emirates: A Modern History.* 2nd ed. London: Hurtwood Press, Ltd., 1994.

Algar, Hamid, trans. and annotator. *Islam and Revolution: Writings and Declarations of Imam Khomeini.* Berkeley: Mizan Press, 1981.

Aras, Bulent, and Fatih Ozbay. "Dances with Wolves: Russia, Iran and the Nuclear Issue." *Middle East Policy* 13, no. 3 (2006).

Bakhash, Shaul. *The Reign of the Ayatollahs.* New York: Basic Books, 1990.

Balfour-Paul, Glen. *The End of Empire in the Middle East: Britain's Relinquishment of Power in Her Last Three Arab Dependencies.* Cambridge, UK: Cambridge University Press, 1991.

Beehner, Lionel. "Russian-Iranian Arms Trade." *Council on Foreign Relations,* January 1, 2006 at www.cfr.org.

Beeman, William. *The "Great Satan" vs. "The Mad Mullahs": How the United States and Iran Demonize Each Other.* Westport: Greenwood Publishing Group, 2006.

Bill, James. *The Eagle and the Lion: The Tragedy of American-Iranian Relations.* New Haven and London: Yale University Press, 1988.

Brinkley, Joel, and Stephen Engelberg, eds. *Report of the Congressional Committees Investigating the Iran-Contra Affair, with the Minority Views.* New York: Random House, 1988.

Brzezinski, Zbigniew, and Robert Gates. "Iran: Time for a New Approach." *Council on Foreign Relations,* 2004.

Brzezinski, Zbigniew, Brent Scowcroft, and Richard Murphy. "Differentiated Containment." *Foreign Affairs* 76, no. 3 (1977).

Buchta, Wilfred. *Who Rules Iran? The Structure of Power in the Islamic Republic.* Washington DC: The Washington Institute for Near East Policy and the Konrad Adenauer Stiftung, 2000.

Byman, Daniel. *Deadly Connections: States that Sponsor Terrorism.* Cambridge, UK: Cambridge University Press, 2005.

Carter, Ashton B., and William J. Perry. *Plan B for Iran: What If Nuclear Diplomacy Fails?* A Report Based on a Workshop Hosted by the Preventive Defense Program of Harvard and Stanford Universities, May 22, 2006.

Chubin, Shahram, and Sepehr Zabih. *The Foreign Relations of Iran.* Berkeley and Los Angeles: University of California Press, 1974.

————. *Iran's National Security Policy: Capabilities, Intentions and Impact.* Washington DC: The Carnegie Endowment for International Peace, 1994.

————. *Iran's Nuclear Ambitions.* Washington DC: The Carnegie Endowment for International Peace, 2006.

Clarke, Richard A. *Against All Enemies: Inside America's War on Terror.* New York: Free Press, 2004.

Cordesman, Anthony H., and Abraham R. Wagner. *Iran's Military Forces in Transition: Conventional Threats and Weapons.* Westport: Praeger, 1999.

————. *The Lessons of Modern War, Volume II: The Iran-Iraq War.* Boulder: Westview Press, 1990.

Crowe, Admiral William J., with David Charnoff. *In the Line of Fire.* New York: Simon and Shuster, 1993.

Ehteshami, Anoushiravan. *After Khomeini: The Iranian Second Republic.* London: Routledge, 1995.

Feldman, Noah. "Islam, Terror and the Second Nuclear Age." *New York Times Magazine,* October 20, 2006.

Fisher, W.B., ed. *The Cambridge History of Iran.* Cambridge: Cambridge University Press, 1968.

Fitzpatrick, Mark. "Assessing Iran's Nuclear Programme." *Survival* 48, no. 3 (2006).

Fuller, Graham. *The "Center of the Universe": The Geopolitics of Iran.* Boulder: Westview Press, 1991.

Gardiner, Col. Sam. "The End of the Summer of Diplomacy—Assessing U.S. Military Options on Iran." *A Century Foundation Report,* 2006 at www.tcf.org.

Gasiorowski, Mark, and Malcolm Byrne, eds. *Mohammad Mossadeq and the 1953 Coup in Iran.* Syracuse: Syracuse University Press, 2004.

Graham, Robert. *Iran: The Illusion of Power.* New York: St. Martin's Press, 1979.

Hersh, Seymour M. "The Coming Wars." *New Yorker,* January 24 and 31, 2005.

————. "The Iran Plans." *New Yorker,* April 17, 2006.

————. "The Next Act." *New Yorker,* November 20, 2006.

————. "The Redirection." *New Yorker,* March 2007.

————. "Shifting Targets: The Administration's Plan for Iran," *New Yorker,* October 8, 2007.

————. "Watching Israel: Washington's Interest in Israel's War." *New Yorker,* August 21, 2006.

Hunter, Shireen. *Iran and the World: Continuity in a Revolutionary Decade.* Bloomington: Indiana University Press, 1990.

Huntington, Samuel. *Political Order in Changing Societies.* New Haven and London: Yale University Press, 1968.

The Iraq Study Group Report. New York: Vintage Books, 2006.

Kaplan, Lawrence F. "Iran Syria Operations Group." *New Republic,* April 10, 2006.

Katz, Mark. "Putin, Ahmadinejad and the Iranian Nuclear Crisis." *Middle East Policy* 13, no. 4 (2006).

Kechichian, Joseph. "Can Conservative Arab Gulf Monarchies Endure a Fourth War in the Persian Gulf?" *Middle East Journal* 61, no. 2 (2007).

Keddie, Nikki R. *Modern Iran: Roots and Results of Revolution.* New Haven and London: Yale University Press, 2003.

————, ed. *Scholars, Saints and Sufis: Muslim Religious Institutions since 1500.* Berkeley, Los Angeles, and London: University of California Press, 1972.

Keddie, Nikki R., and Mark J. Gasiorowski, eds. *Neither East Nor West: Iran, the Soviet Union, and the United States.* New Haven and London: Yale University Press, 1990.

Kelly, J.B. *Arabia, the Gulf and the West.* London: George Weidenfeld and Nicolson Ltd., 1980.

Kemp, Geoffrey. *Iran's Bomb: American and Iranian Perspectives.* Washington DC: The Nixon Center, 2004.

Kerr, Paul. "Divided from Within." *Bulletin of the Atomic Scientist* 62, no. 6 (2006).

————. "The Iran Nuclear Crisis: A Chronology." *Arms Control Association* at www.armscontrol.org.

Lake, Anthony. "Confronting Backlash States." *Foreign Affairs,* March/April, 1994.

Lenczowski, George. *American Presidents and the Middle East.* Durham and London: Duke University Press, 1990.

————, ed. *Iran Under the Pahlavis.* Stanford: Stanford University Press, 1978.

————. *The Middle East in World Affairs.* 4th ed. Ithaca and London: Cornell University Press, 1980.

————. *Political Elites in the Middle East.* Washington DC: American Enterprise Institute for Public Policy Research, 1975.

Leverett, Flynt. "Dealing with Tehran: Assessing U.S. Diplomatic Options Toward Iran." *A Century Foundation Report,* 2006 at www.tcf.org.

Long, David E., and Christian Koch, eds. *Gulf Security in the Twenty-First Century.* Abu Dhabi: Emirates Center for Strategic Studies and Research, 1997.

Marshall, Joshua Michael, Laura Rozen, and Paul Glastris. "Iran-Contra II: Fresh Scrutiny on a Rogue Pentagon Operation." *Washington Monthly,* September 2004.

Mattair, Thomas R. "Containment or Collision?" *Middle East Insight* 11, no. 5 (1995).

————. "Exiting Iraq: Competing Strategies." *Middle East Policy* 13, no. 1 (2006).

————. "Horizons for Cooperation in the [Persian] Gulf: The View from Washington." *Iranian Journal of International Affairs* 7, no. 3 (1995).

————. "Interview with U.N. Ambassador Kamal Kharazi of Iran." *Middle East Policy* 3, no. 3 (1994).

————. "Mutual Threat Perceptions in the Arab/Persian Gulf: GCC Perceptions." *Middle East Policy* 14, no. 2 (2007).

————. *The Three Occupied UAE Islands: The Tunbs and Abu Musa.* Abu Dhabi: The Emirates Center for Strategic Studies and Research, 2005.

Menashri, David. *Revolution at a Crossroads: Iran's Domestic Politics and Regional Ambitions.* Washington DC: The Washington Institute for Near East Policy, 1997.

Nader, George. "Interview with President Ali Akbar Hashemi Rafsanjani." *Middle East Insight* 11, no. 5 (1995).

Nasr, Vali. *The Shia Revival: How Conflicts within Islam Will Shape the Future.* New York: W.W. Norton and Company, 2007.

Navias, Martin S., and E.R. Hooton. *Tanker Wars: The Assault on Merchant Shipping During the Iran-Iraq Crisis, 1980–1988.* London: I.B. Tauris and Company Ltd., 1996.

The 9/11 Commission Report: Final Report of the National Commission on Terrorist Attacks on the United States. Authorized Edition. New York: W.W. Norton and Company, 2004.

Noyes, James. *The Clouded Lens: Persian Gulf Security and U.S. Policy.* 2nd ed. Stanford: Hoover Institution Press, 1982.

O'Sullivan, Meghan L. *Shrewd Sanctions: Statecraft and State Sponsors of Terrorism.* Washington DC: Brookings Institution Press, 2003.

Pahlavi, Shah Mohammad Reza. *Answer to History.* New York: Stein and Day, 1980.

———. *Mission for My Country.* New York: McGraw-Hill, 1961.

Pape, Robert A. *Dying to Win: The Strategic Logic of Suicide Terrorism.* New York: Random House, 2005.

Parsi, Trita. *Treacherous Alliance: The Secret Dealings of Israel, Iran, and the United States.* New Haven and London: Yale University Press, 2007.

Perry, William J. "Gulf Security and U.S. Policy." *Middle East Policy* 3, no. 4 (1995).

Podhoretz, Norman. "The Case for Bombing Iran." *Commentary,* June 2007.

Pollack, Kenneth M. *The Persian Puzzle: The Conflict Between Iran and America.* New York: Random House, 2004.

Porter, Gareth. "Burnt Offering." *The American Prospect,* May 21, 2006.

———. "Cheney-Led 'Cabal' Blocked 2003 Nuclear Talks with Iran." *Inter Press Service News Agency,* May 28, 2006.

———. "How Neoconservatives Sabotaged Iran's Help on al-Qaeda." *Inter Press Service News Agency,* February 23, 2006.

———. "The Iran Attack That Wasn't." *American Prospect,* August 2, 2007.

———. "US 'Surges,' Soldiers Die, Blame Iran." *Asia Times,* August 16, 2007.

Posen, Barry. "We Can Live with a Nuclear Iran." *New York Times,* February 27, 2006.

Quandt, William B. *Peace Process: American Diplomacy and the Arab-Israeli Conflict since 1967.* 3rd ed. Washington DC and Berkeley: Brookings Institution Press and University of California Press, 2005.

Ramazani, Ruhollah K. *The Foreign Policy of Iran: A Developing Nation in World Affairs, 1500–1941.* Charlottesville: The University Press of Virginia, 1966.

———. *Iran's Foreign Policy, 1941–1973: A Study of Foreign Policy in Modernizing Nations.* Charlottesville: The University Press of Virginia, 1975.

———. *The Persian Gulf: Iran's Role.* Charlottesville: The University Press of Virginia, 1972.

———. *The Persian Gulf and the Strait of Hormuz.* Alphen aan den Rijn: Sijthoff and Noordhoff, 1979.

———. *Revolutionary Iran: Challenge and Response in the Middle East.* Baltimore: The Johns Hopkins University Press, 1986.

———. "The Shifting Premise of Iran's Foreign Policy: Towards a Democratic Peace?" *Middle East Journal* 52, no. 2 (1988).

Rebuilding America's Defenses: Strategy, Forces and Resources for a New Century, Project for a New American Century, September 2002 at www.newamericancentury.org.

Reidel, Bruce. "Al-Qaeda Strikes Back." *Foreign Affairs* 86, no. 3 (2007).

Roberts, Paul Craig. "The War on Truth and Liberty: The Neocon Threat to Our Freedom." *Counterpunch,* June 12, 2007.

Roosevelt, Kermit. *Countercoup: The Struggle for the Control of Iran.* New York: McGraw-Hill Book Company, 1979.

Rozen, Laura. "Three Days in Rome." *Mother Jones,* July–August 2006.

Samuels, David. "Grand Illusion." *Atlantic,* June 2007.

Sher, Neal M. "Comprehensive U.S. Sanctions Against Iran: A Plan for Action." *American Israel Public Affairs Committee,* April 2, 1995.

Sick, Gary G. *All Fall Down: America's Tragic Encounter with Iran.* New York: Penguin Books, 1986.

———. *October Surprise.* New York: Random House, 1991.

———. "The Truth About Iran." *Foreign Affairs* 85, no. 6 (2006).

Slavin, Barbara. *Bitter Friends, Bosom Enemies: Iran, the U.S., and the Twisted Path to Confrontation.* New York: St. Martin's Press, 2007.

Sokolski, Henry, and Patrick Clawson, eds. *Checking Iran's Nuclear Ambitions.* Carlisle, PA: Strategic Studies Institute of the U.S. Army War College, 2004.

———. *Getting Ready for a Nuclear Ready Iran.* Carlisle, PA: Strategic Studies Institute of the U.S. Army War College, 2005.

Takeyh, Ray. *Hidden Iran: Paradox and Power in the Islamic Republic.* New York: Henry Holt and Company, 2006.

Telhami, Shibley. *The Stakes: America and the Middle East.* Boulder: Westview Press, 2002.

Tira, Oded. "What to Do with Iran?" December 30, 2006 at www.ynetnews.com.

Twinam, Joseph. *The Gulf, Cooperation and the Council: An American Perspective.* Washington DC: Middle East Policy Council, 1992.

U.S. Department of State. *Patterns of Global Terrorism 1993.* Washington DC: Department of State, April 1994.

U.S. Directorate of National Intelligence. *Prospects for Iraq's Stability: A Challenging Road Ahead.* Washington DC: Office of the Director of National Intelligence, January 2007 at www.dni.gov.

———. *Prospects for Iraq's Stability: Some Security Progress but Political Reconciliation Elusive.* Washington DC: Office of the Director of National Intelligence, August 2007 at www.dni.gov.

———. *Regional Consequences of Regime Change in Iraq.* National Intelligence Council, Washington DC, January 2003 at http://intelligence.senate.gov/prewar.pdf.

U.S. Office of the President. *National Security Strategy of the United States of America.* Washington DC: The White House, 2002 at www.whitehouse.gov.

———. *National Security Strategy of the United States of America.* Washington DC: The White House, 2006 at www.whitehouse.gov.

———. *Report of the President's Special Review Board (the Tower Commission Report).* Washington DC, February 26, 1987.

Yetiv, Steve A., and Chunlong Lu. "China, Global Energy and the Middle East." *Middle East Journal* 61, no. 2 (2007).

Index

About the Author

THOMAS R. MATTAIR is an independent scholar based in Washington, DC. He has published, lectured, and served as a consultant throughout the United States and the Middle East. He has also served in senior positions at the Emirates Center for Strategic Studies and Research in the United Arab Emirates and at the Middle East Policy Council in Washington. Dr. Mattair began his career as a professor at Kent State University, the University of Southern California, and Cornell University.